401 Questions
Every
Entrepreneur
Should Ask

PEMBINA TRAIL

BY

JAMES L. SILVESTER

FOREWORD BY TIMOTHY M. KAINE, GOVERNOR OF VIRGINIA

D1399481

CAREER
PRESS

Franklin Lakes, NJ

401 QUESTIONS EVERY ENTREPRENEUR SHOULD ASK
EDITED AND TYPESET BY ASTRID DERIDDER
Cover design by Rob Johnson/Johnson Design
Interior images courtesy of Art Explosion
Printed in the U.S.A. by Book-mart Press

To order this title, please call toll-free 1-800-CAREER-1 (NJ and Canada: 201-848-0310) to order using VISA or MasterCard, or for further information on books from Career Press.

The Career Press, Inc., 3 Tice Road, PO Box 687,
Franklin Lakes, NJ 07417
www.careerpress.com

Library of Congress Cataloging-in-Publication Data

Silvester, James L.
    401 questions every entrepreneur should ask / by James L. Silvester.
        p. cm.
    ISBN-13: 978-1-56414-901-5
    ISBN-10: 1-56414-901-3
        1. Business planning—Handbooks, manuals, etc. 2. Business—Handbooks, manuals, etc. 3. Entrepreneurship—Handbooks, manuals, etc. I. Title. II. Title: Four hundred and one questions every entrepreneur should ask.

HD30.28.S4345 2006
658.4′01—dc22

2006016818

Dedication

I dedicate this book to my deceased parents, Louie and Ruth Silvester, to whom I owe so much. Even though I lost them early in life, I am thankful every day that I had these two extraordinary individuals to guide me. I also thank my wonderful wife of 28 years, Debbie, who had to tolerate me through this project. And to the best kids in the world: Katie, who is serving her country in the Peace Corps in China; Jonathan, who is just starting out with a bang in the corporate world; and Nicholas, who is about to join the United States Navy. My father-in-law and mother-in-law, also two great people, have supported me as well. I feel them to be my stand-in parents and just downright good people. I can't forget my sister Fran; we've been through much together in life. And last but not least, my granddaughter Madison. Her cute smile and the ever-present twinkle in her eyes always brightens my day.

Thanks to Tris Colburn, my literary agent, and Michael Pye at Career Press, for believing in me at this stage in my life, and making this book possible. I would also like to acknowledge the efforts and contributions of my employees and editors, Jason Tevalt and Ariel Shry.

Mom and Dad, I did something right, for I feel that I am truly the luckiest and wealthiest person in the world to have all these wonderful people in my life.

Contents

Foreword

BY

TIMOTHY M. KAINE, GOVERNOR

Commonwealth of Virginia
Office of the Governor
Timothy M. Kaine, Governor
April 19, 2006

It is with great pleasure that I write a foreword for James L. Silvester, a distinguished Virginian, and his new book *401 Questions Every Entrepreneur Should Ask*. Mr. Silvester is a noted expert on entrepreneurship and business operations. Entrepreneurship is literally the lifeblood of the American economy. The innovation and dynamism of entrepreneurs creates new jobs, new opportunities, and new investments. Entrepreneurship fuels economic growth in our country. Without entrepreneurship, the United States would not be known as the land of opportunity.

This important book lays out critical questions to ask based on Mr. Silvester's decades of professional and educational experience as a noted business consultant as well as popular seminar speaker. This book is the third installment of Mr. Silvester's books providing a how-to guide for aspiring entrepreneurs. As Governor of Virginia, I spend much of my time working as the state's chief economic development officer working to attract new jobs and new investments. Entrepreneurship makes these opportunities for our state and for our people possible. We are very fortunate to have an entrepreneurship expert like Mr. Silvester call Virginia home.

I am confident that aspiring and experienced entrepreneurs alike will find this new book very useful in helping them make good decisions for their business, avoid consequences, and be as successful as they can be. I can think of no more important contribution to our economic growth than helping entrepreneurs succeed. I commend Mr. Silvester for this important book and recommend it to anyone starting or considering starting a business.

—Sincerely,
Timothy M. Kaine

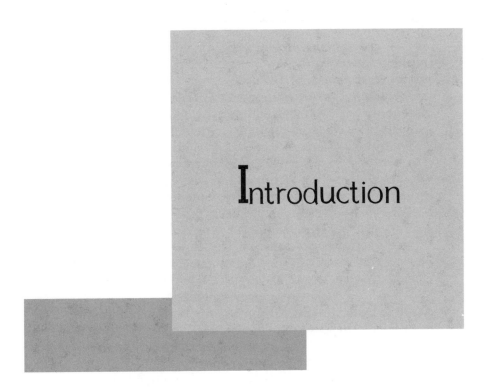

Introduction

Our parents taught us to study hard, work part-time while in school, participate in sports, and join various clubs in high school and college. They taught us that these things would lead to good, steady, and secure jobs throughout life—but they were wrong! There is no security left in Corporate America. As international competition ravages our mainline companies, as Wall Street insists on more streamlined firms, and as more white collar jobs are outsourced to India, the so-called secure jobs here in America are disappearing.

After decades of hearing about Japan, Korea, and Germany, America again reins supreme in terms of the world economic output (30 percent of global output), while many of our competitor nations falter or grapple with low growth situations and look to the United States for support and leadership.

For many years, some universities offered one or two courses in entrepreneurship. Now we see masters and bachelor degrees in entrepreneurship becoming commonplace. We are even beginning to see large corporations try to emulate entrepreneurship within their ranks (sometimes referred to as *intrapreneuring*).

The nation's entrepreneurial sector, which makes up millions of small businesses, has been the engine of economic growth over the past 20 years. Almost all of the 37 million jobs that have been created by the United States economy since 1980 have been a result of entrepreneurial start-ups and growth, while mid-sized and large companies have been stagnant in terms of job creation.

Even though Congress and the various states have been slow to recognize and acknowledge the contributions of small enterprises to the overall economic picture, things are starting to change for the better. We are starting to see real entrepreneurial incentives appear.

We even hear talk about the giant corporations trying to go small. A term called *corpreneuring* has also recently emerged. This concept is the efforts of these giants to relegate their various departments, divisions, and subsidiaries into entrepreneurial units, each with its own identity, capital resources, and profit/loss responsibility. Their objective is to increase overall corporate profitability.

Most experts suspect this new emphasis on going small on the part of giant corporations is just another fad, and the harsh realities of corporate administration will once again take hold. But the silver lining is the comfort of knowing these corpocrats realize the potential value of successful small businesses, and just cannot stand the fact that they must surrender profits to entrepreneurs.

Recognizing the business climate to be more risky than ever in these turbulent economic times, I set out to provide a valuable reference source for both beginning and seasoned entrepreneurs. *401 Questions Every Entrepreneur Should Ask* is my newest work in my how-to trilogy of entrepreneurial self-help books, and perhaps the most important. The book reviews the operational environment of the entrepreneurial firm. It poses a series of more than 400 questions that every entrepreneur should ask. Each question poses thought-provoking issues that induce answers to the questions, and then goes on to explain the business consequences to expect if any question is answered in the negative. The book then develops further and instructs the entrepreneur on how to correct or avoid the potential negative consequences.

—James L. Silvester
Stephens City, Virginia

Author's Note: The data used in this book are mostly from my own files while serving as a professor of entrepreneurship and director of a Small Business Institute (SBI). Additionally, I drew selected material from a few U.S. Small Business Administration (SBA) publications, including the internal training manuals that are used to train SBI directors.

Do
You
Have
What It
Takes?

CHAPTER 1

SAME OLD THEORIES

Many people have suggested that successful entrepreneurs have particular traits or characteristics that lead to their business fortunes. Terms such as *first born, tall, gambler, partly insane,* and *egotistical* have all been used to describe what it takes to be successfully self-employed. Some have even suggested that there is a direct link been sexual virility and success in small business! Of course, most of these theories have been set aside and disregarded as hogwash.

If you look closely, success comes in many different packages. Tall people, short people, young people, old people, educated, uneducated, white, Hispanic, black, male, female, egotistical, introverts—the list could go on forever. What we do know is that being the child of an entrepreneur tends to give an advantage, as does your socioeconomic background. I believe that the socioeconomic factors will become less important as our nation continues to break down the walls of discrimination, and the wealth of our productive endeavors spreads throughout society.

11

To truly understand entrepreneurial success, one must understand the motives and attitudes that drive individuals to take the leap. Motives can be varied; some are simple, some complex, and some cast in stone (such as the child who inherits a business). For the sake of simplicity, we will define *motives* as external forces conditioning behavior, and *attitudes* as internal forces conditioning one's behavior. Both mix to create a human point of view, and therefore determine subsequent response.

MOTIVES

Why enter the ranks of the self-employed? The motives are different for everyone, but usually include the desire for economic independence; the desire for job security; the desire for wealth, power, and fame; the desire to carry on a family business; the desire to keep what you really earn; or the desire for change. Or perhaps it's just the right time to take the plunge. Since entrepreneurship seldom produces massive wealth, fame, or power, let's concentrate on those motives that matter the most.

Economic security

Corporate America no longer offers job security in the traditional sense. Gone are the days when we all went to college and got a job with a big company and then got on the fast track to an ever-increasing rank and salary. In the 1980s, 1990s, and continuing into the new century, international business competition, corporate consolidation, corporate corruption, outsourcing, and downsizing put an end to that era. Ten of millions of jobs, both blue and white collar, have been permanently eliminated.

Many individuals believe entrepreneurship provides a safe haven in terms of job security. Some have acted on that belief and have joined the ranks of the self-employed, while others continue to dream. Given the high level of employment cutbacks in large- and medium-sized firms, sometimes self-employment becomes the only alternative. Some see it as insulation against future layoffs. Consequently, many business executives and hourly workers are seriously pursuing small business enterprises. Quite a few are now running side businesses out of their homes, hoping to someday generate a full-time operation.

Independence

Self-employment provides a degree of personal and economic freedom not found when working for somebody else. As the old saying goes, "There's nothing like being your own boss."

Potential profit

Where you find the potential for risk, profit opportunities also exist. You get to keep what you earn, except what must be paid to various taxing authorities. In other words, instead of selling yourself for wholesale to some employer who will mark up your services and resell it for retail and pocket the profit, you get to sell yourself for what the market will bear, and keep the profits for yourself.

Quality of life

Many individuals find a high degree of fulfillment in self-employment. Some successful entrepreneurs have reported an enhanced self-image and positive attitude, along with other psychological rewards.

Good economic environment

With recession nowhere in sight and continued economic expansion underway, it is an ideal time to be starting a small business. This is also true of service enterprises, which comprise most of the nation's small firms. The service field will continue to be the fastest-growing sector of the economy.

Consumer and business confidence

Despite some consternation, buyers and sellers are generally positive about the nation's economic prospects. If this positive attitude continues, economic growth will follow suit.

Continued low inflationary expectation

For the time being, inflation is still under control, and that's a positive note for investors, managers, and consumers. High inflation erodes confidence in the economy, and recession normally follows to correct spiraling prices.

Lower interest rates

Despite recent increases in interest rates, these rates are still at historic lows. Moderate economic activity, shrinking federal budgets as a percent of Gross Domestic Product (GDP), and low-to-moderate inflation are all merging at the same time to create a unique and promising interest rate environment. These events will continue to free up capital resources for investment purposes.

Federal budget

The latter half of the 1990s saw the federal budget in balance and producing large surpluses. The early years of the 21st century saw a return to large budget deficits, largely due to a new administration, a change in fiscal policies, and a moderate recession. However, it must be pointed out that the current deficit is now moderating, as robust economic activity ensues, with accompanying increases in tax receipts. Also, despite the return of large budget deficits, those deficits as a percent of Gross Domestic Product (GDP) are at historic lows. We must remember that during the Reagan years, deficits soared while interest rates dropped. But let's not confuse the issue with extremes—high or low deficits versus their effects on interest rates. Many people take the position that budget deficits are irrelevant to interest rates; that inflation is the key. There is a direct relationship between long-term interest rates and inflation, with both going up in unison. And the Federal Reserve will hike short-term interest rates to slow the economy in an effort to reduce inflationary pressures caused by an overheating business cycle.

I take a dual position. Acknowledging that there is a relationship between interest rates and inflation, you must recognize that at times the federal government will arbitrarily raise short-term interest rates in order to attract enough foreign investors to fund its budget deficit, especially during times when the dollar is falling in value against world currency exchanges.

Good tax environment

Recent tax cuts have ushered in an era of capital gains reduction and numerous tax breaks for the entrepreneur. Increasing favorable write-offs for healthcare, equipment purchases, and investment in research and development have proven valuable to both startup and seasoned entrepreneurs.

New emphasis on small firms

Governments are starting to realize the importance of the small business sector. Consequently, more governmental resources and favorable tax legislation are being directed to the small business community. Governments now see the entrepreneur as the single most important economic factor that is adding to the wealth stock of the nation.

PITFALLS TO CONSIDER

We have discussed your motives for pursuing entrepreneurship. As with anything in life, no matter how attractive, there are multiple downsides to self-employment.

International trading giants

The European Union, India, and China all pose an economic threat to the global dominance of the American economy. The 25 countries of the EU have a GDP equaling that of the United States. China's economy is now 60 percent the size of the United States's and growing at a 9.5 percent annual rate. By that measure, it will surpass the United States as the world's largest economy in 2012. India is competing on every level with the United States in the medical, scientific, telecommunication, and heavy machinery fields. This situation surely provides some great business opportunities. Outsourcing products and services to India and China has been a boon to many American companies by increasing their profits. Even small firms can do well by doing business with China, India, and the EU. Obviously, they offer huge and expanding export markets that can be exploited. However, as the United States loses its grip on global economic dominance, it will lose its ability to control events to the advantage of its domestic firms and citizens. As overall systemic economic opportunity shifts to other trading blocks in the world, there will be fewer opportunities at home. To what extent this will create domestic political and economic instability is being quietly debated today. It is safe to say that firms of all sizes need to be ready to compete in a truly global marketplace.

Constantly changing buying motives of potential customers

Changing economic conditions caused by such factors as deflation, inflation, compressed economic cycles, international events, competition, or unanticipated shifts in stock and/or bond values, and so on, can all have a significant impact on a small firm.

Number of business failures

The failure rate for small businesses is very high, even in the best of economic times. It does pulse back and forth somewhat, depending on the economic condition at hand.

Possibility of losing money

Where you find potential reward, the possibility of risk is always present. An individual can lose a considerable amount of money if the business is a losing proposition and one fails to bail out in time to cut large losses.

Psychological damage

Business failure can produce negative psychological effects that may haunt you for a long time to come. Some people will completely avoid a second try at self-employment.

Long hours

Contrary to popular belief, most successful entrepreneurs put in 12-hour days. Most work just as hard as corporate executives.

Medium income and age

Successful small business entrepreneurs make, on average, about the same as a mid-level manager in a large corporation. According to the researchers Willard & Shullman, the average small business owner works 52 hours per week. The median age of the small business owner is 43, as reported by *Inc.* magazine.

Income variation

Income derived from your own business will be less regular than the receipt of a salary or wage from an employer. If you are starting a new business, the first six to 12 months might be bad, because the operation is functioning at a loss. Even after business income is generated, variations in profits can be expected because of many factors.

THE RIGHT STUFF

Trial by trait

While there are no ingrained traits that guarantee entrepreneurial success, possessing certain qualities surely enhances the possibility of success. One recent study by William E. Jennings titled "A Profile of the Entrepreneur" highlights some interesting findings. Many small business owners were queried and asked to rate what traits and attitudes were important to successful entrepreneurship. The study points out the most important attributes are perseverance, desire, and willingness to take initiative, competitiveness, self-reliance, a strong need to achieve, self-confidence, and good physical health.

Drive
- Responsibility: the ability to make sure things get done.
- Persistence: the willingness to see things finalized.
- Health: having physical and mental stamina.

Initiative
- The ability to take charge when necessary and be the first to act.

Vigor
- Having the limitless vitality needed to succeed.

Thinking ability
- Originality: the ability to create new ideas and approaches.

- Creativity: the ability to think and explore in unorthodox ways; also initiative.
- Critical sense: the ability to make intelligent comparisons and comments.
- Analytical sense: the ability to reason in practical, theoretical, and abstract terms.

Human relations ability

- Sociability: the ability to get along with others, including peers, in a number of settings (home, work, politics, international relations, and so on).
- Cooperation: the willingness to work with others in a constructive manner.
- Tactfulness: the ability to hold or water-down discomforting comments or actions.
- Cheerfulness: the willingness to laugh and smile even when the going gets rough.
- Consideration: the ability to appreciate the value of other people's time and money.
- Personal relations: the ability to get along with people.
- Ascendancy: the ability to govern and control wisely without excessive ego involvement.
- Emotional stability: having the appropriate maturity level for the task.
- Cautiousness: the ability to give serious evaluation before taking risks.

Communications ability

- Oral communications: the ability to speak in a clear, concise, and logical manner.
- Verbal comprehension: the ability to listen, absorb, and understand the conversations of others.
- Written communication: the ability to write in a clear, concise, and logical way.

Technical knowledge

- The information an entrepreneur possesses about the physical process of producing the goods or services and the ability to put the information to use in a creative manner.

If you have most of the aforementioned characteristics, or believe you can learn them as needed, then entrepreneurial success can be achieved. When analyzing yourself, stay away from lofty estimations of your abilities. Be candid about your personality and capabilities. If deficiencies do exist, it's better to know them before moving head first into a prolonged venture that will consume your time and money. Many mistakes and emotional scars can be averted if you understand your limitations and move to correct them before getting in too deep.

WHEN IN DOUBT, LOOK ABOUT

The man

Of course, you could say that all of this is just my opinion. As both an independent businessman and former college professor of entrepreneurship, I have always taught others to look beyond a single individual's stated positions or opinions. It never hurts to look around for other thoughts on important issues—such as entrepreneurship—particularly when it impacts you directly.

In that vein, let's explore the research and findings of Lysander Thomas White. Although having passed away in 1966, this man did more in terms of entrepreneurial research than any person before or after him. Even though his findings are old, the basic premise of his principals and findings still hold true today.

Lysander Thomas White was born in 1895. He started his career in the energy industry, spending almost 30 years in the petroleum sector with Cities Services. There he studied the operations of small oil jobbers. He was instrumental in establishing several petroleum management institutes to help these jobbers engender the cooperation of vocational schools, colleges, and universities throughout the country. Upon retiring in 1961, White moved to Washington, D.C., and became a noted consultant, speaker, and advocate for small business concerns.

In addition to working in cooperation with and under contract for numerous government agencies and professional associations, he was a recurring speaker for the Harvard Business School, the University of Wisconsin, and the University of California. He also conducted entrepreneurial research for the states of Virginia, Wisconsin, Illinois, Ohio, Michigan, and Florida.

What does it take to be an entrepreneur, according to White? Here are the characteristics he thinks are most important:

- The ability to get along with people. You must have customers, suppliers, and employees. A surly or introverted person will lose out. A pleasant, outgoing person attracts other people. A willingness to provide service is what brings in sales.
- Health and energy. You must have not only the willingness, but an actual ability to work hard.
- A strong desire to build and create. True entrepreneurs want to create a lasting business. They consider it their legacy.
- An optimistic spirit. Pessimists don't take chances. Risks are inherent in business.
- A sense of organization. An entrepreneur must maintain an attractive place of business and an orderly and tidy inventory. The entrepreneur must keep a number of records, and must be able to direct the people under him or her, frequently delegating duties.
- Some business background. You don't have to be strong in all phases of business management. You can look to experts, but you need a basic understanding of functions, such as selling, accounting, purchasing, finance, and so on.
- Drive. You must have ambition plus determination to get ahead, to concentrate on the business, to enlarge it creatively, to live with it, to fulfill a competitive interest.
- Confidence. Shrinking violets do not, as a general rule, do well in business.
- Self-reliance. A willingness to shoulder responsibility, to make decisions, and to stand by them.
- Independence. A desire to master your own destiny and be your own boss.
- Willpower. The strength to see a thing through, rather than to vacillate or to procrastinate.
- Patience. Business has many irritations and frustrations. If you can't take these, or if you are inclined to fly off the handle easily or become upset about small pressures, don't go into business.
- Ability to take worries or to leave them. Responsibilities and anxieties go hand-in-hand from time to time.
- Integrity. Honesty is the best policy in business. It's hard to fool the public permanently. The smart angle promoters don't last long.
- A feeling for community service. No business can remain isolated for long.

Important Questions to Consider

#1. ARE YOU A GOOD LISTENER?

If you are not listening, there will be a lack of communication between you and your customers, suppliers, employees, vendors, and creditors. Additionally, you won't pick up on your competitors. All in all, this will keep you out of touch with the market for your product or service.

Corrective Measures:

You must realize the value of input from all sources that affect your business, particularly your competitors. Observe, listen, keep your mouth shut, and act when necessary.

#2. DO YOU WELCOME THE RAPID CHANGES TAKING PLACE IN YOUR SOCIETY; READILY ADJUSTING YOURSELF AND YOUR MANAGEMENT STYLE TO THEM?

If you do not, you will be unaware of the latest business trends and applications, and risk marketing products and services that are slowly losing their demand and appeal in the marketplace. You may also be utilizing and applying obsolete methods of business operation.

Corrective Measures:

You need to research the present status of your product/service line, equipment, and methods of operation and management, as it relates to your marketplace. Modify these as needed to particular management methods.

#3. HAVE YOU GIVEN SERIOUS THOUGHT TO ATTENDING A SEMINAR GIVEN BY YOUR TRADE ASSOCIATION, A COLLEGE, OR OTHER ORGANIZATIONS?

You will lack the skills needed to compete in an increasingly competitive marketplace and become stagnant in terms of learning and flexibility. You can bet your competitors will be taking advantage of seminars being offered!

Corrective Measures:

Attend the appropriate seminars and involve yourself in these activities with an open mind. Network with others in your industry, even competitors, and utilize what you learn to your firm's advantage. Nobody can take it away once it's in your head. And what's in your head can not be made an issue in any court, according to the Trade Secrets Act.

#4. UNLESS YOU DEPEND PRIMARILY ON TOURIST TRADE, DO YOU MAKE AN EFFORT TO KNOW YOUR CUSTOMERS PERSONALLY? THEIR FAMILIES? THEIR LIFESTYLES? DO YOU GREET THEM AS FRIENDS?

If you do not, bad customer relations will ensue. Also, there will be a lack of knowledge of your customers' needs and desires, thereby decreasing your customer base, especially if your competitors take more of an interest than you. There will be an overall loss of customer goodwill.

Corrective Measures:

Research and study your individual customers when possible. Get to know them. Be friendly. Use this enhanced knowledge to make sales.

#5. ARE YOU A COOPERATOR, EXERCISING LEADERSHIP IN COMMUNITY AFFAIRS, RATHER THAN A LONE OPERATOR?

If not, you may hinder the growth of your community by not providing your input and expertise, especially if that expertise is of a unique and/or creative nature. In addition, at a critical juncture in your company's history (when community support is needed), you may lack the advantage of community support because you failed to develop good contacts in the past.

Corrective Measures:

Actively participate in community affairs. Express your opinions in friendly but assertive manner. Solicit community input and support when and where appropriate.

#6. HAVE YOU WORKED RECENTLY WITH LOCAL GOVERNMENT OFFICIALS AND OTHER BUSINESS LEADERS TO IMPROVE THE SPECIFIC AND OVERALL BUSINESS CLIMATE IN WHICH YOU OPERATE?

If not, don't bark about having no input in promoting positive growth or when a piece of bad legislation sneaks through that's harmful to business interests. Likewise, you may forgo the opportunity to support and participate in worthwhile high-profile community projects.

Corrective Measures:

Get to know the politicians and bureaucrats who are the movers and shakers. Work with them and other businesspeople who are involved to determine how to promote proper growth. If your business owns real estate holdings, take some extra time and work closely with the zoning and planning officials. Not only will this give you an advantage when you need their cooperation on zoning issues, but it will also help to ensure a proper growth mix across the board, which is good for everybody. And if you still don't like the way things are handled, run for public office! Small business people often make good political leaders.

Strategic Planning Imperative

CHAPTER 2

THE PLANNING PROCESS

Not only do you need to have identifiable goals and objectives, but you also need to have a comprehensive plan of action. I call this the strategic plan. Very few individuals have become successful entrepreneurs without knowing where they are going and how they are going to get there. If you are still working for someone else, set a timetable for breaking away and taking the plunge. However, if you are currently an entrepreneur but lack goals and specific plans, now is the time to sit down and do some thinking.

Know your goals

Here is a list of some common goals that you may consider. Please be advised that this is not a complete list. These ideas are offered as a guide only. Great care should be taken when delineating your own goals. Every individual situation is different and requires careful consideration and unique planning.

■ I want to be self-employed within the next 18 months.
■ I would like to provide for all of my family's needs within two years.
■ I want to be financially independent within 10 years of starting my own business.
■ I would like to employ my spouse and/or children.
■ I would like to pass on a viable business to my heirs.

Your goals should be structured so that there stands a reasonable chance of attaining them. Goals that are unrealistic will only lead to frustration and depression. In addition, keep them simple and to the point. Make sure they can be reviewed and evaluated as time progresses.

What is strategic planning?

Once your goals have been visualized, the next step is to formulate various plans of action that will provide you with a roadmap into the realm of entrepreneurship. Action plans are multi-purpose guides that will point you in the right direction and ensure a higher degree of success than you might otherwise expect.

Strategic planning is simply a procedure by which you take a look at your enterprise in terms of its complete external environment and surroundings, particularly as it relates to its markets, and then plan out a course of action utilizing your internal resources. In reality, the strategic planning process is a series of planning stages that, once understood, mastered, and organized, becomes your strategic plan. The stages are:

■ Short-term plans: These plans are designed to lead to the successful culmination of goals that must be achieved within one year.
■ Intermediate-term plans: These plans provide a roadmap to the successful culmination of goals that must be achieved within one to five years.
■ Long-term plans: These action plans are structured to help you culminate goals that are slated to be achieved in a time span exceeding five years.
■ Contingency plans: These action plans are trigger mechanisms designed to react in the event that one or more forces (external to the enterprise) threaten its existence.

More than 35 years ago, very few firms planned for the unanticipated. Economic and financial cycles were fairly predictable. The Arab oil embargo in 1973, the oil scare of 1979, the terrorist attacks of September 11, 2001, and the hurricane season of 2005 changed all of that. Any American firm, large or small, is faced with many external forces, also known in management circles as *uncontrollables*. These forces fall outside the direct control of managers, and sometimes even the whole political process.

Planning is the most important part of the decision-making process. Planning is a must for any size firm. Even the smallest entrepreneurial enterprise must ultimately embrace planning in order to survive highly competitive environments. Planning is a dynamic process that must be reviewed and modified on a regular basis. A 20-year long-range plan that was developed in 1995 should not look the same as it did 10 years ago. If it does, you are heading for trouble. This kind of inflexibility will lead to grave miscalculations in the marketplace.

THE ULTIMATE STRATEGIC PLAN

A business plan has traditionally been viewed as a document used in raising capital to start or expand a business endeavor; however, it does have another purpose, which is largely ignored. The business plan is first and foremost a strategic planning device. The secondary function is to raise capital. The preparation of the plan forces its author and designer (the entrepreneur) to evaluate the prospects for success or failure in the marketplace.

Creation of a good business plan is a grueling process that takes months to complete. The final plan, ranging anywhere between 30 and 100 pages in length, is the ultimate testimony as to whether your product or service will be successful in the marketplace. This process forces you to look at everything related to the business venture beginning at the present and extending 10 years into the future. Capital requirements, competition, and operational considerations are but a few things reviewed and dissected in the business plan.

Constructing a business plan is similar to taking out an insurance policy. It will minimize your risks. Whether you are just starting your entrepreneurial enterprise or already in operation, it is essential to develop a business plan. In the process, both opportunities and hazards will be identified. The plan may convince you not to pursue your venture any further, in which case it has done you a favor. On the other hand, the business plan could verify the need for a particular product or service, but at the same time it may force you to change your attitude toward distribution, marketing, warehousing, or other factors that relate to existing products/services.

The importance of a properly constructed business plan cannot be emphasized enough. Whether your proposed venture or existing operation is a small part-time operation or of substantial scale, develop a business plan to learn where you stand. It is the ultimate strategic planning document. Be advised that you may want to seek professional assistance in the construction of your business plan if you have never constructed one before.

Environments that matter; external and internal factors

External factors are those that affect the market served by your business, but are generally beyond your control. Internal factors are resources within your control that you have at your disposal to react to—or eliminate—threats caused by the external forces. The following are typical external factors and forces:

- government policies and regulations
- business trends
- changes in population characteristics and profiles
- economic fortunes of customers
- changes in buying habits
- competitive pressures and conditions
- economic cycles
- state of technology
- changing demand patterns
- industry trends
- unions
- inflation
- international events
- competitors

The following are typical internal factors and forces:

- promotional plans
- expansion plans
- capacity restrictions
- new product introductions
- product cancellations
- sales force changes
- pricing policies
- profit expectations
- market expansion to new customers or territories

Important Questions to Consider

#1. DO YOU HAVE A WRITTEN STATEMENT OF YOUR FIRM'S MISSION OR PURPOSE?

Without a vision, you cannot establish goals and objectives. You will lack the ability to predict future directions and orientation.

Corrective Measures:

As an entrepreneur you must establish realistic (but uncomplicated) mission statements by outlining what must be accomplished and how to carry it out. After which you must articulate these visions to all employees and constantly evaluate them to ensure proper direction.

#2. HAVE YOU ESTABLISHED OVERALL, AS WELL AS DETAILED, OBJECTIVES?

Your business needs definable goals to achieve in terms of both broad and specific objectives. Lacking these, your business will lack direction, which could hamper its ability to avoid and overcome obstacles.

Corrective Measures:

Sit down and establish goals and objectives both broad and specific in scope. Make all facets of your organization, including your employees, aware of these benchmarks. Detail these goals and objectives in a fashion that will be easy to understand. Most importantly, always monitor results, and alter goals and objectives as internal and external factors demand.

#3. HAVE YOU DONE ANY LONG-RANGE PLANNING FOR GROWTH?

If not, your business will lack structured direction. Moving in the wrong direction could compromise survival in our increasingly competitive marketplace. Profit opportunities will be lost. Nowadays mistakes are more costly and less forgiving than in the past.

Corrective Measures:

Develop long-range planning procedures. Review this planning function periodically and modify the process when appropriate. In addition to your day-by-day activities, find time for advance planning.

#4. ARE YOUR PLANS CONSISTENT WITH BOTH EXTERNAL AND INTERNAL FORCES THAT AFFECT YOUR BUSINESS?

If not, the prior external forces list could overwhelm your business, and the internal adjustments necessary to deal with the external threats may come too late.

Corrective Measures:

Develop your plans taking into consideration both external and internal factors. Stick with these goals and objectives until internal factors can no longer compensate for changes in external forces, thus forcing you to alter your plans. In other words, you must periodically evaluate external forces and modify your internal plans to adjust to the external forces.

#5. DO YOU ACTIVELY ASSESS YOUR COMPETITORS FOR CLUES AS TO WHAT THEY WILL DO NEXT?

Your competitors can be a great source of information, and it's generally free. Don't let your competition get the jump on market opportunities by being satisfied with preserving equality with your competitors. Failure to learn from your competitors can be costly in terms of lost opportunities and mistakes.

Corrective Measures:

Keep a close watch on your competitors at all times for any changes in tactics and strategies. Ask questions of your customers about your competitors. Even ask your friendly competitors. You will be surprised how much you can discover through loose lips. Listen, learn, and adapt when necessary. Move ahead with new ideas to improve service and sales when appropriate. Try to beat your competitors to the punch if it's not too risky.

#6. RECURRING CRISES FORCE YOU TO MAKE CHANGES THAT MAY NOT BE CAREFULLY AND THOUGHTFULLY ANALYZED. DO YOU HAVE PLANS FOR THOSE TIMES?

If not, unplanned and rushed decisions may be faulty and costly. Impulsive decisions generally lead to organizational confusion.

Corrective Measures:

A well-planned business is prepared to face and handle any crisis quickly and decisively through the strategic planning process; well-trained staff and consultants will also help in the time of a crisis. Good management runs one step ahead of a crisis and will anticipate various crises and have contingency plans in place. If the same recurring crisis comes along on a frequent, yet unpredictable basis, at least you can learn how to deal with it.

#7. IS THIS YOUR ATTITUDE TOWARD PLANNING?

a. It must be done for successful growth.

If not, your attitude denotes a lack of overall direction, and organizational drift will occur. This will lead to employee and vendor confusion as to the true direction of the firm. Organizational resources will not be optimized, thereby leading to missed opportunities and mistakes in judgment. Your business will suffer at the hands of better-prepared competition.

b. It is necessary in all circumstances.

If you answered no, keep in mind that planning ahead is necessary in every business in order to remain competitive. If you don't, you won't compete over the long haul. Your market share and profits will suffer, particularly during downturns in the economy. Recoveries will be harder and more painful as time goes on.

c. It is needed even if my operation is small.

No operation is too small for planning; even the home-based business. It takes planning and goal-setting to make a business successful. It is not a matter of how large or small the business; lack of planning will lead to competitor encroachment on your market share, missed opportunities, errors in judgment, lack of overall direction of the firm, and so on. Organizational confusion and drift will ensue.

Corrective Measures:

Engage in long, intermediate, and short-term planning in addition to crisis planning. Make sure that adequate resources are available to support planning endeavors. Involve your employees in the planning process at their various levels within the firm. Most importantly, communicate the planning process to all employees to ensure that everybody understands its purpose and objective.

#8. IN ADDITION TO DAY-BY-DAY ACTIVITIES, CAN YOU FIND THE TIME FOR ADVANCE PLANNING?

Too many interruptions for unimportant things waste valuable management time. In addition, your unwillingness or inability to delegate responsibilities to others in order to help with the workload will consume valuable time needed for planning purposes.

Corrective Measures:

Keeping operations well-managed and organized will free up planning time. Avoid and discourage unproductive interruptions. Having a well-trained staff to help with daily activities will also open up time for planning. A special time each day should be set aside for planning purposes. It doesn't take up as much time if you do a little planning every day.

#9. HOW DO YOU PREDICT FUTURE DEVELOPMENTS?

a.   By personal observations of informal (non-numerical) methods?

Remember that ignoring your gut reaction can be costly. Intuitive decisions are considered valuable decision tools nowadays.

Corrective Measures:

Informal observation is considered a credible research method. Apply it, but do so correctly. Use the data collected from informal means in concert with the results of other methods more scientific in nature.

b.   By formal (numerical) methods?

Numbers don't always tell the whole story, but they are a good guide. Historical numbers can be used as a tool to calculate probable future events. You may be overlooking important potential outcomes if you ignore numerical methods of prediction. Also, you may lose your basis of carrying on rational discussions with bankers, investors, vendors, employees, and so on. in terms of performance regarding financial statements and market trends.

Corrective Measures:

Use numerical methods of prediction in conjunction with empirical and other informal approaches. Collect your numbers by engaging in primary research methods— collect hard numbers yourself or by hiring third party research firms, if the budget allows. Also, collect secondary predictive numerical data from existing industry and government sources. It is less costly and time-consuming. Generally, using a lot of inexpensive secondary data in combination with a little primary data will do the trick. Read, absorb, and use what numerical information is collected, no matter what method is employed or what combination is used.

#10. DID YOU PREDICT THE CURRENT STATE OF ECONOMIC CONDITIONS?

If you didn't, start paying attention. Reacting too late (in terms of expense control) to economic and/or industry slowdowns can be costly in terms of reduced profits or even business survival itself. Conversely, reacting too late to economic expansions will result in missed profit opportunities. Profit margins are generally the greatest just after recessions, at the start and early stage of the economic rebound cycle.

Corrective Measures:

Pay attention to economic indicators. Read the trade journals related to your industry as well as general business news. Keep abreast of those economic indicators sensitive to your particular industry. Also, seek advice from experts within your industry and from people who have an understanding of general economic conditions.

#11. DID YOU PLAN FOR TECHNOLOGICAL CHANGES, WHICH MAY AFFECT YOUR BUSINESS?

If not, you will eventually cease to exist. Sales will suffer because your products, services, methods, equipment, and pricing will become obsolete and you will not keep up with, or ahead of, the competition. Your product or service offerings to the market will become less and less attractive and more and more expensive as time progresses.

Corrective Measures:

Anticipate and allow for technological changes. Study the impact of these shifts and changes on your business. Establish a research and development (R&D) budget. A very small investment in R&D can pay big dividends, even for the smallest firms. Innovate when necessary in terms of product/service development. To the degree possible and affordable, always take advantage of the latest technical improvements, methods, and R&D tax credits within your industry.

#12. DO YOU CONSIDER SOCIAL TRENDS?

Without consideration of social trends, you may find your business losing ground to competitors who take note of fads, general trends, and changes in societal norms. Unwillingness to observe and change to accommodate social trends will render your products or services obsolete and eventually damage your business in terms of revenues and profit, thereby compromising its survival.

Corrective Measures:

Pay attention to all the social trends that affect your industry and business. There's money to be made with successful planning in regard to shifting attitudes and fads within your industry. Consider the demands of special groups you may have ignored in the past. They can be sources of additional revenues and profits. Be willing to change marketing and merchandising plans and procedures to accommodate changing social trends.

#13. Have you made predictions on how changes in government policies may affect your business?

Government policy changes affect everything from interstate trade to local licensing. Not anticipating and planning for such changes can leave you unprepared to alter your internal management structure to accommodate forthcoming legal and regulatory changes. Violation of any law can mean punishment and/or fines being imposed.

Corrective Measures:

Read, listen, learn, and do a lot of checking on all new laws and policies being proposed, particularly the ones that will affect your industry and business. Governments, be they local, state, or federal, change policy on a constant basis. New regulations are introduced and older ones terminated. Watching this process will ensure your continued compliance.

#14. When you find that change is called for, do you act decisively and creatively?

If not, potential problems will become real problems, and these real problems can become uncontrollable. The longer you wait to rectify problems and difficulties, the more difficult the cure.

Corrective Measures:

Analyze all problems carefully. Decide on a course of action and then move quickly and decisively. Don't be afraid to take new and creative measures in dealing with problems if the methods are well-thought-out and evaluated.

#15. Do you categorize the elements of your firm's internal environment into manageable groups?

If not, managerial and operational confusion on a department/division scale will ensue, leading to operational stalemates. Breakdowns in internal communications between operational units will occur on a frequent and recurring basis. Problems will go unresolved, with mounting consequences to your business.

Corrective Measures:

Anticipate, review, and examine the firm's external environment as it relates to each individual department or division. Analyze the correct internal environment needed to meet these threats. Then establish the appropriate management functions per department/division to minimize or eliminate threats that may be present or anticipated. Communicate to all employees within these operational units (and others who need to know) the logic behind any of your decisions.

#16. HAVE YOU BROKEN DOWN YOUR GOALS AND OBJECTIVES INTO SUFFICIENT DETAIL, SO EACH EMPLOYEE CAN DO HIS OR HER SHARE?

If not, then you are compromising your ability to achieve stated goals and objectives. Your employees will be unsure of what is expected of them, preventing then from producing at optimal levels and achieving benchmarks.

Corrective Measures:

Establish goals and objectives in sufficient detail so that there are no misunderstandings as to what is expected of each person. Make sure you communicate clearly what is to be expected of each employee. Then monitor all results on an individual basis, and modify the goals and objectives if needed.

#17. IS PROJECT PLANNING AN INTEGRAL PART OF YOUR ESTIMATING PROCESS?

If not, your project costs may exceed expectations. Time may be incorrectly estimated and appropriate personnel not available when necessary, or time and effort may be inappropriately applied. These factors can spell disaster for small firms operating on a bid basis, in which your gross revenues are locked in and cannot be adjusted.

Corrective Measures:

Constantly review, measure, and evaluate cost appraisals and estimations to keep costs within estimated project range. Keep projected completions on schedule with an accurate estimate of the time involved. Record all project data for future reference in costing decisions. This historic data is important to your future project cost estimating system.

#18. IS YOUR HOME OFFICE OFTEN MORE CORRECT ON ESTIMATES OF TASK DURATION THAN YOUR FIELD PERSONNEL AND PROJECT MANAGERS?

If not (which is often the case when managing field operations) the home office may not have a realistic view of the overall field project. Home offices generally do not have realistic views of local workers and their abilities. In addition, being separated from field operations, the home office may not be sensitive to the negative impact of such things as foul weather, poor site conditions, field labor problems, and so on.

Corrective Measures:

The home office needs to be sensitive to field input. Maintain a good and close working relationship with field personnel in terms of information flow.

#19. IS YOUR FIELD COST AND TIME REPORTING SYSTEM DESIGNED TO WARN YOU EARLY OF SCHEDULE AND COST OVERRUNS SO YOU HAVE THE TIME TO TAKE CORRECTIVE ACTION?

If not, the cost for travel, labor, materials, and other expenses may exceed the original estimates very quickly, thus compromising profits, and the project at large. Also, scheduling problems will cause hostility between employees, management, and contractors, causing costly delays in terms of project execution.

Corrective Measures:

Develop an appropriate project cost and time reporting system. Ensure that the system is coordinated between field personnel and the home office. Actively involve the appropriate personnel in setting up an accurate and frequent project reporting system. Select someone to be in charge of this process. Working closely with all relevant project employees allows for quick problem identification and resolutions to avoid or minimize difficulties.

#20. DO YOU RELY ON BOTH FIELD AND OFFICE STAFF FOR PROJECT SCHEDULE AND COST REPORTS?

If not, field and office personnel might lack communication. You may not be getting all the necessary information for accurate reporting. There may be no standard or consistency in reporting.

Corrective Measures:

Have frequent project meetings between field and office personnel. Appoint one well-trained and reliable employee (it could even be you as owner-manager) to be in charge of all reports and scheduling. Charge that person with circulating all the relevant reports to the right people.

#21. IN SCHEDULING PROJECTS, DO YOU EMPLOY ADVANCE PLANNING TO ASSURE AN ADEQUATE SUPPLY OF WORKING CAPITAL?

Inadequate funding can delay the completion of your project or plan of action. That can be costly in terms of failed milestones and resource utilization. Customer goodwill could be negatively affected, not to mention monetary penalties and fines imposed by contract agreement because of schedule delays.

Corrective Measures:

Do a detailed projected financial plan for each project and estimate capital requirements. Set up a list of all potential problem areas that may require additional funding, and then budget the project. Analyze and correct variances between amounts budgeted and actual results on a regular basis.

#22. DO YOU GIVE YOUR MANAGERS THE OPPORTUNITY TO PARTICIPATE IN PLANNING FOR VARIOUS PROJECTS? DO YOU INFORM YOUR MANAGERS AND EMPLOYEES ABOUT WHERE THE PROJECT FITS IN YOUR BUSINESS PLAN?

If not, they will not fully understand what is expected of them and what the final outcome should be. The finished project may not be anything like the original plan. Lack of close communication with your people in reference to project management will lead to project down time, labor problems, miscommunication, and so on, and have a detrimental impact on client goodwill.

Corrective Measures:

Let your project managers and employees get involved at all levels of the planning stages so they can be fully aware of every detail and what is expected of them. Spend time making sure you listen to their ideas and others that will directly affect the outcome of the project. This is not wasted time, and could ultimately affect project productivity, project outcome, and employee morale in very positive ways. When and where appropriate, spend additional time getting to know contract laborers and craftsmen and listen to their ideas.

#23. DO YOU HAVE SOMEONE READY TO TAKE YOUR PLACE IN CASE OF AN EMERGENCY?

If not, the business could come to a grinding halt. Critical decisions may not be made, thereby compromising continued existence. The business may cease to exist altogether.

Corrective Measures:

A well-trained administrative assistant can carry on in your interim absence. Delegate authority on a continuing basis to ensure that others can make critical decisions in your absence. A good key-man insurance policy will provide enough money for a replacement, whether family, partner, or employee, to fund continued operations or initiate a new start.

#24. ARE YOU GROOMING SOMEONE TO ASSIST AND SUCCEED YOU AS GENERAL MANAGER?

If the answer to this question is no, then your business lacks management depth. If illness or death strikes, no one would be available to assume leadership and carry on business activity. Also, as your business grows, task-handling can become too burdensome and time-consuming for you to handle alone.

Corrective Measures:

An administrative assistant would give you time to manage and expand your company the right way. Also, new blood could introduce and advance new ideas within your company that may develop into revenues and profits. In addition, an heir apparent can be groomed to assume command one day. In the alternative, an exit strategy that minimizes taxes and optimizes payout should be planned well in advance.

Organizational Structure

CHAPTER 3

EVALUATION IS NECESSARY

Legal forms of organization

It is vitally important that entrepreneurs select the correct form of legal structure. Whether a new business or an existing operation, the legal form will determine to a great extent the way in which business is conducted, not to mention tax affairs. It will also affect the degree of freedom to operate within the total business environment. Selecting the most appropriate form of legal organization is easier said than done. Many aspects must be examined, taking into account both personal and business considerations.

There are seven kinds of legal structure in general use today. They are: sole proprietorship, general partnership, limited partnership, corporation, subchapter S corporation, limited liability company, and business trust. Each has unique characteristics with certain advantages and disadvantages that need to be evaluated. The form which best suits you and your business needs should be selected.

Sole proprietorship

More than 95 percent of all businesses in this country are classified as proprietorships. This is the simplest form of legal structure, generally requiring only a local business license to operate. The owner usually serves as manager. The primary advantages of this structure are:

■ Easy to form. Establishing a sole proprietorship is simple and inexpensive, requiring little or no government approval. Check with the local court clerk to determine if there are any licensing requirements.

■ Owner keeps all of the profit. The owner is entitled to all profits generated by the business.

■ Freedom from government regulation. Most government agencies direct their regulatory efforts toward large corporate entities, although the government paperwork requirement for small businesses has increased somewhat over the last decade. Whatever the case, small firms are expected to comply with all local, state, and federal regulations, even though governmental policing is held to a minimum.

■ Low taxes. The owner of a sole proprietorship is taxed as an individual, at a rate normally lower than the corporate tax.

■ Complete control. The owner makes all the decisions and determines management policy.

■ Quick decision-making capability. One person can make quicker decisions than a number of individuals.

■ Little working capital needed. In many cases, a sole proprietorship can be operated with limited capital requirements.

■ Easy to terminate. A sole proprietorship can quickly and easily cease operations without red tape.

Disadvantages of the sole proprietorship form of legal organization are as follows:

■ Lack of continuity. If the owner becomes ill and/or dies, the business may terminate.

■ Unlimited liability. The owner is legally responsible for all debts of the business without question. If the business fails and there are debts outstanding, creditors may sue the owner to satisfy their claims. The owner's personal assets could be at risk. Certain types of loss (physical, personal injury, theft) can be prevented by maintaining adequate insurance programs.

- Capital starvation. Some proprietorships have difficulty raising money because of the limited funding alternatives available to this legal form.
- Owner spread too thin. The owner has to wear many hats, performing a number of diverse business functions (marketing, purchasing, and bookkeeping).
- Lack of expertise. Generally, a proprietorship is a one-person show, with limited experience in many facets of business operations.
- Difficult to transfer ownership. Selling all or part of a sole proprietorship can be equated to the difficulty involved with the transaction of real estate. In many cases real estate is involved.

General partnership

A partnership is defined by the Uniform Partnership Act as an association of two or more persons to carry on as co-owners of a business for profit. Most general partnerships are evidenced by a written agreement called Articles of Partnership. Though these articles are not required by law, most individuals involved in partnerships agree it is in the best interests of all to have a written agreement. In addition, the articles should be recorded with the clerk of the local court as a matter of public record for the protection of all individuals associated with the partnership. Articles of Partnership are designed mainly to spell out the contributions made by each partner to the business, whether by money or property, and the responsibilities of the partners in the firm. The following are the different types of partners that may be involved in partnership activities:

- Ostensible (general) partner. Active in the business and publicly known as being a partner.
- Active partner. Active in the business and may or may not be publicly known as being associated with the firm.
- Secret partner. Active in the firm but not presented publicly as a partner.
- Dormant partner. Inactive in the firm and not presented publicly as a partner.
- Silent partner. Inactive in the firm but can be presented as being associated with the partnership.
- Nominal partner. Not a partner in the firm but held out publicly to be a partner, usually for prestigious reasons. In some cases, these partners can be held liable for partnership activity if their names are used to represent the firm.

■ Sub partner. Not a partner but contracts with an active partner so as to participate in the partner's business and profits.

■ Limited partner. Not involved in managing the partnership, therefore his or her liability is limited to the amount invested and no more.

Here are some of the more common components of a general partnership:

■ name of the partnership
■ purpose
■ date of formation
■ address
■ name and address of partners
■ duration of the partnership
■ contributions made by each partner
■ how business expenses are handled
■ division of profits and losses among partners
■ duties and responsibilities of each partner
■ salary and/or draw of each partner
■ procedure for selling partnership interest
■ method of accounting and record keeping
■ handling the death of a partner
■ how to change the partnership agreement
■ how to handle disagreements
■ dealing with absence and disability
■ required and prohibited actions
■ protection of remaining partners if a partner dies
■ provisions for the retirement of partners

Here are the advantages to the general partnership form of legal structure:

■ Easy to form. Procedures and expenses are minimized.

■ Enhanced capital availability. Two or more people will be providing and searching for capital. In addition, funding sources are more likely to entertain financing requests because of the broader capital base.

■ Low tax rate. General partners are taxed as individuals. The individual tax rate is normally lower than that of a corporation.

■ Better decision-making capability. Two heads are better than one.

■ Higher quality employees. Partnerships tend to attract better employees because of the possibility of becoming a principal in the firm.

- Managerial flexibility. Generally, important decisions can be made quickly, although not as fast as in a sole proprietorship.
- Limited government interference. Like sole proprietorships, partnerships are normally free of extensive governmental scrutiny, although compliance with regulations is a must.

Disadvantages inherent in the general partnership include the following:

- Unlimited liability. The general partners are personally liable for the debts of the partnership. General partners can legally bind each other. This is why it is extremely important to know intimately the partners involved in the firm. Make sure all general partners are credible.
- Lack of continuity. Normally, a general partnership has a limited life and is terminated on the date specified in the Articles of Partnership or upon the death of a general partner. Termination can be avoided by stating in the articles that the partnership is perpetual.
- Divided authority. General partners may disagree, causing organizational disharmony.
- Profits divided. Profits are shared by all general partners.
- Scarcity of suitable partners. Appropriate partners can be difficult to locate.

Limited partnership

Basically, limited and general partnerships share the same characteristics, with a few distinct differences worth noting. A limited partnership is defined as an association of at least one general partner and one limited partner. The limited partner is an individual who only invests capital and does not participate in managing the firm. In fact, the limited partnership form of business organization is viewed by many as a capital generating mechanism used quite frequently in real estate, oil and gas development, and mining deals. Very attractive tax benefits can be passed to investors involved in a limited partnership agreement.

The main thing to remember is that the general partner in a limited partnership has unlimited liability for the debts of the business without question. On the other hand, limited partners are not liable for partnership debts if they do not participate in managing the business. Their personal assets are not at stake if the limited partnership incurs debts. They can only lose the amount invested and nothing more. Keep in mind that recent court rulings have determined that limited partners who actively get involved in management functions and affairs are not, in fact, limited partners and should be considered general partners, thereby assuming unlimited risk for the debts of the partnership. Once a limited partnership generates profits, the general partners are normally rewarded by receiving between one and 20 percent of all income produced after expenses are paid. The remaining 80 to 99 percent is divided among the limited partners. Percentages may vary among different propositions.

Corporation

The corporation is the most complex legal structure discussed thus far. In 1819, Chief Justice Marshall defined a corporation as an artificial being, invisible, intangible, and existing only in contemplation of the law. Consequently, the corporation is a legal entity separate from the people who own or operate it.

Corporations are normally formed subject to approval of the state government in the state in which the corporation will reside. If doing business in a number of states, the corporation needs to get the approval of each state and will be classified as a foreign corporation within those borders.

In order to form a corporation, an organizational meeting must take place. The organizer(s) must draft a corporate charter, also known as Articles of Incorporation which outline the powers and limitations of the proposed corporation. The charter is then submitted to the secretary of state in the domicile state for approval. If the charter is disapproved, the secretary's office will probably recommend changes in the articles of incorporation so as to facilitate a positive decision. Typical articles of incorporation would include the following elements:

- name of the corporation
- purpose
- life of the business
- location
- incorporator(s)
- capital structure
- capital requirement
- preemptive rights
- initial directors
- internal affairs
- charter changes

After the charter is approved by the state, stockholders need to have a meeting to adopt corporate by-laws and elect the board of directors. The board will in turn appoint the corporate officers. The by-laws are designed to serve as internal regulations that govern the operation of the corporation by establishing rights and limitations. Some by-laws will duplicate provisions of the articles of incorporation (charter) and state law. The corporate form of legal structure has definite pros and cons. These are the advantages:

- limited liability
- ease of transferability
- legal entity
- diversified management
- continuous life
- ease in raising capital

The corporate structure can present a number of difficulties to its owners and managers. Here are some of the most common difficulties:

- government interference
- double taxation
- corporate formation
- charter restrictions
- records
- possible liability

FORMING A CORPORATION

It is not really difficult to form a corporation in most states. In fact, many entrepreneurs form their own without legal assistance, thereby saving hundreds or even thousands of dollars. Generally, states will assist in incorporation by providing booklets, forms, and samples to use in the process. Some states actually promote individuals to incorporate within their boundaries by using various incentives. For example, Delaware, Nevada, and Wyoming are very popular incorporation states because of low taxes and a friendly attitude toward corporations. Also, two of these states have no corporate income taxes.

If you want to incorporate in the aforementioned states, here are their contact addresses. They will be more than happy to provide you with the necessary forms, publications, and instructions:

State of Delaware, Division of Corporations
John G. Townsend Building
401 Federal Street Suite 4
Dover, DE 19901
Phone: 302–739–3073
Fax: 302–739–3812
E-mail: DOSDOC_WEB@state.de.us

Nevada Secretary of State
101 North Carson Street
Carson City, NV 89701
Phone: 775–684–5708
Fax: 775–684–5724
E-mail: sosmail@sos.nv.gov

Wyoming Secretary of State
The Capitol Building; Room 110
200 West 24th Street
Cheyenne, WY 82002
Phone: 307–777–7311
Fax: 307–777–5339
E-mail: corporations@state.wy.us

Normally, individuals can incorporate their businesses and expect no legal problems. However, there are instances in which the complexities of the business might necessitate an attorney being involved in the incorporation process. For example, a firm with many investors and/or engaged in interstate commerce might consider using legal assistance in putting the corporation together. The entrepreneur will have to decide if an attorney is needed.

Subchapter S corporation

A number of years ago, Congress recognized the need to increase the flexibility of small firms that use the corporate form of legal structure. Therefore, the subchapter S corporation was created and designed to permit small business corporations to be treated as partnerships from a tax perspective, thereby eliminating double taxation. A standard corporation is taxed on two occasions. It must pay tax on its business income, and then shareholders (owners) are taxed on the portion of net profits distributed and paid as dividends. Subchapter S provisions allow shareholders to absorb all corporate income or losses as partners and report it as individual taxpayers. In essence, the subchapter S corporation is not affected by corporate income taxes, thereby eliminating the double taxation feature of standard corporations. Aside from being treated as a partnership from a tax standpoint, the subchapter S and standard corporation share most of the same pros and cons, with a few exceptions. A corporation must meet certain requirements before the subchapter S alternative becomes feasible:

- The corporation must be a domestic entity (incorporated within the United States).
- The corporation can only have one class of stock.
- Only individuals, estates, and certain tax exempt organization under federal code 401(a) and 501(c)(3) can be shareholders. Also, business trusts under federal code 1361(c)(2)(a) can be shareholders.
- The corporation cannot be part of another organization.
- The number of shareholders may not exceed 100.
- The corporation cannot have any nonresident alien shareholders.
- 20 percent or more of its revenue must be domestically generated.
- No more than 25 percent of the corporation's gross income can be derived from passive investment activities.
- A corporation must first be filed at the state level, calendar year only corporations with fiscal years ending in a date other than December 31 must apply to the IRS for permission or under the provisions of IRS code section 444.

To obtain subchapter S corporation status, a general, for-profit corporation must first be formed by filing articles of incorporation with the appropriate state entity, usually the Office of the Secretary of State. Once the corporation has been formed, you must file Form 2553 with the IRS.

If the corporation meets all of the above requirements and wants to adopt the subchapter S option, it must do so within 75 days of starting business activity. In the case of an existing firm, adoption must be executed sometime within the initial 75 days of the firm's fiscal year. All shareholders in the business must give consent to electing the subchapter S structure. Their willingness will be evidenced by signing IRS Form 2553, which can be obtained by writing the local or regional IRS office. The adoption will remain effective until the corporation decides to cancel the status or the IRS revokes it because the firm has failed to maintain the required conditions. Cancellation will prevent the firm from adopting the sub-S structure a second time in the near future. There is a waiting period of several years before the status can be renewed.

Subchapter S corporations do provide a few very attractive benefits to family corporations. Recent tax legislation has made it extremely advantageous to establish retirement programs under subchapter S provisions. In addition, family members who are shareholders can shift income from one member to another in order to minimize the tax bite. For example, a father in a high tax bracket can shift income to his son whose tax rate is lower, thereby reducing the tax burden on the whole family.

The major negative aspect of the subchapter S legal structure is its limitation on the number of shareholders it can assume (100 maximum). If the corporation is in an expansion mode and needs to raise additional funds over and above the financial capabilities of its present shareholders, the subchapter S status may have to be forfeited. The firm's management will need to evaluate the benefits of receiving the additional capital versus the cost of dropping the subchapter S form of legal organization. In addition, many states refuse to officially acknowledge the subchapter S form; therefore, corporate income or loss is not given preferential treatment under the income tax codes of the hostile state, although federal income tax advantages still exist.

Section 1244 stock and capital gains

Before forming a corporation, it is wise to remember that certain tax incentives are available to make a business an attractive investment to prospective investors who may want to purchase stock (ownership) in the enterprise. When the directors have the first board meeting, they should consider the election of a section under the Internal Revenue Code 1244 that allows an investor to treat a loss in small business stock as an ordinary instead of a capital loss, thereby enhancing its positive tax impact. In order for a corporation to qualify its shares as section 1244 stock, it must approve the concept at the first director's meeting and before the issuances of any equity. Also, the shares issued can only be common stock and must be sold by the firm in exchange for money or property subject to a promulgated plan, with a few restrictions. Another legal limitation states that the amount of capital received for the shares may not exceed certain dollar limits that have been set forth.

In addition, recent reductions in the capital gains tax are making investing in small firms very attractive once again. However, even though the rates have been reduced back down to the 1980 levels, some asset holding periods have been extended. This was done to reduce speculation. For stock to qualify as IRC Sec. 1244 stock, the following requirements contained in Reg. Sec. 1.1244 must be met:

- The stock may only be common stock.
- The corporation issuing the stock must qualify as a small business corporation at the time the stock is issued.

- A taxpayer must transfer money or other property to the issuing corporation in exchange for the stock.
- The corporation must pass a gross receipts test at the time any loss on the stock is sustained by a shareholder.
- Except for the gross receipts test, each requirement must be met at the time the stock is issued.

Limited liability company

This relatively new organizational structure, also known as an LLC, incorporates the best of the seven traditional forms of legal organization. It gives you the opportunity to avoid double taxation. Income and loss flow through to the owners' personal tax returns, eliminating corporate taxation. Also, there are no restrictions on the number of owners and their nationality, as is the case with subchapter S corporations. And there is ease of transferability of ownership.

Also, an LLC eliminates the need for a general partner, which a limited partnership must have. No one within the LLC structure has to sustain personal liability. In fact, that is its greatest feature. Most of the 50 states that have enacted LLC statutes have made it impossible for the owners of the LLC to be held personally liable for the actions of the LLC. In others words, the owners cannot be personally sued if something goes wrong with the LLC. The exception to this rule is if the members of an LLC engage in proven criminal behavior within the LLC. Then the personal guarantee protections are null and void.

A limited liability company is formed by applying to the state in which you want to conduct business. Soon there will be a Uniform Limited Liability Company Act, in which all of the states with limited liability company codes will agree to general standards of application. This will allow a limited liability company to transact business in other states without having to form an LLC in that state, and still provide its owners the same degree of legal protection afforded any LLC.

Business trusts

This a little-known form of legal entity most commonly used to jointly hold real estate assets. Having the similarities of both a limited partnership and limited liability company, its primary purposes are the avoidance of double taxation, limiting personal liability, and maintaining the anonymity of its organizers, investors, and involved third parties. This legal form does not have to be publicly recorded, as is the case with an LLC.

It is advisable to carefully review all forms of legal structure and analyze how they might relate to your particular situation. Spend a few dollars and ask your accountant for some input and then have your attorney look things over. Many people lack the legal and accounting expertise needed to make a sound judgment about legal structure.

Internal forms of organization

The internal method and structure you use to run your company is as important, if not more important, than the legal form you select. Sometimes called informal organization, it is considered by most management experts as the real management system. Most companies, both large and small, are either decentralized or centralized. A decentralized organization is one in which the authority to make decisions is freely delegated down to other employees within the company. Conversely, centralization means that decision power is vested in the hands of one person, or very few people, if it is a larger company.

The determining factor in whether a company is decentralized or centralized is generally the make-up of top management. In other words, is top management dictatorial in nature or laissez-faire (hands-off), or somewhere in between? Most companies are somewhere in the middle but lean in one direction. Generally speaking, the more dictatorial a company, the more likelihood it will be centralized in nature. And as you might guess, the more laissez-faire companies tend to be decentralized.

There is no set model of success here. There are as many successful stories for decentralized firms as there are for centralized ones. However, by the very nature of economics, as firms grow bigger, most are forced into a decentralized posture. Those that resist suffer in terms of contracting markets, revenues, and profits.

Whatever the case, your organization must be clearly identified and outlined to all outside (creditors, vendors, customers) and inside (employees) parties that do business with you. Take particular care in letting your employees know where they stand within the company and their exact duties and responsibilities.

Important Questions to Consider

#1. HAVE YOU CONSIDERED WHAT LEGAL FORM YOUR BUSINESS WILL ADOPT?

Believe it or not, there is a correct and proper legal form you should choose for your business. Failure to do so could put you in harm's way in reference to legal liability, unwarranted taxes, and the inability to raise capital resources.

Corrective Measures:

Read up on the various legal forms, particularly those that may relate to your particular circumstances. You will find that trade journals and general small business magazines provide some good insight on this topic. Most importantly, and as stated earlier, spend a few dollars and get some good legal and accounting advice.

#2. WHAT IS THE NATURE OF LIABILITY FROM A PERSONAL STANDPOINT?

This a very important question, particularly in the litigious society we live in today. Every businessperson can expect at least one major lawsuit in the span of his or her lifetime. So be prepared before the hammer falls. Failure to prepare can lead to loss of personal assets.

Corrective Measures:

Seek legal counsel on this one. Particular attention must be paid to the type of products and/or services you are selling. Some lead to more lawsuits than others. Sometimes insurance is not enough. Insurance companies are getting very particular about coverage, and will try to find any excuse not to cover a claim against your business. This is why most states have developed new forms of legal structures, such as limited liability companies, to help entrepreneurs fight off nuisance claims.

#3. WOULD THE BUSINESS CONTINUE IF THE ENTREPRENEUR OR OTHER KEY PRINCIPALS OF THE FIRM BECAME ILL AND/OR DIED? IS IT IMPORTANT THAT IT DOES CONTINUE?

Some legal structures lend themselves more easily to continue existence in the events that the owner becomes ill, dies, or leaves the business. Some structures automatically terminate should a partner, shareholder, or member resign. Maybe you are so important to the business that it won't survive your death or prolonged illness.

Corrective Measures:

Be diligent and seek legal advice. Many things must be taken into consideration. Is this venture a one-of-a-kind situation, in which the sale of the asset there is no longer a need for a legal structure? Is the venture set up for investing in reoccurring opportunities as they appear? Is the business set up as an ongoing operation? Generally the more technical ability an owner or key employees possess that is pertinent to the business, the greater the threat to the firm should one or more of these employees die, become ill, or leave the firm. If survivability is feasible in the aftermath of such an event, then proper planning is needed.

#4. Which legal structure would allow the greatest flexibility in management?

The key word here is flexibility. Some legal structures, by their very nature, lend themselves to more flexibility in management than others. Corporations are more flexible than sole proprietorships and partnerships because they are not limited to a certain number of owners/managers. Generally, the more populated an organizational structure, the more flexibility in management you can exercise (if you have the luxury of time). However, the reverse can hold true if you are in a business needing quick management decisions because of rapidly changing external factors, such as a competitor lowering prices. In this case, one or two key managers generally respond more quickly than the management team of a corporation.

Corrective Measures:

You must decide which is more important to the business, and balance the management style against the need to make quick decisions. Dictatorships can react quicker than democracies in most cases. Again you can't let the legal structure drive the business, unless there are very sound overriding legal reasons to do so.

#5. Can additional capital be easily sought if needed?

Failure to take this into consideration in the early stages of your business operation can lead to missed opportunities and stymied growth.

Corrective Measures:

Careful planning is needed. The type of enterprise you are running is also important. A small mom-and-pop retail operation's need for capital is different than that of a medium-sized business distribution business. Even a small real estate development company will have different capital needs than a service station. Some firms, both large and small, are driven by the need to raise capital on a continuing basis. The corporation form of legal structure is a good way to raise capital because the shares of stock are easily transferable. Just sign over a stock certificate. Limited partnerships, limited liability companies, and business trusts are almost as easy. Sole proprietorships and general partnerships can be more difficult. The name of the game is to determine whether you will need capital in the future, how much, and how frequently you need it. Get input from both your CPA and attorney.

#6. CAN ADDITIONAL EXPERTISE BE ATTRACTED IF NEEDED?

There is generally a direct relationship between the size of a company and its ability to attract qualified expertise. Corporations tend to be larger businesses, but that is not always the case. However, your legal structure can hamper you in attracting good people, in particular if you are a sole proprietor. Prospective employees will view your company as having limited opportunities in terms of upward advancement.

Corrective Measures:
Consider changing your legal structure to accommodate ease of transferring partial ownership to good employees, either as an employee buy-in or as a bonus. Corporate and limited liability company structures can accomplish this quite nicely. This will stimulate employee productively and positive involvement in the business. The word will get around and good people will come knocking at your door.

#7. DOES THE DEGREE OF REGULATION HAMPER BUSINESS ACTIVITY?

Again, the larger the business, the more regulation you will endure. The more complex the legal structure, the more the regulation. The industry you are in will also affect the degree of regulation. All regulation hampers business activity.

Corrective Measures:
You can't avoid all regulations, but you can attempt to minimize its effects on your operation by the legal structure you choose. Breaking your company down into smaller independent operating units that are separate businesses may help. Trying to keep your business

something less than a corporate form will also help. This is one of the reasons limited liability companies came about. As a hybrid between a corporation and a small legal structure, the benefits of both can be achieved.

#8. WHAT LEGAL FORM CAN BEST FULFILL THE GOALS OF THE ENTREPRENEUR AND BUSINESS?

Only you know this for sure. There are many variables to consider. Avoiding this analysis can prevent you from reaching benchmarks for your business. For example, you can be subject to double taxation under one form of legal structure as opposed to another.

Corrective Measures:

Seek counsel from others in your business and from outside advisers. A good source would be successful competitors that are about your size. Find out what structure they use. Factors such as growth and profit estimates will affect your decision as well as tax impact, management exit strategies, and continuity of the business in the event of crisis impacts on the business. No single best answer will suffice. Your answer will come from studying the unique aspects of your business and then getting input from your advisers. Basically, let the nature of the business venture drive the type of legal structure you need, as opposed to letting the legal structure drive the venture. In a few cases this is not possible, but sometimes several or more legal structures can be interwoven to achieve maximum effect.

Chaos or Control?

CHAPTER 4

One of the most difficult things to do in business is to foster and maintain discipline. This includes the discipline to construct, manage, control, and measure the proper internal systems and procedures that will ensure optimal operational management.

The use of correct systems is crucial to overall productive entrepreneurial management. It is absolutely essential that the best systems and procedures are applied even to a single managerial policy. The best systems and procedures are those that gather information and data on an ongoing basis, and then builds upon those collections to further and consistently refine the systems and procedures. Then they truly become useful management tools.

Systems and procedures (often referred to as standard operating procedures or SOPs) are simply organized common sense. A more appropriate and formal definition may be the organization of company policies, records, data files, forms, and equipment in such a manner that will streamline, simplify, optimize, and standardize operations within a firm. The objective is to focus the company's primary functions such as marketing, finance, manufacturing, shipping, and so on, by means of routine methodology (systems and procedures—SOPs) and stimulate those policies into concrete action.

A system is a number of procedures designed to accomplish an outcome. By using systems and procedures, a task can be accomplished with less effort and more effectiveness. SOPs make up more than just normal office routines related to accounting procedures, inventory control, and manufacturing processes. They are tools by which you can convert broader company policies into outright action and execution.

Records come in numerous forms, depending upon the type of operation and the nature of the systems themselves. They are used to record facts for future use. For example, sales feedback that analyzes sales by area, product, and type of customers are records that can be used in making marketing decisions in the future.

A system is a smaller part of the overall enterprise. It holds the organization together; guaranteeing an order and method that will be used throughout all operations of the firm. When managers follow a system, records will be maintained and stored by procedure.

When SOPs are tested and performing well within your business, you can begin to operate by the exception principle of management. Your employees will have guidelines and guideposts by which to run the day-to-day operations of your business. Consequently, you will be freed up from the mundane issues within the business and only manage the bigger picture issues with the operation. It also frees up your time to spend on more important factors within your business, such as opening new markets, finding new vendors, or identifying less expensive sources of capital.

INSTALLING SYSTEMS AND RECORDS

Where systems will be required

Before implementing a records system, its purpose and the particular systems and procedures using the records should be considered. The abilities of your employees who will be responsible for the systems must also be carefully reviewed. SOPs are generally necessary in the following operational areas:

- education and training
- equipment utilization
- office management

- plant operation
- production coordination
- records and data management
- research and development

In building an effective set of SOPs, detailed information and data will need to be extracted from the following functions within the business:

- cost accounting
- finance and credit
- general accounting
- inventory control
- production
- purchasing
- quality control
- sales
- warehouse and shipping

DESIGNING A SYSTEM

When developing a new system to achieve a particular management policy, you must consider the following items in great detail:

- system objectives
- system requirements
- employee skill level
- system policy
- system details
- system cost
- system effectiveness
- interrelationships
- forms, records, and reports

Gathering and analyzing such information requires time and money. Study the result and use it as the basis for a new program or system, or to update an old system. Any new or modified system should do the following as a bare minimum:

- provide accurate, adequate, and timely information and data
- be simple, inexpensive, and easy to change
- provide for management by exception
- help plan for the future

The role of total systems management

Modern computerization and data management/accounting software has given rise to the ability of a small firm to totally integrate its internal procedures and control. Data flow all the way from the raw materials loading dock to the customer shipping dock can be integrated and managed to increase organizational productivity and profitability.

Conclusion

The SOPs and supporting records and systems you establish and the overall effectiveness of your decisions will depend on the information and records your company generates. You should review these systems frequently to make sure the data being generated is both accurate and reliable. You should make modifications as your business grows and policies change. Also, you must develop records and systems that will assist in making the most productive use of your time and that of your employees. You must keep yourself updated and abreast on current computer hardware and software and how they relate to your particular industry and particular company. Most trade associations within your industry will have great recommendations on issues ranging from standard SOPs to use within your business to suggesting what computer hardware and software to use to support your systems and records.

You will also need to constantly update the managerial skills of your employees, in particular those who will manage your systems and records. Believe me, the best rewards are the extra time gained and money saved for managing more productively and the achievement of both business and personal goals.

Important Questions to Consider

#1. ARE ALL SYSTEMS AND PROCEDURES UNDER THE CONTROL OF ONE INDIVIDUAL OR DEPARTMENT?

If they are not, there will be a lack of uniformity in procedures. Various departments and systems may not be appropriately compatible with each other and may cause conflict. There may be duplication of procedures when it is not necessary. Multiple individuals involved in the management of SOPs will lead to communication breakdowns and organizational confusion.

Corrective Measures:

SOPs should be under the control of one designated individual within the company, or division/department if a larger firm, in order to ensure proper conformity in terms of work flow and problem resolution. Periodically review procedures for effectiveness to ensure that they are not obsolete and in need of modification or elimination. Update procedures as changes warrant.

#2. ARE FORMS AND RECORDS CONTROLLED IN YOUR FIRM?

Without proper attention and periodic review, a massive proliferation of forms will occur in most firms, regardless of size or industry. Forms may continue to be used long after their operational usefulness to the company. Records may be kept longer than needed, thereby wasting space, which is a cost factor. This can lead to unnecessary clerical expense and management effort, not to mention reporting errors throughout the company's management information system.

Corrective Measures:

Review your forms yearly to see if they are still needed. Review forms to see if any can be combined; combine or eliminate forms where possible. Investigate whether automated data processing and/or storage could be cost effective in keeping in terms of forms management.

#3. ARE YOUR NUMBERING AND REFERENCE SYSTEMS CONSISTENT, COMPATIBLE, AND EASY TO UNDERSTAND AND USE?

Nothing is more frustrating, expensive, inefficient, and draining (from a management prospective) than a confusing, duplicating, or inadequate control system that will not match up numbers and reference codes to invoices, bills of lading, or shipping documents. Time will be wasted in managing incorrect information. Data can easily be miscoded and training employees to use your current system could be costly in terms of inefficiencies.

Corrective Measures:

Immediately review and evaluate your current system. If necessary, design an effective and efficient system that works for your business. Then train all your employees to understand and use it properly. Be sure the new system is computer compatible.

#4. Have you investigated the use of system packages for your accounting functions, inventory control, material requirements, and similar activities?

Whether your management information system is specifically designed for your particular company or purchased from a third-party vendor, it is important to ensure that all software function in unison to support each other. Using separate programs to support different business functions within the business is inefficient, costly to maintain, and will lead to significant computer downtime. The ability to coordinate information in an efficient and timely manner will suffer. Most importantly, you may be spending too much time and money using a system that could otherwise be designed, purchased, and operated more efficiently. Your less-than-integrated systems are not as flexible or versatile, and generally lack important features.

Corrective Measures:

Have a computer software development company demonstrate various package system alternatives to see if one meets your needs. Purchase only if you find it to be beneficial and it provides adequate training and support. You may want to consider a computer consultant. Many small firms can save lots of money by spending a few hundred dollars for sound advice.

#5. Do you regularly revise forms and records which involve obligations and commitments to outsiders?

Times change, and so do the terms of operation with outside third parties who do business with your firm. Whether the changes are positive or negative to the company, periodic and timely assessment of forms and existing records is necessary to ensure that commitments and obligations, be they governmental or private in nature, meet with the desired intent given where your company finds itself at the moment. You may find you are making obligations/commitments that are not needed or desired. Or the terms of the obligations may be, or have become, more expensive than you previously thought. Some obligations and commitments may be obsolete or not needed due to recent product/service improvements or other factors, such as changes in the competitive environment.

Corrective Measures:

Evaluate all contracts and forms related to obligations and commitments on a periodic basis. Make sure your control forms are giving you the information that would assist you to make a change when necessary. For example, do you have forms that would alert you to a sudden increase in liability insurance premiums for your business? Create, implement, evaluate, and modify your control forms in reference to your company's obligations and commitments.

#6. ARE YOUR PRODUCTION ACTIVITIES AS UP-TO-DATE AS YOUR KNOWLEDGE OF TECHNOLOGY AND COMPETITIVE ORGANIZATION?

If not, your costs of production may be disproportionately higher than other facets of your business operation. Additionally, you may not be producing as good a product as the latest technology will permit, thus allowing your competition ever increasing shares of the marketplace.

Corrective Measures:

Evaluate the latest technology to determine potential improvements for your production. Implement the latest improvements if it would be cost effective and further production efficiencies.

#7. DO YOU KNOW HOW PRODUCTION ACTIVITIES PROVIDE "THRUST" FOR YOUR ORGANIZATION?

If not, certain areas of production within your company may not be running efficiently. One section may be out of synchronization, waiting on another section to produce as quickly.

Corrective Measures:

Evaluate and cost out current and proposed production activities applicable to your business. Decide which ones would be beneficial to your company and implement the ones that would increase efficiency.

If you are a manufacturer, understand that production efficiency is the fuel that feeds your company's fire, and thus profits. Even small changes may pay big benefits.

#8. Are your production activities flexible so that you can react to a variety of circumstances?

You may experience delays in production if breakdowns occur and you don't have a backup plan of action, such as shifting production internally if possible, or contract manufacturing (outsourcing your production). Also, you may not be able to increase production on short notice if increased demand occurs, or be able to modify and change your process quickly enough to accommodate changes in demand.

Corrective Measures:

Determine how flexible you can afford or need to be. Create a plan of action for if your production goes down. Also, determine a time factor and a game plan for increasing production, if demand warrants an increase.

#9. Do you have adequate data on costs of operations so that break-even points can be calculated for a variety of individual and simultaneous production runs?

If you don't, minimum and smaller production runs may be more expensive than you realize, thus compromising your profit margins. Higher production runs, even with overtime, may be more cost effective. Without break-even data, your pricing may not be adequate.

Corrective Measures:

Assemble break-even data on production runs of various sizes and compare this information with industry norms. Modify your production and implement any new methods that help production efficiency.

#10. Are your production and related operations capable of the following:

a. Providing the standards in components and manufacturing techniques which are important to your customers?

b. Maintaining quality consistent with production costs and sales prices?

c. Furnishing services which compliment the production aspects of your products?

d. Meeting customer shipping dates on time?

If you answered no to any of these questions, you are endangering your customer goodwill. Your product or service will get an undesirable reputation over a period of time, thus compromising your markets. Customers will switch to competitor products or services, rather than continuing or expanding a business relationship with your company.

Corrective Measures:

Set standards of performance that will impress your customers. Be sure service is available and advertise it as a selling point. Design and build value-added quality into your product or service, and then promote it as a selling point. Review and develop proper production and shipping coordination to meet customer shipping dates.

#11. Does your production control system provide timely, accurate data on all stages and aspects of the production processes?

If not, you may be overproducing, resulting in excessive and/or wasteful inventories, which is a negative cost factor. Costly delays in production may occur because of the use of inefficient methods. Additionally, underproduction may occur, which can have devastating effects on customer goodwill, particularly if late shipments occur because of the underproduction.

Corrective Measures:

Set up a system to get timely data feedback. Cross check the system to ensure that data is accurate. Be sure the system gives fast and accurate data on each phase of production. Use this information to improve production capability in terms of avoiding costly delays, overproduction, and underproduction. If these events occur, you need to know why and then forecast how to deal with the fallout. Some of these events will be recurring and others nonrecurring. The trick is to know which is which per production run or by customer, and then plan ahead. Generally, it is well worth the money to procure professional accounting assistance when developing production control systems.

#12. Do you really know what aspects of production and operations produce the major portions of profit for your firm?

If not, you may be concentrating your resources and efforts in the wrong areas. Costly inefficiencies will ensue, and you may make decisions that will damage your more profitable operations. Also, you could be hurting the employees who benefit you the most, thus hurting morale and productivity.

Corrective Measures:

Set up an internal control system that shows you the costs and efficiencies of each operation within the business. Study the data to learn which production operations are the most profitable and why. Determine where inefficiencies exist and then move to correct them or minimize their effect on the company.

#13. Do your budgets provide rewards for improved performance?

If not, your employees will lack the will and desire to improve in their jobs. Employee productivity will lag, and it could even have a negative effect on morale. There may be too many employees on the payroll because the lack of performance incentives is holding back those employees who would be stimulated and more productive with an incentive program in place.

Corrective Measures:

Budget additional monies for incentives that reward enhanced and ongoing improvements in performance. Research other incentive methods appropriate to your industry and business. Implement them if they make sense.

#14. Do you express your plans in terms of a budget, covering sales, stocks, markups and expenses?

Lack of careful budgeting may allow ongoing losses in critical profit centers, or even the business as a whole. Your business could be in financial trouble before you are aware of this fact. Mistakes could be made in determining exact problem areas.

Corrective Measures:

See that each profit center is placed on an operational budget, and the company as a whole. Constantly review your budgets and make changes where necessary in order to control costs. Always evaluate your budget estimates against actual expenditures. Use this information for future budgeting and planning purposes.

#15. Do you set up your budget for relatively short periods?

If not, it may be difficult to see what seasonal factors may do to your business. Some parts of the year may require special planning. This is particularly true in the agricultural industry.

Corrective Measures:

Budget for relatively short periods, when appropriate. Analyze the budget versus actual expenses over these shorter budget periods and adjust accordingly. Most experts recommend at least quarterly budget planning, but play it safe and do it monthly.

#16. Do you make an organized, planned effort to determine the potential sales of your product or service in your immediate community?

If not, and most of your sales are concentrated outside your immediate area, you may be missing some great sales opportunities for your products or services right under your nose. And let's not forget the public relations and political value of doing business in your own community.

Corrective Measures:

Review your goods and/or services often to see if they could be sold within your community. Determine whether any new developments have arisen in the community through which you could expand your market potential. If so, develop a game plan to exploit them.

#17. In controlling your operations, do you frequently compare actual results with the budget projections you have made, and do you then adjust your marketing promotion and expense plans as indicated by the deviations from these projections?

If not, you may be overspending in various areas, or not generating the revenues needed to cover costs, and not be aware of these factors until the checks start bouncing. Additionally, you may not realize which areas of expenditures pay the best returns for dollars spent.

Corrective Measures:

Review the budget projections versus the actual expenditures frequently. Decrease expenses where needed, and/or increase revenues, if possible. Don't be afraid of spending money to take advantage of opportunities that will reap benefits—even if it means busting the budget. Just remember to get back a return that covers the budget overrun plus some profit.

#18. Do your key employees have a voice in formulating budget plans concerning them?

If you don't let them participate they may feel ignored, unappreciated, and unhappy. They may see areas within the business where funds could be better spent, thus saving you money, and enhancing profits for the company.

Corrective Measures:

Allow your employees to participate in the budget process to see if their suggestions correlate with your goals and objectives. Allow them to give you suggestions and critique your budget proposals. You will find that some employees can be quite creative in terms of cutting costs.

#19. Do you think in terms of ratios and percents, rather than exclusively in dollars-and-cents?

If not, you may be deceived into thinking big money means big net profit, when quite often that is not the case. You may not realize when an increasingly higher percentage of cost is yielding decreasing rates of marginal returns. Also, you may not realize when a small investment in expenses could yield a high percentage of return.

Corrective Measures:

Be sure you understand the concept of ratios and percentages. Review key business ratios to understand how they can give you insight into running your operation. Apply and review data from your business in the ratio and/or percentage format on a frequent basis. Both Dun & Bradstreet and Robert Morris Company can assist you in this area by providing the raw ratio data for your industry and business, as well as providing numerous publications on how to use ratio analysis.

Big Government

Chapter 5

The dreaded tax monster

You should never have any problems paying your taxes. You must develop a system designed handle all federal, state, and local tax obligations. "Taxes" is not a bad word. Don't let it become a nightmare scenario of anxiety and confusion. Planning, controls, and the correct procedures for collecting taxes, safekeeping funds, and paying to the proper taxing authorities will make life a lot easier.

Managing taxes

The successful management of your tax obligations will encompass the following:

■ Always keep abreast of your total tax liability.
■ Know what different kinds of taxes need to be paid.
■ What are the dollar amounts per category?
■ When are they due per category? Different taxes have different due dates.

- Set aside the money to pay the various taxes in specified tax accounts.
- Pay taxes on time. Late penalties can very expensive.
- From time to time, get expert advice from a qualified licensed professional.

Trustee and debtor

You will play two distinct roles in managing your tax situation. You are a trustee, and at the same time a debtor. As a trustee, the taxing authorities give you the responsibility to collect the taxes due and to pay them to said authorities on a timely basis; so be diligent in this regard! When you do not pay these taxes, it is viewed as violating a trust between you and the taxing authority. The monetary penalties are severe and can even be considered criminal in nature, leading to jail time. You can also be held personally responsible for the taxes, interest, and penalties due for late tax payments.

As a debtor, you hold liability for the various taxes and payments to various tax authorities as part of your overall business obligations. Be they income taxes paid quarterly, excise taxes paid monthly, or real estate tax paid once a year, they are all tax obligations that bear the burden of penalties, personal liability, and potential criminality if not managed in good order.

Be you a trustee or debtor, the critical issue for you is the duty and obligation for collecting taxes on behalf of taxing authorities and paying those taxes when due. The way you think and manage your taxes should be standard operating procedure within your business, and needs to be flexible enough to accommodate the various taxing jurisdictions.

Tax overview

The form of business you operate determines what taxes you must pay and how you pay them. The following are the four general types of business taxes:

- income tax
- self-employment tax
- employment tax
- excise tax

BE BUSINESSLIKE

In managing your tax obligations, always exercise good business principles. Manage taxes as you would other aspects of your business. Always report and pay taxes when due. Failure to file or pay taxes when due can bring stiff penalties (fines and/or jail sentences) and interest on the tax money due. You can be held personally responsible for taxes due by your business. In addition, criminal charges may be imposed. Have cash on hand when a particular tax is due. Put the funds in a separate bank account on a regular basis.

If you use employee withholding trust funds for operating capital, it is a very expensive form of borrowing. Most borrowers of withholding taxes think they will return the money in short order, but they don't. It will generally take the Internal Revenue Service eight or nine months to catch up with offenders. By this time penalties and interest have assessed to a point where the effective cost of borrowing this money is anywhere between 25 and 48 percent. It is easy to tap into these withholding funds for operational capital. The funds are just sitting there for the taking! But the consequences are far reaching, and can even lead to jail time in extreme cases.

In closing, always pay taxes by check with your tax account number and type of tax paid written on the check and check stub of each check. In the case of direct transfer via electronic funds transfer (EFT), make sure your check register, general journal, and general ledger contain the same information.

THE DREADED REGULATOR

Laws and regulations

The following are common types of codes, laws, and regulations. This is just general information and not intended as a replacement for good legal advice. Competent legal advice should always be sought for:

- licensing
- government regulations
- regulations for consumer protection
- laws protecting the environment
- laws encouraging competition
- labor relations

Important Questions to Consider

#1. Is the person who prepares your payroll kept up to date on maximum wages for payroll tax purposes?

If not, incorrect tax amounts could be withheld from your employees' pay. You as the employer may be held liable for incorrect withholding.

Corrective Measures:

Keep up to date on withholding regulations and guidelines through contact with appropriate government agencies, their publications, and your accountant. Have your payroll calculations double checked internally to stop and correct errors. If some of your sales are subject to state and/or local sales tax, apply the same procedures as you would with your withholding taxes.

#2. Do you adequately differentiate between taxable and nontaxable sales?

If you do not, you will not know how much of your sales revenue is subject to tax collection and payment, thereby placing you at risk in terms of overpaying, hence lost profits or underpaying, thus creating a tax liability, along with penalties and interest. If you are audited by the tax authorities, you may have no way to prove that you collected and paid tax on the correct amount of sales. Worst of all, you may charge tax on sales which should be nontaxable, which raises the price of your products or services, thereby making you less competitive in the marketplace.

Corrective Measures:

Be sure you know which types of transactions are taxable and which are not. Set up your invoicing and accounting system to clearly differentiate between taxable and nontaxable sales. Get help from a professional. Collect, record, and pay sales taxes accordingly.

#3. Do you have detailed equipment records?

If not, you may not be receiving the proper deductions for depreciation expenses on your tax returns. If you claim too little, this could reduce your cash flow. If you claim too much, you may be building up a tax liability that comes back to haunt you. Your balance sheet may not accurately reflect equipment assets. In case of an audit, you may have difficulty proving values claimed.

Corrective Measures:

For each piece of equipment, be sure to keep complete and accurate records. Be sure that you update depreciation annually with correct balance sheet and income statement figures. If you buy equipment during the year, be sure to create a detailed record for each item purchased. Request from your accountant depreciation formulas that can be used and have this person explain the depreciation process to you, so no unwarranted surprises surface at tax time or during an audit, should that occur.

#4. HAVE YOU DISCUSSED WITH YOUR ACCOUNTANT AND ATTORNEY WAYS IN WHICH YOU MAY REDUCE YOUR FEDERAL INCOME TAX?

If not, you may be unaware of changes in accounting methods which could save you money on taxes. You might be able to make other changes in your corporate or operational structure to create tax savings which are not presently apparent. Also, you may not know about recent tax law changes that could save money.

Corrective Measures:

Regularly consult with your accountant and attorney and ask for ideas about tax savings. Be willing to make accounting, operational, and corporate structural changes if necessary to reduce your tax liability. Generally, the few dollars you pay for this periodic review is worth the investment.

#5. IF YOUR BUSINESS IS A PARTNERSHIP OR A CORPORATION, HAVE YOU ARRANGED FOR CONTINUATION OF THE BUSINESS IN THE EVENT OF YOUR DEATH?

If not, the person or persons you want to assume your ownership may be unable to do so. The business may have to be dissolved because of legal problems resulting from your death. Your heirs may suffer unforeseen and burdensome financial and legal consequences.

Corrective Measures:

Prepare a plan of succession with the help of your attorney and accountant. Make sure this plan is in writing and is understood and accepted by all principals and significant third parties. Provide financial support (such as building cash reserves or key-man insurance) for heirs left behind.

#6. I~F~ YOUR BUSINESS IS A CORPORATION, IS YOUR STOCK S~ECTION~ 1244 ~STOCK?~

If not, and your company fails, you may not be able to claim the loss on your personal income taxes against ordinary income. You would have to claim it as a capital loss, which would mean a significant reduction in tax benefit in most cases. Also, Section 1244 stock is an investment inducement. Because of the treatment of potential losses described above, without 1244 stock, potential investors may be less likely to provide capital.

Corrective Measures:

Consult your accountant or tax attorney regarding shares which may qualify as 1244 stock. If your stock qualifies, find out how you can claim losses against your ordinary income, and what limits apply.

#7. I~F~ YOU HAVE A PENSION PLAN OR A PROFIT SHARING PLAN, HAVE YOU CONFERRED WITH YOUR ATTORNEY REGARDING THE REPORTING REQUIREMENTS TO THE FEDERAL AND STATE GOVERNMENT AS WELL AS TO YOUR EMPLOYEES?

If not, you may be fined for failure to report correctly, in addition to losing some potential tax benefits as well. This is also a red flag area for federal and state auditors. In rare cases, you may fine yourself open to suit by your employees.

Corrective Measures:

Check with your attorney and/or accountant to make sure you are meeting the current requirements. Periodically check back with them to see if any changes in reporting requirements have occurred. Comply with the changes immediately.

#8. I~F~ YOU PROVIDE WARRANTIES, HAVE YOU HAD YOUR ATTORNEY CHECK THE WORDING OF THESE WARRANTIES TO COMPLY WITH CURRENT LAWS?

Because warranty agreements are legal contracts, you may inadvertently leave yourself open to suits. Also, you may be promising more than the law requires, thereby increasing your warranty costs unnecessarily.

Corrective Measures:

Have all existing warranties reviewed by your attorney. Immediately make any recommended changes to the warranties to protect yourself from potential legal actions and other unnecessary claims. Periodically review your warranty package with your legal counsel and trade association if possible.

#9. IF YOU OFFER CREDIT, HAVE YOU ARRANGED TO GIVE CUSTOMERS THE NOTICE REQUIRED UNDER THE CONSUMER CREDIT PROTECTION ACT AND OTHER APPLICABLE LOCAL, STATE, AND FEDERAL LAWS RELATED TO THE GRANTING OF CREDIT?

If not, that's a big mistake! Savvy customers of today may sue for inadequate notice. You cannot legally impose service charges without adhering to the terms of this act. You may not be able to enforce collection procedures on overdue accounts.

Corrective Measures:

Again, consult with your attorney and/or appropriate government agencies regarding the requirements under this and other consumer credit acts. Instruct yourself and others in your credit department regarding the appropriate procedures to be followed. Be sure that required notices are given to all of your customer accounts and all other requirements are fulfilled. Periodically review changes in consumer credit laws and modify procedures accordingly when appropriate.

#10. HAVE YOU CONSIDERED WHETHER ANOTHER TYPE OF BUSINESS ORGANIZATION, FOR INSTANCE A CORPORATION FORM, WOULD LIMIT YOUR LEGAL LIABILITY?

Your current organization may not give you enough protection in the event of legal action against you, such as product liability suits, employee suits, or vendor suits. Your personal assets may be in jeopardy in the case of legal action against your business.

Corrective Measures:

Discuss with your attorney the pros and cons of the various forms of legal organization. Refer back to Chapter 3, where we discuss the various forms and their particular advantages and disadvantages. Determine whether you need to change your form of organization, and do so if need be. Arrange personal assets and/or adopt the legal organization that provides the optimal protection in terms of both personal and tax liability. You may find you have to pay a little more tax to get a little more legal protection, and a little less legal protection for a smaller tax burden. Your attorney and/or accountant can sort it out for you. Today there are new legal forms that can generally fit the bill by finding a balance between personal legal liability and tax liability.

#11. ARE YOU FAMILIAR WITH THE INDEX OF LAWS REGULATING BUSINESS IN YOUR STATE?

If not, you will be unable to find legal information critical to your business. Also, you may not be up to date on recent changes in state laws. You will be unable to make quick reference to immediate legal issues facing your business.

Corrective Measures:
Check with your local library to locate a copy of your state's law index, and then locate the sections regulating your business. Review these sections carefully. Also, ask your attorney to make this information available to you, since he or she is likely to have a legal library and can make reference checks.

#12. HAVE YOU REVIEWED STATE AND LOCAL LAWS WITH AN ATTORNEY TO FIND OUT HOW THEY AFFECT YOUR BUSINESS OPERATIONS?

If not, the business may not be operating in accordance with the applicable laws that apply to your business. You could be spending time and money trying to comply with laws that do not affect your business. You may not be in proper compliance even with laws you know about.

Corrective Measures:
Discuss with your attorney and/or state and local officials any and all laws which apply to your business. Be sure you understand the implications and ramifications of these laws. Make any changes necessary in your business to achieve full compliance with the applicable laws.

#13. DO YOU KNOW IF YOUR STATE OR LOCAL GOVERNMENT HAS AN ADMINISTRATIVE AGENCY THAT REGULATES YOUR BUSINESS?

If your answer to this question is no, then you may be subject to certain administrative regulations you don't know about, and thus you will find your business in a state of noncompliance. You may also be subject to special licensing or reporting requirements through this agency. Additionally, you may not be aware if your business is eligible for certain kinds of assistance through such an agency.

Corrective Measures:
Find out what state or local agencies may regulate your type of business and what regulations may apply to your situation. Comply with their regulations at once. Determine if the agency offers any special services useful to you.

#14. IS YOUR BUSINESS LOCATED IN A STATE OR MUNICIPALITY WHERE THE ADMINISTRATION OF REGULATION IS DYNAMIC, AGGRESSIVE, AND PRO-BUSINESS?

If not, your business operations may be limited by overzealous regulators and/or outdated regulations. The business may find itself in an area that is negative toward business development and growth. Your business may not be receiving attractive services and tax incentives available in other states.

Corrective Measures:
Find out what other areas in your state, or other states, have more favorable business climates. Consider the value of moving your business to one of these areas. Make the move if the advantages outweigh the disadvantages. Become politically active to modify and/or change existing laws that may affect your business or the business community at large.

#15. ARE YOU AWARE OF AND IN COMPLIANCE WITH CURRENT ENVIRONMENTAL REGULATIONS, BOTH STATE AND FEDERAL?

If not, you will not be aware of the recent changes in these regulations that may affect your business in a favorable or negative way. Noncompliance will surely occur and you may be fined or have your business closed down. You may be subject to serious legal penalties and personal liability imposed by federal, state, and/or local authorities.

Corrective Measures:
Be sure you are fully informed of all federal, state, and local environmental regulations and laws which currently apply to your business. Develop methods and procedures to ensure that you can fully comply with these demands. Follow up to make sure that all of your employees are educated about proper compliance, and stay within the required guidelines and milestones.

#16. Do you have current information on what you must do to comply with equal opportunity legislation?

If not, you may be subject to fines or other litigation for noncompliance. Employees and/or potential employees (rejected job applicants) may bring suit for lack of compliance. Criminal charges may also ensue.

Corrective Measures:

Find out about current equal opportunity regulations which apply to your business. Change any operations or procedures so that you are in compliance with the requirements under law.

#17. Have you taken steps to ensure you are in compliance with federal and state requirements for minority quotas in your work force, should they apply to your business?

You may be subject to quotas and not know it. Quotas, laws, and regulations are changed periodically, and may be different if your work force has grown. You may be subject to employee and/or governmental litigation if you are not in compliance.

Corrective Measures:

Even though federal quota systems are slowly being phased out, many states still maintain quota standards, as do some private firms. Inquire about quota laws and regulations. Ask state and government agencies and/or your corporate attorney for guidance. If you are not in compliance, take immediate steps to correct the problem. Periodically inquire about any changes in the regulations.

#18. Do you check periodically to determine if the labels on your merchandise satisfy the various laws and regulations?

If not, you may be violating numerous laws and regulations and may be liable. Labeling laws are frequently changed and you may no longer be in compliance. Costly litigation could occur. You could be restrained from selling your products.

Corrective Measures:

Keep abreast of all labeling laws and modifications. Your trade association should provide assistance in following changes. Modify your labeling immediately when necessary. Seek help from your attorney if you are unsure of legal interpretations and ramifications.

Inventory, Equipment, and Location

CHAPTER 6

NEED FOR PROMPT ACTION

Inventory problems often require prompt corrective action. In many businesses, the market life of inventory is short, and if inventory is insufficient when market demand peaks, sales and profits are lost. If inventory is excessive when demand declines, the excess must be cleared, often at sharply reduced prices.

These distinct problems are particularly sensitive in certain businesses. The market life for the latest hit record may be just a few months. For seasonal greeting cards, the market life is just a few weeks, and for fresh fruit, produce, and baked goods, the market life is measured in mere days.

Inventory is the single largest asset in many retail and wholesale operations. Control of this investment is vital. It will eliminate a number of the problems associated with capital shortages and will provide financial recourse to permit expansion of operations for increased sales and profit.

Controlling inventory levels

You can provide a suitable assortment and supply to meet market requirements while minimizing the risk of excessive investments simply by controlling the inventory levels in your business. This can be accomplished by:

- Investing in inventory wisely so that excessive capital is not tied up. Excessive space is not required, and the investment does not force unnecessary borrowing and interest expense.
- Creating and maintaining accurate, up-to-date records to help identify and prevent shortages and to serve as a database for decisions.
- Taking prompt action to correct inventory imbalances.

Inventory management

Inventory management can be briefly described as:

- Acquiring an adequate supply and assortment of merchandise that customers can then purchase from you.
- Providing safety stocks to meet unexpected demand or delays in inventory replenishment.
- Maintaining clear, correct, and current records.
- Purchasing the proper assortment of goods in quantities that will maintain inventory levels consistent with business requirements while providing adequate safety stocks.
- Reducing excessive inventories promptly, so that the dollars realized from clearing overstocks can be invested in merchandise with a greater market potential.

Inventory investment control

Inventory investment control is accomplished in two ways:

- Prompt elimination of overstocked items.
- Inventory replenishment in anticipation of customer demand.

Whenever a particular item is overstocked, the overstock should be reduced as promptly as possible. Naturally, the most effective and profitable way is to sell it to customers, even at a discount. However, there are other possibilities. There may be a wholesale market available for certain kinds of inventory. Excessive consumer goods inventories are often sold to bargain basements or warehouse sales to a competitor. You can even arrange wholesale sales to a competitor. Frequently, it is wiser to scrap inventory that shows no sales activity for an extended period of time. In this way, you reduce a misleading overstatement of inventory on your books. At the same time, you make space available for inventory that can be sold at a profit.

Inventory replenishment

Your ability to anticipate customer demand for certain items will help you plan your inventory purchases so that sufficient stocks are on hand to accommodate sales volume (without excesses that cause other problems). Adhering to procedures for inventory replenishment is the key to successful inventory management. Planning your purchases will also help you avoid shortages that can only be filled through forfeiture of discounts or absorption of premium shipping charges. Determining purchasing requirements involves answering two questions:

- What should you buy?
- How much should you buy?

Both questions can be answered by establishing an inventory target for an item you carry to be expressed as daily, weekly, or monthly amount of sales.

Sales forecasting

The first step in estimating expected sales in upcoming months is to calculate—from inventory records—actual sales during an appropriate review period. For example, if you want to determine an appropriate inventory level for ski boots on October 1, it will be of little value to consider sales in July, August, or September. Average monthly sales for the entire year will tell you little or nothing either. A more suitable review period would be the months of October, November, and December of the previous year. In addition, if your sales showed a year-to-year growth rate, you should adjust your review period sales for the average sales growth that your business has experienced in the previous year.

LOCATION

One of the first things you need to consider in structuring your business is finding the appropriate location and a suitable physical plant or office that will allow for an efficient operation and future expansion. The most important factor in selecting real estate is location. A good location will do more for you than even the most ambitious advertising campaign.

While location is a vital concern for retailers because they rely a great deal on visibility and exposure to their target markets, location also plays an important role in success of service and manufacturing.

They need to keep operating costs down, and that means locating near key suppliers in an area that will be cost efficient and zoned for manufacturing. You can also learn a great deal about your location by looking at some danger signals:

- The local unemployment rate.
- The necessity for high school and college graduates to leave town to find suitable employment.
- Declining retail sales and industrial production.

Favorable signs are:

- The opening of chain- or department-store branches.
- Branch plants of large industrial firms located in the community.
- A progressive chamber of commerce and other such civic organizations.
- Good schools and public services.
- Well-maintained business and residential premises.
- Good transportation facilities to other parts of the country.
- Construction activity accompanied by a minimal number of vacant buildings and unoccupied houses for sale.

Site location

Site location is an important factor in determining success, not only for retail businesses, but also for wholesaling, service, and manufacturing businesses as well. According to studies conducted by the Small Business Administration, poor location is among the chief causes of all business failures. When determining a site for a retail operation, you must be willing to pay for a good location. The cost of the location sometimes reflects the volume and/or quality of the business you will generate. Never select a location merely because the facility is open and available. Base your selection of site on the market information you've obtained and the potential in that area.

There are many types of service-oriented businesses, and just as many parameters used in choosing an appropriate site. The most important factor you have to consider for a service location is the type of customer you will attract and how you will service them. Manufacturers will usually be restricted to industrial areas by the zoning laws of most cities. Your main tasks in examining these sites will be to determine the suitability of shipping and loading facilities, the distance to key suppliers of raw materials and to markets, the availability of cheap fuel, and the skill of the support staff in the local area. Among the factors to consider when pinpointing an exact location for your business are:

- anticipated sales volume
- accessibility to potential customers
- rent-paying capacity of the business
- restrictive ordinances
- traffic density
- parking facilities
- proximity to other businesses
- side of the street
- history of the site
- terms of the lease

EQUIPMENT

If you are just starting out or buying an existing operation, having the right equipment is essential to your business enterprise. Whether you are a small service firm or a large manufacturing operation, the right equipment mix is important. Take stock of your situation. There is a tendency for most people to go out and buy the latest technology and gadgets, but maybe used equipment will fit the bill, particularly when it comes to office equipment.

In reference to production equipment, you must balance the cost and efficiency of operation. Technical improvements in such things as production speed, reduced energy consumption, and reduced floor space may more than offset the increased cost. In some cases that may not hold true. Have your accountant assist you with that cost/benefit analysis. Generally, when it comes to computers and communications, the latest technology is both less expensive and more productive, but there is still a right mix.

I remember a $10 million client who had the latest computer hardware and software, not to mention the latest in cell phone technology. The problem was that half of the data stations within the firm were either not used or underused, and 30 of the 95 cell phones he was paying for were sitting idle!

In reference to purchasing an existing business, the same rules apply. You may be stuck with some old equipment that needs updating. But I hope your acquisition price adequately discounted for that situation. The moral of the story is that there is a correct equipment mix for every business of every size in every industry. Do your homework and seek out your trade association and accountant for further input. Many trade associations maintain information and data on equipment mixes. Some larger ones have trained specialists that can assist you with your equipment decisions, or at least point you in the right direction.

Important Questions to Consider

#1. IS YOUR OPERATION CONVENIENT AND EASILY ACCESSIBLE TO YOUR TARGET MARKET?

If not, the cost of transporting and distributing your goods could be devastating, causing you to lose customers.

Corrective Measures:

Compare the area with previous businesses and their success/failure rate. Move closer to your markets if necessary, or consider alternative distribution systems.

#2. IS YOUR CUSTOMER SERVICE TAILORED TO EACH CLIENT IN TERMS OF PROXIMITY TO MARKET?

If not, the concept of individual attention for individual needs is not being considered, and the lack of flexibility could result in a loss of business.

Corrective Measures:

Modify your standard procedure for allowances to various clients, strive for service flexibility, and if possible, adapt the basics to everyone's needs.

#3. ARE YOUR SOURCES OF MATERIALS AND SUPPLIES RELIABLE AND CONVENIENT?

If not, you could be creating a production backlog. Using disreputable suppliers can delay deliveries and impede sales, resulting in a loss of goodwill with your customer base.

Corrective Measures:

Use only reputable suppliers. Determine their reputation by checking with other business associates for references and implementing a trial relationship with the supplier before committing to any long-term contracts.

#4. ARE TRANSPORTATION FACILITIES SUCH AS ACCESS, PARKING, LOADING, AND LIGHTING DEVELOPED AT YOUR SELECTED LOCATION?

If not, a lack of parking and easy access will cause clients to shop elsewhere or never see your place of business. Improper lighting can bring on a higher crime rate within your area. A combination of these factors may cause financial hardships due to lack of sales volume.

Corrective Measures:

Check with other businesses in the area for their concerns. Make a complete study of the area to determine aforementioned needs and perform the modifications, if appropriate. In cost analysis of construction and remodeling, always take into consideration the necessary requirements to ensure profit.

#5. IS A TRAINED LABOR SUPPLY AVAILABLE?

If not, the job cannot be performed properly, and additional unanticipated training could cause major delays, which may result in a loss of revenue and profit.

Corrective Measures:

Check with job services and government agencies to ensure that potential labor exists. Contact high schools, vocational schools, and local colleges to assess their training capabilities, and check into government-sponsored training programs.

#6. HAVE YOU REVIEWED YOUR PRESENT OR PROSPECTIVE OPERATIONS SITE WITH REGARD TO THE FOLLOWING FACTORS:

a. size and expansion possibilities?

Government regulations may limit your expansion plans and you could encounter interference from other businesses that are competing for the same area.

Corrective Measures:

Make your long-range plans and goals based on an accurate location analysis, check on government, state, and local zoning regulations and retain a well-qualified attorney to safeguard your interests.

b. water supplies?

An inadequate supply could impede production. Water that needs chemicals added or removed may involve extra expenses.

Corrective Measures:

Check with municipal suppliers to ensure their supply availability and confirm cost estimates; also have the water tested to ensure your standards.

c. utilities?

An unrealistic estimate of utilities can result in excessive spending; government restrictions may be involved, or the existing utility service may be inadequate for your needs.

Corrective Measures:

Determine which utilities, particularly power, will meet your needs, and then check with similar users to determine any potential problem areas. Finally, consult with utility companies on costs for installation and services, including potential cost increases in the future.

d. waste disposal?

Facilities for proper disposal may not be available and the cost of building an adequate system can be astronomical. Also, government regulations may require a large financial commitment.

Corrective Measures:

Check municipal or landfill regulations regarding the type of system needed, then study all types of regulations and laws and make adjustments as needed. Also, make sure that there are alternatives in case the present system is inadequate.

e. drainage and soil conditions?

Soil that hasn't been analyzed can settle and erode around your work site and under the foundation, causing added expense at later dates. In addition, improper drainage can weaken the foundation and increase your maintenance costs.

Corrective Measures:

Retain engineers who are experts in their field to research all possible conditions and alterations, and then consult the proper authorities regarding any problems and plans.

f. land and development costs?

Developing a location may involve so much time and extra funds that it is uneconomical to cultivate and your land costs may exceed the acceptable range for a profit margin.

Corrective Measures:

Obtain sites that are reasonable in terms of cost. Compare other similar businesses in regard to their initial investments and margins related to land development costs. Consult your local planning officials for tips and ideas.

#7. HAVE YOU NOTICED ANY RECENT TRENDS RELATIVE TO YOUR LOCATION, SUCH AS POPULATION SHIFTS, GROWTH OF SHOPPING COMPLEXES, HOURS OF OPERATION, TRAFFIC FLOW, OR PROPERTY MAINTENANCE?

If not, be aware that decreased population, traffic flows, etc. in an area may result in a decline of sales and profit; just as increased population, traffic flows, etc. may cause problems for other types of businesses, such as manufacturing.

Corrective Measures:

Read and keep up with your local papers, council meetings, and other information pertaining to your area. Listen to your customers and their ideas and needs.

#8. HAVE YOU ANALYZED PLANT LOCATION AND FACILITIES TO DETERMINE WHETHER OR NOT OPERATIONS ARE EFFICIENT?

If not, keep in mind that obsolete and inefficient facilities are expensive to maintain and replace, causing your productivity to suffer. Manufacturers may incur excessive costs in transportation of raw materials to the plant or shipping of finished goods to market, if location is too distant from vendors or customers.

Corrective Measures:

Analyze your delivery and shipping needs before the establishment of your business. Be sure that machine placement, utilization, and material flow are understood as necessary components of a healthy business operation. Relocate your operations if necessary.

#9. ARE YOU ABLE TO MAKE A SOUND DECISION ABOUT MACHINE AND EQUIPMENT OWNERSHIP FOR MANUFACTURING VERSUS PRODUCING PRODUCTS ELSEWHERE?

The costs of manufacturing (workman's compensation, labor, coverage for machine operators, and so on); maintenance of facilities and equipment to meet OSHA standards; fire insurance and any storage requirements may outweigh the costs of purchasing products from other sources.

Corrective Measures:

Research similar operations to determine the requirements for finished and in-service goods, especially if providing seasonal products, and how they operate. Become familiar with the total manufacturing process and any potential changes or innovations expected in your industry. Do a study of all costs involved in manufacturing the products compared to a contract purchase of the same finished goods for resale or use. Make your production decision based on this analysis: Is it cheaper to contract out or not?

#10. DO YOU REGULARLY ASSESS THE POSSIBILITY OF PLANT AND EQUIPMENT OBSOLESCENCE?

Increased productivity may be lost if faster, more efficient equipment is not acquired and utilized. Employee morale on the production line may be lowered by the company's refusal to acquire more up-to-date equipment. The quality of your product may not be competitive with other producers if your equipment is obsolete.

Corrective Measures:

Researching new equipment availability will help you to determine any benefits or disadvantages of acquiring additional or replacing existing equipment. Employees will strive to keep abreast of the latest production techniques if equipment and training are made available to them. Budget planning to include funds for possible replacement or expansion of equipment will help keep products competitive.

#11. HAVE YOU CONDUCTED A FACILITIES MIX ANALYSIS FOR YOUR FIRM?

If you don't explore your complete facilities needs and make-up, you may find your facilities don't allow for optimum production and/ or service. Enhanced profit opportunities will suffer.

Corrective Measures:

Explore short-term and long-term combinations for changes that would be desirable and appropriate. If you are acquiring new facilities, conduct a careful study before making a final selection. Work to initiate a proper mix.

#12. DO YOU MAINTAIN THOROUGH LIFETIME RECORDS ON ACCUMULATED COSTS FOR ALL PLANT AND EQUIPMENT FEATURES?

If not, it will be very difficult to determine replacement capital needs and future budgetary requirements. A lack of records documenting the accumulating lifetime costs for specific plant and equipment features will make it difficult for you to make valid decisions regarding continuation or expansion plans in those areas.

Corrective Measures:

Maintain separate records on each type of plant equipment to include the cost of operation, annual cost of repairs, insurance costs, depreciation expense, and so on.Ensure that your records for all of the above agree with those of your supplier, for greater accuracy in planning future investments.

#13. HAVE YOU DEVELOPED DATA FOR CONSIDERING THE POSSIBILITIES OF PLANT AND EQUIPMENT FAILURES AND THEIR COSTS?

If not, unanticipated plant and equipment failures could result in lost contracts and a loss of goodwill. Unanticipated breakdowns could create a need for borrowing additional capital for repairs and/or replacements that your business can ill afford. Trained employees will seek employment elsewhere as a result of hours lost due to downed equipment.

Corrective Measures:

Prepare a contingency plan for back-up equipment (in order not to necessitate employee layoffs) and locate other sources that can temporarily fill gaps to keep current contracts. Maintain adequate retained earnings or a line of credit with leading institutions to ensure quick repair or replacement of equipment.

#14. DO YOU KNOW THE IMPORTANCE OF THE PLANT AND THE EQUIPMENT IN THE OVERALL SUCCESS OF YOUR FIRM?

Inadequate knowledge of facilities and equipment can slow production, create unanticipated expenses for repairs, replacement, and storage, and can give a negative image to both your prospective consumers and employees.

Corrective Measures:

Study your product or process layouts. Worker machine sheets and time motion studies should determine the best use of plant and equipment. Prepare flow diagrams, showing the relationship of individual processing and production operations in sequence and with interacting functions.

#15. DOES YOUR PLANT LOCATION AND INTERNAL LAYOUT MINIMIZE BOTH THE COST AND TIME REQUIRED TO LOCATE, PROCESS, AND DELIVER THE MATERIALS USED IN YOUR OPERATION?

Poor location of your business in relation to supplies of raw materials, resources needed for processing, and ease and minimal cost of delivery can determine the difference between your business being profitable or unprofitable. A poorly planned layout of your plant can also cost in terms of time and labor efficiency in reference to material handling.

Corrective Measures:

Most cost-effective plant locations can be determined by evaluating prospective site opportunities in terms of labor supply, union activities, living conditions, cost of supplies, and delivery. Plant layout should be developed on the basis of the type of product or process—whether the product or process layout is appropriate. A three-dimensional layout will demonstrate the interaction of equipment, personnel, and services.

#16. DO YOU CONSIDER BOTH CONSUMER AND WORKER SAFETY AND WELFARE IN THE SELECTION OF: EQUIPMENT, OPERATIONS LAYOUT, MATERIALS USED, AND WORK PROCEDURES?

Failure to provide a safe working environment can make an employer liable for damage suits brought by the injured employee. Failure to utilize safety and loss-prevention measures can increase the cost of compensation premiums. Failure to ensure high-quality materials and procedures can result in liability for damage suits.

Corrective Measures:

Be aware of and follow up on all safety regulations as required by government regulation agencies. Take adequate measures to ensure worker safety and welfare. Use acceptable quality materials and standards of production, even if it requires a small loss in profit margin.

#17. DO YOU ATTEMPT TO:

a. Balance workstations?

Failure to distribute tasks in an orderly and systematic manner can result in downtime and lost productivity and dissatisfaction among employees.

Corrective Measures:

Implement the use of process flow charts, operation charts, and worker machine charts to maintain a proper flow between workers.

b. Minimize interferences?

Failure to operate at a demand capacity in every area will result in lost opportunities and increased costs.

Corrective Measures:

Use workload analysis to determine if the present system and distribution of tasks is efficient, and to determine future workload demands and changes that may be necessary.

c. Provide flexibility?

If your employees are trained to only perform certain tasks, then absenteeism and/or unexpected demands in one area can create a slowdown in production.

Corrective Measures:

Cross train your employees to provide flexibility in the coverage of all tasks, thus providing smoother operations.

#18. DOES YOUR OPERATIONS LAYOUT PROVIDE ATTRACTIVE AND PLEASANT SURROUNDINGS, ADEQUATE LIGHTING, AND AN UNCLUTTERED APPEARANCE FOR BOTH YOUR EMPLOYEES AND CUSTOMERS?

Unattractive and unpleasant work environments can have a negative impact on your employees' performance and morale. Your potential consumers may be negatively influenced when plant operations appear to be unclean or unorganized.

Corrective Measures:

Provide adequate lighting and custodial services in work areas and insist that employees do their share to maintain a neat and orderly work area.

#19. DO YOU EFFECTIVELY USE THE CURRENT SPACE?

Inappropriate use of display or selling space may result in lower sales. Poorly planned traffic patterns in selling areas will discourage customers from spending time in your place of business, causing you to lose potential sales. If your current space is not utilized for the production or sales of your most profitable products, you may be paying excessive costs for under-utilized space.

Corrective Measures:

Analyze your records to determine which products are the best sellers or attractions to your business. Plan your use of space accordingly, and modify where appropriate.

#20. Are your fixtures and equipment adequate and up-to-date?

If not, your reluctance to invest in adequate and up-to-date equipment can result in a lesser-quality product, diminished quantity of production, and lower sales volume. It also projects a poor image to your existing and prospective employees, customers, and vendors.

Corrective Measures:

Budget your available working capital to allow for necessary changes and improvements as needed. Research your competitors and other similar firms in your industry to keep abreast of current changes. Formulate and implement an equipment replacement policy.

#21. Except for merchandise that needs special protection; does your layout encourage self-selection, making it easy for the customer to handle the goods?

A layout that does not allow the customer a hands-on inspection of the goods will discourage sales, especially if the goods are widely available in competing stores. A layout that does not allow self-selection will also cost more in employee time.

Corrective Measures:

Plan your layout to encourage self-selection by consumers. Provide as much information as possible to the consumer in a visual form to minimize the need for service on the sales floor. Use other point-of-purchase methods.

#22. Are goods that the customer may not be specifically looking for (but is likely to buy impulsively) displayed near your store entrances and at other points that have heavy traffic?

Failure to place impulse merchandise near the entrance and check-out lines (and other points of heavy traffic) will result in missed sales opportunities.

Corrective Measures:

Place impulse merchandise in strategic locations where they will be highly visible and attractively displayed; always keep these items well stocked.

#23. ARE YOU CONTINUALLY ON THE LOOKOUT FOR OPPORTUNITIES TO IMPROVE YOUR LAYOUT AND MERCHANDISE ARRANGEMENT TO EXPOSE MORE GOODS TO CUSTOMERS IN AN ATTRACTIVE WAY?

Failure to keep up with buying trends and up-to-date merchandising and layout techniques will result in a loss of sales and customer goodwill.

Corrective Measures:

Utilize all selling space to the maximum by displaying as many of your goods as possible without a cluttered appearance. Update and modify your layout and display strategy by observing your competitors and keeping abreast of the latest trends through industry trade publications and communicating with relevant trade associations.

#24. ARE YOUR CASH REGISTERS WELL LOCATED?

Poorly located cash registers can lead to increased traffic problems, including waiting lines.

Corrective Measures:

Place cash registers near your exits to create an easier flow of customers from the store after purchases have been made. Plan your location of cash registers so that exiting traffic does not interfere with the entrance to the sales floor. Equip your store with enough cash registers and cashiers to handle an average number of consumers without causing excessive delays at checkout.

#25. ARE CLERICAL OR OFFICE ACTIVITIES KEPT OUT OF VALUABLE SELLING SPACE?

Non-selling activities that use space that would be better utilized for sales creates both a loss in sales as well as customer confusion.

Corrective Measures:

Plan or remodel your existing layout so that office and maintenance areas are located away from the sales floor. A second floor or basement location could be utilized for these purposes, thus making all main floor space available for sales.

#26. ARE YOUR STOCK AREAS AS CLOSE AS POSSIBLE TO THE SELLING AREAS THEY SERVE?

Any stock areas that are located away from your selling areas will create more difficulty in regard to re-stocking your displays and sales areas in a timely manner. It could also create time-consuming waiting periods for your customers who have requested merchandise from the storage area.

Corrective Measures:

Plan your layout so that stock areas are as close to the selling areas as possible for each type of merchandise.

#27. DO YOU HAVE FLEXIBLE SHELVING AND BIN PARTITIONING SO THAT STORAGE SPACE CAN BE PROPERLY ADJUSTED TO THE MERCHANDISE?

Non-movable and non-adjustable shelving will create a lot of wasted storage and display space as your business conditions change. This type of shelving may not accommodate new generations of products.

Corrective Measures:

Plan your initial purchases or replacement of inflexible storage with more flexible types whenever possible.

#28. DO YOU RECEIVE, CHECK, AND MARK INCOMING GOODS AT CENTRAL POINTS RATHER THAN ON THE SELLING FLOOR?

If not, receiving and pricing procedures done on the selling floor will create disorganization and confusion. This makes the sales procedure more difficult for both your salespersons and the consumers.

Corrective Measures:

Allow sufficient space in a lesser-used area of your store for the receiving and pricing of your merchandise.

#29. HAVE YOU ESTABLISHED THE PROPER ORDER QUANTITY FOR SPECIFIC MATERIALS?

If not, inaccurate record-keeping and ordering procedures will result in the overstocking or understocking of your merchandise and/ or raw materials, tying up your potential revenue and space with surplus inventory or creating shortages and delays in meeting consumer demands.

Corrective Measures:

Use accurate records of inventory and sales to project your future ordering needs and reorder points. Synchronize your supply and demand.

#30. IS YOUR MAJOR CONCERN WITH THE UNIT COST OF MATERIAL IN-PLACE?

If the unit cost of material in-place is not determined as a basis for determining profits, unrealistic figures may be used in the analysis, thereby creating financial problems when planning future purchases of materials. Your inventory prices will also be inaccurate.

Corrective Measures:

Keep accurate records regarding the receiving and inventory of materials (including costs) in order to have accurate information when projecting future needs. Adjust your unit costs to reflect new prices on incoming inventory.

#31. DO YOU TAKE MEASURES TO ENSURE THAT MATERIALS WILL BE DELIVERED AT THE PRICE ORIGINALLY QUOTED?

If consistent policies are not established in your ordering procedures, such as prior bids followed by a written purchase order or responsibility for shipping costs, then your suppliers are not bound to a set price, and overcharging will occur.

Corrective Measures:

Check merchandise received against the quantity, quality, and specifications as stated on the written order. Check the charges against the quotation stated in the original bid and challenge all extra charges.

#32. ARE PRODUCTS CLEARLY LABELED BY THE MANUFACTURER?

Insufficient labeling of your products can lead to inappropriate purchases or misuse of products by your customers. This could lead to customer dissatisfaction and/or possible liability suits in the case of injury or damage to the user.

Corrective Measures:

Ensure that products are clearly labeled as to their content and purpose. Give instructions for use and precautions that should be taken to prevent accidental misuse. Always attempt to pass any potential liability claims back to the manufacturer if you are a third-party seller.

#33. DO SUPPLIERS BACK UP THEIR WARRANTIES?

If suppliers do not back up their warranties, the purchaser (the customer or you) will have to bear the cost of repairs or replacement of the defective merchandise.

Corrective Measures:

Carefully read all warranty information provided with the merchandise, preferably before the transaction takes place. Complete any paperwork that is required to put the warranty into effect and return it promptly to the manufacturer. Do not hesitate to contact the manufacturer if the merchandise appears to be defective when received, or fails to operate as expected within the warranty period. Always insist that appropriate action be taken by the supplier to repair or replace the merchandise as specified in the written warranty.

#34. Do you hold suppliers to meeting their delivery schedules?

Delayed shipments of raw materials or other supplies could result in serious slow-downs in production, sales, and a potential loss of your profits.

Corrective Measures:

Be sure to specify the desired delivery rate in the written contract. Write a penalty clause regarding late delivery in the contract for supplies that are essential to your continuous production or sales activity. In every case, push for delivery.

#35. To avoid buying new machinery, do you occasionally rent construction equipment, or sub-contract work you would normally do yourself?

If not, excessive costs can be involved in the purchase of machinery and equipment that is not used frequently enough to justify the expense.

Corrective Measures:

Rent or sub-contract any work that can be done at a lower cost than the purchase of the equipment and in-house labor would involve. Manage your rentals carefully to ensure that costly idle time can be avoided.

#36. Is equipment generally in good operating order?

If not, equipment breakdowns will cause a slow-down or halt in production. This leads to a significant cost in your manufacturing process in terms of idle capital and labor.

Corrective Measures:

A preventive maintenance policy should be established and incorporated with the routine maintenance program. A capital equipment budget will ensure that equipment turnover is properly executed.

#37. Do you have accurate hourly operating data for each piece of equipment you own or lease?

If not, your own equipment may be costing you more than it should. If you lease equipment, you need to know all associated costs; it may be wiser to buy. Job costing of projects and products will be impossible without such data.

Corrective Measures:

Keep accurate and separate records on all costs for each piece of equipment. Initiate job cost accounting on all projects and/or products.

#38. Are operators thoroughly trained in the safe, effective use of equipment?

Untrained operators are likely to have more accidents and could cause more breakage of equipment. Lawsuits could occur more frequently than would otherwise happen.

Corrective Measures:

Establish employee-training programs to thoroughly acquaint new employees with the equipment they will be using, and train current employees for use of any new equipment that may be introduced to their work area. An evaluation system should be set up to determine the worker's competency before he/she is allowed to utilize the new equipment. Maintain and periodically review the history of each piece of equipment and make changes when necessary.

#39. Do you periodically reconcile the physical inventory with the accounting records?

If not, shortages will occur and if not caught early enough, could result in a loss of sales and profits. You won't be able to recognize what has sold or hasn't, which may cause overstocking or understocking problems, and by not knowing what has sold, you can't determine your real profit or loss.

Corrective Measures:

Devise a system to check physical inventory and do this regularly. Always ensure that physical inventory counts match accounting records.

#40. Do you have a high frequency of stock-outs on certain essential items?

If so, you will lose important sales on a fast-selling item because you lack a proper system. Customers will recognize this frequent problem and take their business elsewhere, causing you to possibly lose sales of other items as well.

Corrective Measures:

Keep a current, up-to-date inventory of what has been sold and try to anticipate reordering periods. Pay particular attention to volume and high-margin items.

#41. If you maintain parts, stocks, or similar items necessary for your services, does your inventory turnover compare favorably with similar businesses in data compiled by such firms as Dun & Bradstreet?

If not, you may be keeping the wrong items in stock. If your service inventory isn't turning over quickly enough, then you have too much of your cash tied up in slow-moving items.

Corrective Measures:

Check your parts inventory turnover regularly and adjust ordering patterns as needed. Try to purchase on consignment wherever you have a return option.

#42. Have your costs of supplies remained a relatively constant proportion of sales?

If your costs increase faster than your sales on a proportionate basis, your profits will decline. Possible factors include theft, waste, or other problems affecting costs.

Corrective Measures:

You may need to adjust your pricing or review your inventory for overstock conditions, then set order points for stock items. Use these order points to control overstocking, as this will cut costs to a minimum. Check for other factors, such as waste on job sites, theft, or the receipt of damaged goods from vendors.

#43. If you maintain an inventory, do you know by what means your inventory is valued?

If you don't know the value of your inventory, you can't figure out your profit or loss. If you don't know your inventory value, your balance sheet will reflect incorrect values. In the case of a disaster, you won't have a proper value of your inventory for insurance purposes.

Corrective Measures:

Values should be added into the inventory listing along with the sale price of the item in order to compare your profit or loss against the reduction of physical inventory. Update and review your inventory on a periodic and regular basis, and adjust financial statements to reflect the changing inventory values.

#44. Do you know what it costs to purchase, process, handle, and stock the product or products used in your business?

If not, then it will be impossible to project what the cash needs are for reordering. Profitability can't be determined without knowing all costs, in particular those relating to warehousing and handling. You may be overlooking hidden costs, such as indirect labor costs.

Corrective Measures:

Understanding all stages of product handling will help you understand the full cost of the product, from purchasing to selling. Analyze the costs at the various stages to identify any areas of cost improvement.

#45. Have you applied an ABC analysis to your product inventory?

If not, you may have too many items that are expensive and cater to a particular class of people, or you may have an overabundance of items that are inexpensive, causing an off-balance in inventory. When reordering, you may have a tendency to reorder merchandise that doesn't move, and that will tie up your cash for too long a time.

Corrective Measures:

An ABC analysis is used for cycle counting, in which all the items in your inventory are counted at least once a year. Classify your inventory according to product and/or customer group. Determine the maximum and minimum inventory levels for the various groups.

#46. Do you know the total cycle times needed for inventory replacements, particularly for critical items?

If not, you may lose customers because of constant stock shortages, forcing them to go to a competitor for the product they need. Vendor problems could occur and make matters worse.

Corrective Measures:

Learn your cycle times and keep accurate records so that you will reorder items in a timely manner to avoid any outages. If you know the length of time to get something shipped, you could please a customer by being able to tell them how long it will take to arrive, and of course, always explain delays to your customers.

#47. Dᴏ ʏᴏᴜ ᴀᴘᴘʟʏ ᴛʜᴇ ᴘʀɪɴᴄɪᴘʟᴇs ᴏꜰ ᴇᴄᴏɴᴏᴍɪᴄ ᴏʀᴅᴇʀ ǫᴜᴀɴᴛɪᴛʏ (EOQ) ᴛᴏ ʏᴏᴜʀ ɪɴᴠᴇɴᴛᴏʀʏ?

If not, ordering too many slow-moving items can cause overstock conditions and tie up your cash. While large-quantity ordering may reduce your unit cost, it may not be advantageous if the item is a slow mover.

Corrective Measures:

Using the economic order quantity approach to inventory replacement will help you keep well-stocked while allowing for maximum cash flow. It will also provide a better approach to inventory recording and evaluation.

#48. Dᴏ ʏᴏᴜ ʜᴀᴠᴇ ɢᴏᴏᴅ, ᴜᴘ-ᴛᴏ-ᴅᴀᴛᴇ, ᴘᴇʀᴘᴇᴛᴜᴀʟ ɪɴᴠᴇɴᴛᴏʀʏ ʀᴇᴄᴏʀᴅs ꜰᴏʀ ᴘʀᴏᴅᴜᴄᴛɪᴏɴ ɪᴛᴇᴍs, ᴡᴏʀᴋs ɪɴ ᴘʀᴏɢʀᴇss, ᴀɴᴅ ꜰɪɴɪsʜᴇᴅ ɢᴏᴏᴅs?

If not, you won't know how long it takes to get a product completed. You can't predict when you're running short of a necessary item, and workers may improvise or be wasteful if they run short, causing productivity to suffer.

Corrective Measures:

By keeping good records of production related to inventory, you can analyze where bottlenecks occur, compare time and cost of production, and determine whether you are producing a product that allows for a consistent profit.

#49. Aʀᴇ ʏᴏᴜʀ ᴘʜʏsɪᴄᴀʟ ɪɴᴠᴇɴᴛᴏʀʏ ᴄʜᴇᴄᴋs ᴜsᴇꜰᴜʟ ᴛᴏ ʏᴏᴜ ɪɴ ᴀɴᴀʟʏᴢɪɴɢ ʏᴏᴜʀ ɪɴᴠᴇɴᴛᴏʀʏ ᴍᴀɴᴀɢᴇᴍᴇɴᴛ?

If you don't check your inventory properly and periodically, you may wind up with your cash tied up and be overstocked. If you don't take inventory frequently, you may not be able to catch the items that need reordering; shortages will be difficult to discover and manage, and you will not know what products are not selling.

Corrective Measures:
Frequent and accurate physical inventory counts give you true values, and by reducing inventory on your records as sales are made, you can reorder before you run short of needed items. Computerize your inventory management in order to make inventory checks easy and cost-effective.

#50. ARE ALL PARTS OF A PURCHASE TRANSACTION CAREFULLY CHECKED AND RECONCILED BEFORE BEING CLOSED OUT?

If not, there may be damages, such as too small a quantity, the wrong item ordered, or the items ordered may be of lesser quality. If the prices are not verified, you may have accepted items that are above the price you expected to pay.

Corrective Measures:
Check prior records for comparison along with shipping receipts for accuracy. Always confirm verbal orders in writing and don't hesitate to return or exchange items that aren't to your specifications. Always verify the final price and compare it with the purchase order to ensure accuracy.

#51. HAVE YOU DEVELOPED REASONABLE COSTS, WHICH ENABLE YOU TO DETERMINE REALISTIC TRADE-OFFS IN YOUR INVENTORY PROGRAM?

If not, some inventory values could be underpriced or overpriced. These factors will complicate accounting reports and could interfere with your inventory selection and proper inventory costing.

Corrective Measures:
Be sure your inventory is consistently valued at either cost or market (whichever is less) and keep accurate, up-to-date records of physical inventory. Selectively trade off between inventories when and where the market and costs permit.

#52. HAVE YOU ORGANIZED YOUR BUSINESS INTO SELLING DEPARTMENTS OR CLASSIFICATIONS?

If not, this indicates disorganization. The customer might assume that some items or services are not available. This could also make reordering and inventory counts difficult, and leads to little or no understanding of what departments, products, or service classifications are generating in terms of revenue and expense.

Corrective Measures:

Classify your merchandise or service in a manner that will help in inventory and reordering, and will aid your customers. Allocate all revenues and expenses to the various departments, products, or service class groups.

#53. DO YOU KEEP SALES, INVENTORY, AND PURCHASE RECORDS BY TYPES OF MERCHANDISE WITHIN YOUR DEPARTMENTS?

If not, be aware that disorganization will complicate your record-keeping. This will not allow you to see what needs to be reordered, or items that are strong or weak. Duplicate ordering could occur, which is costly in terms of inventory carrying charges.

Corrective Measures:

Grouping your records in merchandise categories will help you to determine which classes of merchandise are moving and profitable. It may help you to see which departments are being managed better, and will aid in your overall inventory management.

#54. WITHIN EACH MERCHANDISE TYPE, DO YOU DEVELOP A MODEL STOCK PLAN FOR KEY POINTS OF TIME IN THE SEASON IN ORDER TO MAINTAIN A BALANCE BETWEEN BREADTH AND DEPTH OF ASSORTMENTS?

If not, you may not have enough of the item to meet the demand. You may be too late to order and receive items in time for that particular season, causing you to end up with out-of-season items that won't sell.

Corrective Measures:

Separating merchandise into categories will let you concentrate on the individual items, identifying seasonal reorder points. Order cut-off points will be identified and lessen the risk of overstocking, and tying up cash.

#55. FOR STAPLE AND REORDER ITEMS, DO YOU PREPARE A CHECKLIST (NEVER-OUT LIST) WHICH YOU FREQUENTLY CHECK AGAINST THE ACTUAL ASSORTMENT ON HAND?

Reorders could be duplicated and/or fast-moving items may be overlooked. Having too much can be costly in terms of carrying costs. Inventory imbalances may occur and you'll have excess amounts of some items and not enough of others.

Corrective Measures:

Develop a "never-out" list. Frequently check the list against periodic inventory counts to ensure adequate stock of fast-moving and profitable items. Attempt to achieve an inventory balance, thus ensuring an adequate supply of hot items while resisting the temptation of overstocking the fast movers.

#56. Do you make certain that best sellers are reordered promptly and in sufficient volume, and that slow selling items are processed swiftly for clearance?

If not, you could be stuck with clearance items all the time, when money could be cleared at full price for the best sellers. You could sell out of your best items too quickly, causing your customers to go elsewhere to find the same or similar item.

Corrective Measures:

Monitor your entire stock. Reduce any slow movers for clearance to enhance cash flow. Redirect cash flow to items that move faster and/or generate higher than normal margins. Determine the relationship between volume and margin for each item and make the appropriate profit decisions.

#57. When you go to market or place orders at home for seasonal merchandise, do you use a written buying plan to guide your selection?

A lack of preparation could cause your selections to cost more than you anticipated; or you could buy too much of items not needed, and too little of items more in demand. Some merchandise purchased may not fit into your overall marketing plan.

Corrective Measures:

Have a written plan and budget and stick to it. Always know exactly what you are ordering and the price you're going to pay for it. Use data from previous seasons to guide you in your decision of what and how much of seasonal items you should purchase.

#58. Do you use a reliable system for determining and controlling slow-selling stock?

If not, items may sit for too long, resulting in deterioration of your product(s). Sales may suffer if items are repeatedly placed where customers know the item has been for several months, without being placed on sale. You may accidentally reorder the same stock without knowing the length of time it took to sell the present supply.

Corrective Measures:

Devise a system to keep you aware of slow movers. Always reduce prices on slow movers and group clearance items together. Slow items that are not on sale should be moved periodically to different display areas.

#59. Do you keep separate records on those goods which do not belong in the store or warehouse, such as customer's own goods, goods on consignment, and so on?

If the records are not kept separate, your balances may not match in terms of sales and income.

Corrective Measures:

When goods are placed on consignment, have a written contract specifying the terms. Keep separate daily records and label merchandise for identification of its source. Periodically count other inventory for the record.

#60. Do you determine the amount of your merchandise shortages at least once a year?

If not, your cash and inventory will not balance at the end of the year. If you don't keep records of your total shortages, you will not be able to balance your inventory figures. If records are not kept, you can't justify accounts if audited and any theft problem will not be identified or remedied.

Corrective Measure:

Take a complete physical inventory at least once a year and compare to your sales and purchase records to determine any shortages.

#61. Are you taking adequate safeguards to reduce shoplifting?

If not, expect increased inventory costs and reduced profits. Also, if adequate safeguards are not taken, a habitual shoplifter will think your store is an easy pick.

Corrective Measures:

Cameras or spotters monitoring your business will help prevent shoplifting. People have a tendency to retreat from taking if they know they're being watched. Post signs indicating that shoplifters will be prosecuted to the fullest extent of the law.

When in Doubt, Look About

CHAPTER 7

CONTROLLING FOR PROFITS

Many research studies have shown that some individuals who start their own businesses are not good managers. If these individuals do not rely on outside expertise or qualified employees, they're asking for trouble; many go out of business or are forced to sell. Just remember that a good manager will spot and solve a problem before it can threaten the enterprise. Procrastination is deadly.

The cash flow blues

You wouldn't believe how many entrepreneurs refuse to acknowledge the importance of financial information. Some of these people are operating on the notion that a checkbook is the only thing you need in the way of financial statements! Many entrepreneurs are running $2 to $3 million per year enterprises shackled with the idea that rudimentary accounting systems are enough to do the job. I knew one gentleman who was running a business with four separate departments. He didn't know which department was making or losing money. All funds were put into a general account, without being tagged to a particular department. Expenses were handled in the same manner. When he got into a cash flow bind, he didn't have anything to work with in the form of financial feedback. Upon being hired as his management consultant, I immediately went to work with a CPA to straighten out the books. We were able to set up a manageable financial control system so that revenues and costs could be traced back to the department of origin. In other words, we could track what departments were making or losing money.

What you have to watch at this point is the accounting firm. Make sure that they have experience with entrepreneurial enterprises. Ask about their reputation. Don't ask for references, because they will give you their personal friends and most satisfied clients. Find out for yourself who they serve and then seek those firms out for comment.

Opportunities galore

New products or services are your profit opportunities of the future, just as your current products or services generate today's revenues. All companies, both large and small, fall victim to the product/service life cycle. It basically illustrates that products and services come and go. This underscores the need for your company to be constantly on the lookout for new opportunities. If you refuse to accept this business fact of life, your enterprise will not survive to see the future.

MANAGING FOR SUCCESS

Management is a broad topic covering many different disciplines. It is impossible to discuss all facets of the subject in the confines of this book. However, the important managerial elements of running a small business must be highlighted, and they are broadly reviewed here.

Managing cash and credit

Always remember that money is a commodity that is bought and sold for a price (interest rates). It is one of the most precious resources available to a business, and requires effective management if the firm is to survive and prosper.

Send out invoices consistently and promptly at about the same time each month. The bills should contain all relevant information about the sale (date purchased, cost, account balance, terms, and so on). When income is received from receivables or cash sales, deposit it promptly in interest-bearing checking accounts or other insured accounts that can be drawn on readily. After paying obligations due, put the remaining cash back into the operation immediately, so as to generate additional sales and profits. Idle cash or money sitting in low-yielding accounts is not an example of effective money management.

Make sure that accounts receivable are current and take steps to keep them that way. Past dues can be costly if money must be borrowed or existing funds used to finance operations until accounts are collected. Therefore credit and collection control procedures are critical to successful operation. Grant credit based upon certain conditions that may vary depending on the customer. This can be accomplished by evaluating potential accounts relative to their ability to pay. After that, payment terms and credit limits can be established.

All prospective and existing accounts must be required to fill out a credit application form. The form should include a promise to pay according to the terms of the credit agreement and it can be used to investigate customers' credit history. Make sure the application has a release statement allowing permission to conduct a credit investigation.

If accounts are offered to customers, expect some problems to surface, especially during periods of economic recession. Normally, it is advisable and advantageous to work with slow payers instead of being overly rigid and losing business. Set up procedures for dealing with slow or delinquent accounts. Degrees of slowness should be established with the objective of applying increasing measures of pressure the longer the overdue remains unpaid. Extreme cases may have to be pursued legally.

When the business decides to use credit, always exercise conservatism and precedence. Pay your bills on or before due dates to maintain a healthy credit history. A bad payment record can be expensive in terms of loss of credit privilege and higher interest charged by worried lenders. Take advantage of early payment discounts if they are economically favorable.

In addition, maintaining good relations with all creditors, including bankers, can prove to be beneficial in the long run. Keep them informed as to what is happening with the business. Below are some tips that may help to accomplish this:

- Be candid about positive and negative situations. Many creditors will work with a business in a difficult environment if they are aware of the problems besetting the enterprise and its industry.
- Help the creditors to understand the business and industry. Sometimes ignorance is the biggest stumbling block to effective relationships.

■ Provide insight into management and control functions. This will gain the creditor's confidence and faith in that it shows a willingness to make things operate smoothly and efficiently.

■ Be specific about short-term, intermediate-term, long-term, and crisis planning. Creditors always dislike unanticipated disruptions. Tell them when things are going to take place.

It is not necessary to incorporate the aforementioned tips into creditor relationships, but they will help relieve some of the natural and obvious tensions that exist between borrowers and creditors. An atmosphere of mutual trust and respect will also be fostered, leading to a lasting and growing relationship.

Managing other finances

Existing and prospective small business owners should attempt to understand the financial complexities involved in business operations. A thorough understanding of financial statements will provide a solid foundation for making good business decisions. These statements should be prepared and examined once a month by a competent accountant. Each account within the statements should be shown for the current period and the same period for last year.

Good financial statements will also serve to contain costs. Studying past and present information concerning cost accounts may provide valuable insight into the conditions affecting expense figures.

GROWTH MANAGEMENT

Growing too fast can be as hazardous as a no-growth situation, if not more so. Growth must be implemented and managed carefully to ensure that the business does not expand beyond its ability to control and/or finance operation. Many firms have met with demise because of uncontrollable expansion.

Growth should be mapped out well in advance. Within these plans, a reasonable estimation of resources necessary in carrying out objectives must be evaluated and scrutinized to determine the feasibility of expansion. If resources will be lacking because of internal constraints and/or environmental factors, expansion objectives should be altered to meet with the realities of the situation.

Managing inventory

Proper inventory management can mean the difference between profit and loss, and in some cases survival. Excessive inventories will lock up needed cash that would otherwise be used to generate sales and profits.

If an inventory system is to be effective, its main objectives should be cost containment and efficient delivery. A study of purchase activity relative to finished goods and raw materials will need to be performed in order to accomplish these goals. Once the study and evaluation is completed, a minimum amount of inventory within each item and raw material classification can be stored to satisfy short-term customer orders. In addition, production can be maintained. Here are some additional tips for addressing the inventory problem:

- Compare prices among suppliers.
- Purchasing should be controlled by one individual or department. Duplication of effort is a waste of time and money.
- All finished goods or raw material orders should be confirmed in writing, outlining every cost and condition.
- When goods are delivered, check to make sure that everything is received in proper condition.
- Cross-reference the supplier's invoice with the written quotation. This will avoid overcharges, which occasionally happen.

CONCLUSION

Business analysts report that poor management is the main reason for business failure. Poor cash management is probably the most frequent stumbling block for entrepreneurs. Understanding the basic concepts of cash flow will help you plan for the unforeseen eventualities that nearly every business faces.

Cash versus cash flow

Profit growth does not necessarily mean more cash on hand. Profit is the amount of money you expect to make over a given period of time. Cash is what you must have on hand to keep your business running. Over time, a company's profits are of little value if they are not accompanied by positive cash flow. You can't spend profit; you can only spend cash.

Cash flow refers to the movement of cash into and out of a business. Watching the cash inflows and outflows is one of the most pressing management tasks for any business. The outflow of cash includes those checks you write each month to pay salaries, suppliers, and creditors. The inflow includes the cash you receive from customers, lenders, and investors.

Important Questions to Consider

#1. DOES MORE THAN ONE PERSON HANDLE THE RECEIPT OF CASH AND ALSO DEPOSIT THE RECEIPTS IN THE BANK?

If not, consider having more than one person in charge of the receipt of cash and bank deposits to curb any potential embezzlement.

Corrective Measures:

Limit your cash receipts to the responsibility of two persons. Limit the responsibility of your bank deposits to two different persons, and always compare your cash receipts to the deposit ticket.

#2. IF SOMEONE OTHER THAN YOU WRITES CHECKS FOR AMOUNTS OWED, DOES A DIFFERENT PERSON SIGN THEM?

If not, it increases the chances for embezzlement and more mistakes will occur.

Corrective Measures:

It is best to have one person write the checks and another person sign them. This also gives several people knowledge of your company's financial system, and having more than one person involved provides better control for cash flow and internal control systems.

#3. WHEN YOU SIGN THE CHECKS, DO YOU MAKE CERTAIN THAT ALL OF THE BILLS AND CHECKS ARE BROUGHT TO YOU AT THE SAME TIME?

If not, be aware that sometimes there is a difference between the bill, what was quoted, and what should actually be paid.

Corrective Measures:

Always have the bill before you when writing out and signing the check. Don't pay for unordered supplies or merchandise, and always reconcile your records on a frequent and regular basis.

#4. DO YOU SCRUTINIZE THE BILLS CAREFULLY TO MAKE CERTAIN THAT THE PAYEE, AMOUNT DUE, AND DATE ARE CORRECT?

If not, you could be paying for merchandise that was not ordered. Supplies or items could be purchased from the wrong company, or the check could be written to the right company for the wrong amounts, or vice versa.

Corrective Measures:

Carefully read bills or receipts to make sure these are the correct items ordered. Recheck your bills against checks written before issuing a check.

#5. DO YOU, OR YOUR ACCOUNTANT, RECONCILE YOUR BANK STATEMENT MONTHLY?

If not, then the true balance at any time can only be determined by knowing what previously written checks are outstanding. If you or the bank made a mistake, it won't be corrected and if the checks were written incorrectly, this also will go undetected.

Corrective Measures:

Reconcile your monthly bank statements to keep a correct balance. Correct, in a timely manner, any bank or company mistakes.

#6. DO YOU HAVE ANY KIND OF MECHANICAL CHECK PROTECTION, SUCH AS AN IMPRINTING MACHINE THAT RECORDS THE AMOUNT?

If not, be aware that amounts recorded can be different from the amounts actually written. A person could forget to record a check that was written, and amounts that are written by hand on the check can be more easily changed.

Corrective Measures:

Purchase an imprinting machine to automatically record the checks written, or have your checks generated by computer.

#7. IS A SEPARATE PETTY CASH FUND MAINTAINED FOR SMALL AND IRREGULAR DISBURSEMENTS?

If not, more check writing will result and there will be too many small checks written. Things will be delayed while checks are written and approved for small purchases.

Corrective Measures:

Set up a petty cash fund and limit the amount for any one purchase. List what things can be bought and those authorized to spend from it. Record all disbursements from the fund and always post your petty cash disbursements to the appropriate journals and ledgers.

#8.   ARE YOUR CHECKS PRENUMBERED?

If not, mistakes can happen by duplicating numbers by hand. A lost or stolen check may not be noticed.

Corrective Measures:

Have your checks printed and prenumbered. Always account for all checks at the end of each month and correlate the check numbers to bills paid.

#9.   DO YOU USE PRENUMBERED DUPLICATE SALES CHECKS, INVOICES, AND RECEIPTS?

If not, it is difficult to keep a concise record of checks, invoices, and receipts. It is also hard to correlate checks, invoices, and receipts with each other, leading inventory control to suffer.

Corrective Measures:

By using a prenumbered system, it is easier to keep track of inventory and sales records. By matching checks with invoices and receipts you know what has been sold and paid for when a question arises. Always try to match your checks, invoices, and receipts on a periodic and frequent basis.

#10.   DO YOU HAVE A CASH REGISTER THAT IS ADEQUATE FOR YOUR NEEDS?

If not, then limited entries for assistance in accounting, recording, and inventory may exist and it will force you to maintain more written records. You are more prone to make mistakes at the point of purchase.

Corrective Measures:

Purchase a more adequate register, and then train your personnel to use the system. You will save time and money by use of the added entries on the register for bookkeeping purposes.

#11.   DO YOU MAINTAIN A CONTROL ACCOUNT FOR YOUR ACCOUNTS RECEIVABLE?

If not, you may be extending more credit than you can afford, thus not having enough cash flow. Credit may need to be extended or reduced, but without a control account you will not know where you stand. You will not be able to age your receivables, making the management of your receivables impossible.

Corrective Measures:
> Set up a control account. Review it periodically as part of your management procedure. Change and modify it when necessary.

#12. Do you receive a periodic list of your accounts receivable showing those which are overdue and the length of time overdue?

If not, overdue accounts may sometimes be overlooked. There can be confusion as to the length of time bills are overdue, causing cash flow to suffer.

Corrective Measures:
> A periodic list of overdue accounts helps you to control credit. Send second and third billings and make personal contacts on a systematic basis. Make a point to pursue the late pays and deadbeats.

#13. Do you keep accounts payable filed by date due in order to take advantage of discounts offered?

If not, discounts can be missed and late penalties sometimes must be paid. It is not easy to determine how much debt is coming due on a given date.

Corrective Measures:
> Set up a file-by-date system to take advantage of early payment discounts when appropriate. Compare discounts to interest paid on bank accounts to see which is the best alternative—to pay now and get the discount, or to keep your money in the bank.

#14. Do you compare current bills for utilities, supplies, and other expenses with the amount budgeted for those items?

If not, then your budget does not mean much. Too little money may be budgeted for these items, causing budgetary shortfalls or too much money may be set aside for these expenses when it is not needed and could be used for other things, causing financial management and planning to suffer.

Corrective Measures:
> By comparing budgeted amounts with utilities, supplies, and expenses, adjustments can be made to halt over-spending or under-spending when appropriate and necessary. Incorporate budget management into your overall planning process.

#15. ARE TIME RECORDS KEPT ON HOURLY EMPLOYEES?

If not, it cannot be determined if each employee is working a full shift. There are no records to refer to when disputes arise, and production costs cannot be accurately determined.

Corrective Measures:

Install a time-keeping system that includes having employees sign in and out with a supervisor. Be sure to appoint supervisors to log hours for each employee.

#16. ARE W-4 FORMS ON FILE FOR ALL EMPLOYEES?

If not, the IRS could penalize your company for this oversight. You cannot legally withhold income tax from employees without this form. Your employees will be confused over taxes owed because this procedure was not followed.

Corrective Measures:

Have all your employees fill out a W-4 form, and then file it for tax purposes.

#17. ARE INDIVIDUAL PAYROLL RECORDS MAINTAINED WHICH SHOW REGULAR AND OVERTIME WAGES, THE AMOUNTS WITHHELD FOR SOCIAL SECURITY, FOR FEDERAL AND STATE INCOME TAX, FOR ANY OTHER DEDUCTIONS, AND THE NET AMOUNT PAID?

If government contracts are involved, you may be violating the contract requirements. If a controversy over a person's pay or withholding develops, it will be hard to resolve. These payments will be difficult to monitor and retrieve at tax payment time.

Corrective Measures:

Set up a bookkeeping system that tracks these records. Make sure your records are updated at the end of each pay period, and keep copies of these for annual tax reporting purposes.

#18. ARE PERIODIC PAYMENTS MADE TO A FEDERAL DEPOSITORY FOR TAXES WITHHELD FROM EMPLOYEES' PAY?

If not, collecting taxes from employees and not paying them to the IRS will cause severe problems with the IRS. This may lead to penalties and interest payments and will force the closing of your business if significant tax liabilities accrue.

Corrective Measures:

Collect and make payments on time to the IRS as required, and keep the IRS abreast of any reasons for noncompliance.

#19. HAVE YOU CONSIDERED THE USE OF AN OUTSIDE SOURCE TO PREPARE PAYROLL AND KEEP RECORDS ON EACH EMPLOYEE?

If not, consider that you may be spending too much time on records and paperwork instead of managing your business. You may not be keeping as good (or as professional) records as an accountant could.

Corrective Measures:

Determine the cost-benefit relationship of having your payroll handled by an accountant or other outside service. If you find it to be cost-effective, follow through.

#20. ARE YOUR RECORDS KEPT ON THE DOUBLE ENTRY SYSTEM?

If not, there is a good chance that accounting mistakes are being made but not detected. You may not have a good way to see the overall picture. Individual account pictures of your business make the audit trail harder to follow.

Corrective Measures:

Consider the double entry bookkeeping system. Get an accountant's advice as to whether it would be applicable to your business.

#21. ARE SPECIAL JOURNALS USED FOR SALES, PURCHASES, AND DISBURSEMENTS?

If not, then key records and transactions can become intermingled with all of your other records. Assembling particular information is often time-consuming and difficult. A general ledger cannot be developed.

Corrective Measures:

Set up special journals for selected transactions that are used to make your business decisions. Post your journal entries to the general ledger at least twice a week.

#22. ARE BALANCE SHEETS AND STATEMENTS OF CHANGES IN FINANCIAL POSITION PREPARED AT LEAST ONCE A YEAR?

If not, you may be in a position to expand and don't realize the potential. You may be able to finance projects or production internally, reducing your borrowing needs. Perhaps you have lost borrowing power and need to seek other financial alternatives.

Corrective Measures:

Have a balance sheet and statements of change in financial position prepared yearly or semi-annually and review it with your accountant.

#23. DO YOU ANALYZE YOUR FINANCIAL STATEMENTS TO DETERMINE ANY TRENDS THAT MAY BE DEVELOPING?

If not, negatively developing trends could spell trouble in terms of future growth and profits if not spotted and addressed. Your expenses may be increasing faster than your revenues.

Corrective Measures:

Review and analyze your financial statements monthly to stop troubling trends that may be developing; then act on the negative trends in an appropriate fashion.

#24. DO YOU HAVE AN ACCOUNTING SYSTEM THAT PROVIDES A VARIETY OF DATA FOR THE ENTIRE RANGE OF MANAGEMENT'S NEEDS?

If not, inadequate data can cause incorrect decisions to be made. Decisions may be being based upon false impressions and not fact. Your overall data may not paint the same picture, as does specific data for different management functions.

Corrective Measures:

Be sure that your accounting system provides all data breakdowns and groupings necessary for managing and use the information provided accordingly. Update the system when necessary to reflect any change in your company.

#25. HAVE YOU HAD AN INDEPENDENT ACCOUNTANT REVIEW YOUR ACCOUNTING SYSTEM AND CHART OF ACCOUNTS WITHIN THE PAST THREE YEARS?

If not, your accounting needs may be obsolete due to company changes. Time and effort may be expanded on unneeded accounting functions when a computerized system may now be cost-effective for your business.

Corrective Measures:
Have an accountant review the effectiveness of your present accounting system and change it if necessary.

#26. HAVE YOU ASKED YOUR ACCOUNTANT TO EXPLAIN THE PURPOSE AND SIGNIFICANCE OF EACH ACCOUNT IN YOUR ACCOUNTING SYSTEM?

If not, you may be accumulating data but not using it, or you may have false impressions of what different accounts mean. You may be making bad management decisions because you are misinterpreting data or posting data to the wrong accounts.

Corrective Measures:
Have your accountant explain each account in your system and be sure you understand how to use these accounts for your management purposes.

#27. DO YOU CONSISTENTLY APPLY BREAK-EVEN ANALYSIS AND OPPORTUNITY COST ANALYSIS TO YOUR PRODUCING ACTIVITIES?

If not, you may be engaging in unprofitable production runs because of low volume. Working overtime to increase production may be unprofitable. You may be keeping inventory levels too high. You may not be aware of other more profitable avenues or options.

Corrective Measures:
Know your break-even point for each production run. Analyze various alternative options; it may be wise to invest your resources elsewhere within the business or outside the firm altogether.

#28. DO YOU HAVE A COST ACCOUNTING SYSTEM?

If not, your company's production operation is flying blind, causing your impressions of what are the most and least costly operations to be wrong.

Corrective Measures:
Implement a good cost accounting system. Evaluate your system on a yearly basis and use its output to enhance profitability on an individual project basis and on a departmental basis.

#29. DO YOU KNOW HOW TO DEVELOP USEFUL DATA THROUGH THE COST ACCOUNTING SYSTEM?

If not, you may not know how costs change for each level of output. You may not realize how different ways of production affect your overall production costs.

Corrective Measures:

Get professional help in developing useful costing data. Be sure you have the critical cost data you need for good management, then analyze and use this data. Modify your costing system whenever necessary.

#30. Can you separate costs to a particular project when several projects are in process at the same time?

If not, you will not know which projects are getting too expensive and which projects are the most profitable. You also won't know which projects need to be adjusted to reflect the proper accounting numbers.

Corrective Measures:

Set up a system that tracks the costs of your individual projects and evaluate these costs in relation to each project.

#31. Is your accounting system adequate for the present business and immediate future?

If not, you may not have all the information you need to manage well, causing your growth to be hindered by your inadequate accounting system.

Corrective Measures:

To be sure your accounting system is adequate for your present need, obtain professional advice. Design a system that will expand with your business or simply change your existing system if possible.

#32. Do you keep careful records of your cash outlays for goods, supplies, and services?

If not, you may be spending more on these items than your records reflect. You may be deceived into thinking that things are being tracked in your budget when they are not.

Corrective Measures:

Set up and use a good record-keeping system for cash expenditures. Also, set a maximum cash amount that can be used for goods, supplies, and services, and review each disbursement consistently.

#33. Do you maintain a cash budget?

If not, you may not have an adequate cash flow or you may have idle cash that could be reinvested into your inventory to create sales and thus profits.

Corrective Measures:

Set up a cash budget and use it to plan adequate cash management. Review the budget constantly against the actual results achieved. Modify your budget when necessary.

#34. Do you keep data on sales, purchases, inventory, and direct expenses for different types of merchandise?

If not, you may not realize what your most profitable items are, or costs may be changing and you don't realize it.

Corrective Measures:

Keep this data, review it, and use it to make decisions about what merchandise should be expanded and which should be reduced. Execute periodic inventory counts with appropriate price data.

#35. Have you carefully considered introducing the retail method of inventory?

If not, you could be overstocked, understocked, or stocking the wrong items to efficiently and profitably handle consumer demand.

Corrective Measures:

Study this method to see if it would be effective in your business, and then obtain advice on setting up and implementing this method if applicable to your business.

#36. Have you analyzed the costs of your business that are fixed for the period, such as rent, and salaries of clerical or supervisory people?

If not, these costs may have increased over time without your realizing it. There may be ways to cut fixed costs that have not been explored.

Corrective Measures:

Review this data quarterly, project future change in salaries and update your budget to incorporate these changes.

#37. HAVE YOU FIGURED OUT HOW MUCH EACH SERVICE CALL OR EACH CUSTOMER SERVICED COSTS YOU IN DIRECT CASH OUTLAY?

If not, these calls may be more expensive than you think, thereby compromising your profits. You may be underpricing your product if service is included in the purchase price.

Corrective Measures:

Tabulate all of the service costs associated with a service call, and then set up a quarterly review system of these costs. Index them to warn you if they exceed a certain percent of your annual business or your cost estimates.

#38. DO YOU KNOW HOW MUCH YOUR FRINGE BENEFITS COST YOU PER EMPLOYEE, PER HOUR?

These costs may be changing more rapidly than you may think and a lack of data relating to fringe benefits could compromise profits and your budget process.

Corrective Measures:

Review your benefits cost periodically and index them so you will be warned if they exceed certain limits. Budget for increases and make the adjustments when appropriate, in terms of cost control.

#39. HAVE YOU DETERMINED HOW MUCH YOU SHOULD BE EARNING, CONSIDERING YOUR INVESTMENT IN THE BUSINESS AND TIME SPENT?

If not, you may be wasting your time and resources in terms of lack of return. You could be misallocating your talents and energies.

Corrective Measures:

Set reasonable goals for what you expect to earn for the amount of time and resources you've invested. Monitor your progress, and make changes in time and resource exposure when appropriate.

#40. HAVE YOU LOOKED AT INDUSTRY FINANCIAL FIGURES FROM YOUR TRADE ASSOCIATION?

If not, you won't be aware if your business is not performing up to the overall industry norm. Your costs may be higher than the industry average, or you may be underestimating your sales potentials.

Corrective Measures:

Review your industry figures periodically. Try to determine why your performance is not up to industry averages.

#41. ARE THE EXPENDITURES OF YOUR FIRM BASED ON ALLOCATIONS ESTABLISHED BY A BUDGETING SYSTEM?

If not, your expenses may be out of control. There may be a lack of data relating to the expenses within your various departments.

Corrective Measures:

Establish and allocate budgets to each major function within your company, then monitor each budget for conformance and variances and act on all variances.

#42. ARE YOUR BUDGETS TIED TO SET AND EQUAL TIME PERIODS, PERFORMANCE STANDARDS, AND INCENTIVES?

If not, your budget will be misleading and hard to relate to other budgets if not structured in equal time periods. If budgets are not tied to performance, then expenses may be excessive or productivity may suffer.

Corrective Measures:

Create a quarterly or semi-annual budget process. This will give you a good indication of your average expenditures. See that your budgets are tied to performance standards, and act on any budget variance immediately.

#43. DO YOU REQUIRE A BUDGET PROPOSAL FOR EVERY PROJECT PROPOSAL ANALYZED?

If not, you may be misled into accepting a poor business venture. Any funds used for a bad proposal would eliminate funds for a more profitable project.

Corrective Measures:

Always include a budget proposal in your project review and monitor the costs of the new venture on a regular basis.

#44. ARE BUDGETS USED TO CONTROL THE AMOUNT AND RATE OF EXPENDITURES?

If not, cash flow problems could occur from excessive and uncontrolled spending, leading to a lack of profitability.

Corrective Measures:

Use your budget to control and monitor the amount and rate of your expenditures. Review your budget periodically to modify your expenses in any areas with spending problems.

#45. Is your checking account balance consistently low?

If you regularly have large checking balances, then your money is not being used or invested for company growth. Incorrect inventory balances will result in a lack of prompt service to your customers.

Corrective Measures:

Use money towards expenses and growth of your company. Maintain an adequate inventory for better service to your customers. Hire more workers or sales personnel.

#46. Bank overdrafts, returned checks, or insufficient funds affect your credibility. Is your planning such that this has never happened to your firm?

If you have frequent occurrences of overdrafts, your credit rating could be jeopardized. Existing and potential lenders may become wary, while vendors may refuse to continue to send you shipments.

Corrective Measures:

Keep a record of cash expenditures and keep an adequate cash balance in your account. If you are in a cash crunch, call your vendor to explain your situation and get an extension. This will promote goodwill and trust between your vendors and your business.

#47. Have you seldom or never used lines of credit to decrease the demands for cash?

Keep in mind that interest will have to be paid on the money that was borrowed, and that the money will have to be repaid on a frequent and timely basis. Acknowledge that repayment could be tough during a period of economic contraction.

Corrective Measures:

Use proper cash flow procedures to eliminate the need for short-term loans when possible. Keep your inventory in line with sales to reduce the lending need. Reduce expenses across the board (this will reduce borrowing needs somewhat) and only borrow when needed.

#48. Have you reviewed the terms offered by your vendors lately?

If not, you may be paying too much for your merchandise and you may not be taking advantage of any discounts or other features. You may also not be taking advantage of any extended time payments.

Corrective Measures:

Review your vendors' terms on a periodic basis and take advantage of them if feasible. Pay your invoices promptly for discounts if it makes sense in terms of offsetting interest earned by keeping the money in the bank instead. Take advantage of any extended time payments.

#49. HAVE YOU DISCUSSED WITH YOUR ACCOUNTANT, FINANCIAL ADVISOR, OR BANKER THE STRUCTURE AND COSTS OF SHORT TERM BORROWING?

If not, you may be paying too much interest if other financing methods are employed. Cash flow may be impeded at times, especially when inventory purchases must be made. A line of credit may not have been established and used when necessary.

Corrective Measures:

Use proper borrowing procedures to secure any short-term borrowing, especially as it relates to inventory. Establish a line of credit to facilitate any short-term operational needs and use long-term borrowing instead of short-term when appropriate. Always treat short-term borrowings as short-term debt to be paid off frequently when you have the resources to do so and used only when necessary to fill short-term funding gaps.

#50. DO YOU INVEST SEASONALLY EXCESS CASH PRODUCTIVELY?

If not, expect a loss of interest, loss of other income opportunities, and a loss of respect within financial circles, especially during economic downturns when your mistakes become very obvious.

Corrective Measures:

Look for the most profitable and secure short-term investments. Seek professional advice from financial consultants, accountants, or attorneys, and be consistent.

#51. ARE WITHDRAWALS FOR PETTY CASH DONE BY CHECK ONLY?

If not, there will be no specific record of any cash withdrawals. You may not be taking advantage of possible tax deductions.

Corrective Measures:

Use proper check-writing procedures at all times, even for your petty cash withdrawals. Keep invoices and records of all petty cash payments and make sure all pertinent information is dated on the checks and check stubs.

#52. Are all payroll checks matched with employees' names, time cards, and personnel rosters?

If not, checks may be issued with wrong amounts and/or to the wrong individual. You may be faced with governmental regulatory and tax problems.

Corrective Measures:

Always use proper payroll procedures. Keep personnel rosters and time cards up-to-date and matched to the proper check. Be sure to withhold the correct tax amounts.

#53. Are blank checks, purchase orders, contract forms, and company securities kept in a safe?

If not, blank checks may be stolen, lost, or forged. Company security documents may also be lost or stolen.

Corrective Measures:

Keep blank checks and other forms in a secure place with limited access. Restrict the access and handling of blank checks only to your assigned personnel. Place your company securities in a safe place. Be sure to keep a duplicate copy of important documents.

#54. Do you require adequate identification of customers who want to pay by check, and those who ask you to cash checks?

If not, you may accumulate bad checks, which will create a cash flow problem if not addressed. Time and profit will be lost in trying to collect on the bad checks incurred.

Corrective Measures:

Establish and use a check cashing SOP. Learn your county and state legal procedures and limitations on collecting bad checks. Set check cashing limits and pursue the deadbeats to the limits of the law.

#55. Have you taken adequate steps to protect your cash from robbery?

An excessive loss of cash could cause business failure, especially for a smaller firm. Your insurance may not pay if steps haven't been taken.

Corrective Measures:

Take out the proper insurance. Install security systems and train your personnel in security measures and procedures. Keep only a small amount of cash on hand by making daily deposits.

#56. Is your postage metered?

If not, you may lose control of postage costs due to excess postage application and employee theft; or you may be using excessive labor for mailing.

Corrective Measures:

If mailings are a mainstay of your business, consider whether investing in a postage meter is appropriate. Use bulk mailing for large mailings when possible and periodically monitor and review all postage-related costs, whether metered or not, to ensure cost effectiveness.

#57. Have you established a line of credit at your bank to permit borrowing at any time for emergency needs?

If not, more time will be required to obtain a bank loan. Your credit with vendors and others may be jeopardized. The money for your inventory purchases may not be available when needed.

Corrective Measures:

Establish a line of credit. Pay off all loans in a timely manner and establish a working relationship with banks by supplying them with a financial statement on a regular basis and keeping your financial sources advised on all matters.

#58. Do you consistently avoid drawing checks to cash and signing blank checks?

If not, there will be no record of payment to specific invoices, tax deductions may be missed, payments may not be posted under the correct expenditures, and if others are involved, theft could occur.

Corrective Measures:

Write your checks for specific invoices and needs. Always avoid writing checks to cash and never sign blank checks. Include invoice numbers and other specific information on all checks.

#59. Have you bonded your cashier and other employees who handle cash and securities?

If not, some types of insurance may cost more or be impossible to obtain and banks may refuse your loans. Insurance will not pay for theft loss.

Corrective Measures:

Require that your cashiers and other security employees be bonded.

#60. DO YOU CONTROL YOUR LIABILITIES WITH THE SAME DEGREE OF CARE YOU DEVOTE TO YOUR ASSETS?

If not, your credit rating may deteriorate and you may not be able to obtain merchandise from your vendors. You may also not be able to obtain loans when needed.

Corrective Measures:

Pay your suppliers on time. Pay all interest and principal payments for short- and long-term notes on time. If possible, pay extra payments on the principle to save you money on interest.

#61. TO PERMIT MODERNIZATION AND EXPANSION OF YOUR PREMISES (IF YOU RENT THEM), HAVE YOU CONSIDERED YOUR LANDLORD AS A SOURCE FOR THE ADDITIONAL CAPITAL YOU WILL NEED?

If not, you may be unnecessarily missing an opportunity for cost effective modernization or expansion and money, for these improvements may cost more from other sources.

Corrective Measures:

Ask your landlord to pay for the improvements. Negotiate a decreased lease term to cover the improvement costs if you finance. Consult your landlord for attractive loan terms if they agree to finance the improvements. Analyze the tax advantages to both or either party; they can be attractive depending upon how the final lease improvement deal is negotiated.

#62. DO YOU MAINTAIN A CLOSE PERSONAL RELATIONSHIP WITH YOUR LOCAL BANKER?

If not, poor communication and infrequent contact could lead to misunderstandings, particularly during difficult times. You may not be aware of special loan rates or options given to your size or type of business or you may not be able to obtain a loan when needed because your banker may not want to take a risk on a company that he or she is unfamiliar with.

Corrective Measures:

Maintain a close business relationship with your banker. Ask your banker about different loan options or opportunities and keep your banker informed of your specific monetary needs. Advise your banker of your company's progress and/or problems on a regular basis. This communication is essential whether the information is good or bad.

#63. ARE YOUR PRICES COMPETITIVE, BASED ON THE QUALITY AND SERVICE THAT GO WITH EACH PRODUCT OR SERVICE SOLD?

Your products or services may not be priced for a quick sale. Losses will occur if the market is not large enough and your products or services are priced high in order to make a profit. Your future market share will suffer despite the quality and service you offer. If you have high quality but poor service without covering your costs of these factors, it will result in substantial losses.

Corrective Measures:

Ensure that your products or services are of top quality and frequently monitor your field dates to insure quality. Price competitively to help maintain a market position. Try to avoid underpricing your product or service to prevent projecting the wrong image.

#64. DO YOU KNOW WHAT PART SERVICE PLAYS IN MAKING A SALE?

If your salespersons cannot answer questions about what they are selling it will hurt your revenues and profits. Service is a key cost feature, and not knowing its impact in the sale function will cause pricing mistakes, resulting in marketing problems.

Corrective Measures:

Properly train your sales personnel in all aspects of salesmanship, particularly as it relates to service. Answer all of the questions about your products, particularly as it relates to service.

#65. ARE THERE ECONOMIES OF SCALE IN YOUR OPERATION, WHICH ENABLE YOU TO SELL LOWER-PRICED PRODUCTION QUANTITIES?

If not, a lack of economies will keep your production costs high, and cause your prices to be high. Your profits will suffer at the hands of those competitors who have an economy-of-scale advantage.

Corrective Measures:

Emphasize quality over price, deliver on time, and always emphasize service.

#66. DO YOU USE A BREAK-EVEN ANALYSIS IN COMPUTING COSTS FOR SETTING PRICE?

If not, your prices may be too high or too low. You may not be taking into consideration all of the costs of your production. You may not understand the relationship between volume and pricing.

Corrective Measures:

A break-even analysis will show you the level of sales needed to cover all of your costs. Make cost and pricing adjustments where necessary.

#67. HAVE YOU DEVELOPED A PRICING STRATEGY THAT ALLOWS YOU TO ADJUST PRICES TO MEET COMPETITIVE SITUATIONS?

If not, the competition will erode your market share, causing your revenues and profits to suffer. It could also cause inventory problems.

Corrective Measures:

Analyze your competitors' price movements and trends. Determine the effects on your products/services in relation to price and make a decision on how to react. Review the decision periodically and modify if needed.

#68. DO YOU ATTEMPT TO MAKE SURE THAT THE PRICE CHARGED REPRESENTS A FAIR VALUE TO NEARLY ALL YOUR CUSTOMERS?

If not, it's possible that you may not be keeping up with the pricing policies of your competitors or any variables in supply and demand. You will experience a lack of appropriate pricing, which balances all factors such as quality, service, or warranties. If your pricing is too high or low, your customer goodwill will suffer.

Corrective Measures:

Even though the prices charged may vary due to supply and demand, your products should be fairly priced and in line with your competitors. Your prices may vary due to costs in production and service, but should still be fairly priced. Establish the same prices for all customers, only allowing variations for volume purchases. If selling your product at a fair price cannot make a profit, drop the product.

#69. DO YOU FIGURE MARKUP AS A PERCENTAGE OF THE SELLING PRICE RATHER THAN A PERCENTAGE OF COST?

If not, your mark-up may be too low. A lack of understanding between the two pricing methods will lead to margin confusion.

Corrective Measures:
> Understand the difference between the two pricing methods, and then select the most appropriate method for each product. Understand that at the same price, the two different pricing methods will indicate different percentage markups.

#70. Do you set price lines and price zones?

> If not, your price setting and methods may be inconsistent among your product groupings and departments; pricing confusion will lead to employee and customer confusion.

Corrective Measures:
> Be consistent in your pricing methods and price-setting within your various product groupings and departments. Minimize employee and customer hassles by establishing consistent and less confusing prices and methods of pricing.

#71. Do you give as much consideration to the adequacy of your dollar markup as to your percentage markup?

> If not, your break-even margin may be too low, compromising your profits. You may be able to move larger quantities at a lower margin, generating high profits.

Corrective Measures:
> No matter what the percentage or dollar markup is, it should be fair to your consumers and competitive. The markup should be enough to cover all of your costs plus an adequate profit for your business.

#72. Are you guided by what you think the typical customer will consider good value?

> If not, your customers will be lost to your competitors who put a higher priority on customer input. You may suffer from a lack of understanding between a market-driven and a cost-driven pricing policy.

Corrective Measures:
> Your customers should always be considered because they will be the ones who ultimately purchase your product. Take into consideration all your costs, and then price your products according to what you think the customer will consider a good value.

#73. Do you practice the technique of average markup, rather than aiming at the same percentage throughout your store?

If not, expect pricing inflexibility to occur. Some prices will be too high or too low on various goods, thereby impeding your sales.

Corrective Measures:

Using the average markup method would be fair to all of your product groups and sub-groups, and a good value to your consumer. Percentages may vary from product to product, depending upon types of products, supply, demand, and other relevant elements such as seasonal factors.

#74. Do you avoid selling new and regular merchandise as loss leaders (items sold at less than cost)?

If not, and you must begin selling certain items as a loss, price hikes will be tough—if not impossible—to implement later, causing profits to suffer and quite possibly projecting the wrong image to your customer.

Corrective Measures:

Never sell your new and regular merchandise as loss leaders. Your company is in business to make a profit and with good sales people and good service all new and regular merchandise should sell for a profit.

#75. Do you keep a record of all your markdowns, and do you analyze them by cause?

Your seasonal markdowns may not be apparent and you may be marking down too quickly or slowly. On occasion, incorrect products may be slated for markdown.

Corrective Measures:

Keep accurate records of all of your markdowns. Analyzing markdown causes will save you time and money and could offer a good reference for future markdowns.

#76. When you have clearance merchandise, does your first markdown normally move a substantial portion of the stock?

If not, your markdowns may be too small, or your sale promotion was inadequate. Be aware of your competitors, as they may also be in the act.

Corrective Measures:

Offer larger, more appealing markdowns and mark down your clearance items often, if only a small amount each time. Sell merchandise as closeout if nothing else works, and try to advertise at various stages of your markdown campaign.

#77. BEFORE YOU MARK DOWN ITEMS FOR CLEARANCE, DO YOU CONSIDER ALTERNATIVE WAYS OF MOVING THEM?

Your profits could suffer because your markdowns involve little or no profit margin. Consistent markdowns will give the wrong image.

Corrective Measures:

Consider a return of the merchandise, or holding the merchandise until the next buying season.

#78. DO YOU HAVE SPECIFIC POLICIES AND PROCEDURES REGARDING WHO IS AUTHORIZED TO PURCHASE GOODS AND SERVICES?

If not, your money can be tied up in excess inventory due to double ordering. Employee theft will occur more easily. You may not be able to keep track of what is really being spent if several people are keeping separate records.

Corrective Measures:

Centralize purchasing under as few people as possible, and make sure a head purchasing agent approves all requisitions. Establish clear, precise, and firm policies on purchasing and the corresponding record-keeping.

#79. HAVE YOU EVER REVIEWED EXISTING PURCHASE PROCEDURES TO SEE IF THEY MEET THE NEEDS OF THE FIRM?

If not and your business is growing, your policies may be too informal. If your business has changed in any significant way, your policies may be outdated.

Corrective Measures:

Review your purchasing policies at least once a year and update them as needed to maintain the proper controls.

#80. HAVE YOU EVER DISCUSSED YOUR PURCHASING FUNCTION WITH OTHERS TO OBTAIN SUGGESTIONS AND/OR TECHNIQUES?

If not, your current procedures may be too cumbersome, too informal, or outdated. Your record-keeping may also be inadequate.

Corrective Measures:

Contact your trade association and request suggestions or information on ways to handle purchasing for your type of business. Ask other people in the same or related businesses what works well for them and what doesn't. You may be able to improve your procedures based upon others' experience, so experiment to find the best procedures for your firm.

#81. Do you request prices from several vendors for each product or service you purchase?

If not, you may be paying more than necessary for your products and not receiving the best product/service for your money. You may be buying an inferior product at superior prices, or you may be unaware of any quantity discounts and special sale prices.

Corrective Measures:

Always compare prices from several different vendors before committing to a purchase. Compare the service, quality, and payment terms to determine the best vendor.

#82. Have you investigated potential vendors to verify that they meet your price, quality, quantity, and service?

If not, what you are being told may not be in line with the vendor's real mode of business, causing you to accept inferior service and quality while overlooking better sources.

Corrective Measures:

Try to visit your current and potential vendors and watch their operations. If you can't visit, ask for customer references so you can get a better picture of their business.

#83. Given large volumes of purchasing for any particular item, do you deal directly with the manufacturer?

If not, you are missing an opportunity to buy direct.

Corrective Measures:

Assess your inventory turnover and buy direct when money can be saved. Regularly review direct buying possibilities to determine if additional advantages warrant this approach.

#84. Do your vendors have regular and competent sales personnel?

If not, you will not know whom to contact in case of problems with your order. You may not be able to get correct information or specifics on products or services.

Corrective Measures:
Deal only with vendors who have competent salespeople and request that only one salesperson be assigned to your account. Request that this person be in touch regularly.

#85. Are shortages, delivery days, or unsolicited gifts causing problems with your supplier?

If so, you may unwittingly find yourself involved in illegal activities. You may be unable to service your own customers because of delays and shortages and any merchandise offered by deviant means may be of lower quality.

Corrective Measures:
Deal only with reputable vendors and stay away from backdoor deals and special favors. If you experience shortages or delivery delays, seek a more reliable vendor. Always check your incoming shipments for quality, quantity, and the prices quoted.

#86. Does your vendor list consist of firms that sincerely want your business?

If not, you may get insufficient service or information, poor quality products, and have trouble returning them. You may be paying too much if they really do not understand your value as a customer.

Corrective Measures:
Compare the service, quality, and price, and try to determine which vendors want your business the most. It may be worthwhile to pay a little more to assure service and quality from a top-notch vendor who really wants your account.

#87. Do your vendors perform services for you, but not for your competitors?

If not, your account may be run-of-the-mill. A lack of communication and rapport with the vendor will cause an inability to obtain special orders or receive emergency shipments.

Corrective Measures:

Work to develop a good rapport with your vendors through prompt or early payment of bills and frequent communication, or simply find another vendor who is more responsive to your needs.

#88. Do your vendors extend themselves for you because you've become a loyal customer?

If not, you will not be informed of specials or discounts. You may experience delays in your shipments or shortages while the vendor emphasizes its newer customers. You may also be sent inferior-quality merchandise.

Corrective Measures:

Look for other vendors who provide equal service. Make a point of asking regularly about any specials and discounts. Confront your vendor immediately about problems with service or quality while emphasizing to the vendor the importance of customers.

#89. Do you buy largely by specification, rather than by brand name or simply by accepting what the vendor offers?

If not, buying brand names may cause you to pay more for items that may not meet your specifications. Brand name products do not always mean the best quality at the best price.

Corrective Measures:

When necessary for technical reasons, always purchase by specification, understanding that different brands can have the same specifications. Don't be lured into buying only name-brand products or other house brands regularly pushed by the vendor. Some vendors may carry off brand products at the same or better quality and at better prices.

#90. Do you make sure you're getting the right quality in your purchases by using a value analysis?

If not, you may be sacrificing volume because of extreme prices on your quality items. You may lose money by replacing low-priced, low-quality items, which do not hold up.

Corrective Measures:

Analyze your stock to make sure price and quality are factored and balanced. At some point, it may be more viable to sacrifice some quality in favor of competitive pricing; however, do not go too far.

#91. Do you have more than one source of supply for any critical item?

If not, and if your one supplier should go out of business or experience shortages, you may not be able to purchase the item and serve your customers.

Corrective Measures:

Research several suppliers for these items. Try to always have at least two sources of supply for critical goods and rotate orders between the suppliers so you can keep a good rapport.

#92. Are you familiar with the transportation rates for your more important purchases?

If not, you may be paying too much in freight costs and not factoring this into the cost of your product or markups. You may not be accounting for these charges in your purchasing budget.

Corrective Measures:

Keep records on the rates and compare them to see that your goods are being shipped in the most economical way. Research other methods or other shipping companies for the best price.

#93. Do you have a market representative who assists you in selecting sources and merchandise, in obtaining low prices, and in promoting merchandise purchased?

If not, you may not be making well-informed purchasing decisions in reference to what sells well and what doesn't, causing pricing and promotional decisions to be incorrect.

Corrective Measures:

If you are having difficulty keeping up with purchasing, merchandising, and turnover, consider hiring a market representative to help you. If your business is smaller and you still need help, designate a knowledgeable employee to assist you.

#94. Have you worked with your buying group to develop and promote private brands?

If not, you may not be obtaining a maximum profit by carrying only name-brand products. Name-brand manufacturers have too much control over their products, so you may not be able to obtain the necessary modifications that might improve your sales.

Corrective Measures:

Work to develop your own in-house or private brand items. Coordinate your efforts and network with others in your field to help finance the costs associated with this approach. Seek the best volume prices on components or raw materials; this will help increase your margins.

#95. Do you have a rule that you or your assigned buyer sees all salespeople who ask for an appointment?

If not, you may miss an opportunity to find a better supplier or new product opportunities, as well as seasonal specials or discounts.

Corrective Measures:

Talk to all salespeople who seek an appointment. Ask about their new products, specials, and discounts, and then compare the information.

#96. Do you concentrate your purchases in each classification with a relatively small number of key resources, rather than spreading them widely over the entire market?

If not, consider that buying small amounts from many suppliers may mean you are paying too much. Your account may be viewed as too small and you may not have the clout to get service in an emergency or in special order situations.

Corrective Measures:

Buy in volume from fewer sources, seeking better prices for larger orders and try to have at least two sources of supply for your critical items. Always be on the lookout for new sources, but keep the alternatives few in number.

#97. In developing a key resource list, do you make a seasonal study of the volume sold of each vendor's goods, including profitability?

If not, you won't know which vendors offer you the greatest sales volume and profits on a seasonal basis.

Corrective Measures:

Include in your key resource list those vendors who offer you the best prices and service for seasonal items as well as regular stock. Do a comparative study of your vendors and your trade with them each year to determine profitability with each. Keep accurate records on buying and sales patterns for all goods, including seasonal ones.

#98. HAVE YOU TRAINED YOURSELF TO KEEP DISTINCT CUSTOMER GROUPS IN MIND WHEN SELECTING MERCHANDISE AND ASSORTMENTS?

If not, you may not be reaching all of your best markets. You may be losing customers by not having the right product mix.

Corrective Measures:

Keep a record of the groups and attributes of buyers who constitute your best market. Plan your purchases taking this data into account. Research the feasibility and profitability of adding products to service special groups or individuals.

#99. WHEN REORDERING NEW ITEMS THAT HAVE SHOWN VOLUME POTENTIAL, DO YOU MAKE IT A POINT TO ORDER A SUFFICIENT NUMBER?

If you are continually out of a new item, you will lose customers. Your profitability will decline if you aren't servicing your customers satisfactorily with volume-generating products.

Corrective Measures:

Keep tabs on any items that become volume sellers. Plan your purchases to include adequate stocks of these items; but do not go overboard and order too much.

#100. DO YOU KEEP UP ASSORTMENTS THROUGH IMPORTANT SELLING SEASONS IN SPITE OF THE PROBABILITY OF MARKDOWNS ON THE REMAINDERS?

If you run out of those stock items early, you may lose the bulk of your seasonal profits. You will lose customers because your stocks are too low to offer a good assortment of merchandise.

Corrective Measures:

Plan your seasonal buying to remain well-stocked, and make sure you keep a wide assortment of goods so customers have choices.

#101. DO YOU PREDETERMINE WHEN FIRST ORDERS ARE TO BE PLACED, WHEN RETAIL SALES ARE TO BE COMPLETE, THE EXTENT OF THE PEAK SELLING PERIOD, THE START OF CLEARANCE, AND DATE OF FINAL CHECKUP?

If not, you may not order stock early enough for timely delivery, causing a poor assortment of goods for the peak of the season. You may not have your markdown sales in time to be competitive, causing your sales to drop.

Corrective Measures:

Be sure you make a dated schedule of all seasonal activities.

#102. ARE THERE NUMEROUS UNNECESSARY DUPLICATIONS IN YOUR STOCK ASSORTMENT BECAUSE YOU DID NOT COMPARE NEW ITEMS WITH ITEMS ALREADY IN STOCK?

If so, you have too much money tied up in excess inventory, and shortages of other items that you do need. You may have to mark down overstocked items and lose profits to generate your cash flow.

Corrective Measures:

Keep accurate records of your inventory. Check this inventory with items being considered for purchase before you buy.

#103. DO YOU HAVE A PLAN WHEREBY GOODS ASKED FOR, BUT NOT IN STOCK, ARE REPORTED TO YOU?

If not, the lack of the needed items could go unnoticed for significant periods of time. If seasonal items, the buying season could pass before you are aware of the shortage and it would be too late to pursue other supply vendors.

Corrective Measures:

Develop a reporting system that signals when you cannot get an item from a vendor. Educate and inform your employees about this system.

#104. ARE ALL YOUR PURCHASE ORDERS WRITTEN ON YOUR STANDARD ORDER FORMS?

If not, your record-keeping may be inadequate, which could lead to internal fraud and theft. You will have difficulty referencing a shipment if there are problems with billing or damage claims.

Corrective Measures:

Make sure all purchases are done on your order forms and make sure your forms are numbered for easy reference. Be sure to match the incoming shipments to the proper order form and assign a specific person to monitor the process. Consider soliciting input from an accountant.

#105. DO YOU TAKE ADVANTAGE OF ALL AVAILABLE DISCOUNTS SUCH AS TRADE, QUANTITY, SEASON, AND CASH, AND DO YOU INCLUDE THEM ON YOUR WRITTEN ORDERS?

If not, you may be paying more than necessary for your goods. You may not be receiving the proper discounts if you do not reference these on your orders.

Corrective Measures:

Keep records of discounts or seasonal deals offered to you by all of your vendors. Be sure to take advantage of all specials and discounts whenever possible and note these on your orders. Check your invoices to see that you received the discounts and/or other special considerations.

#106. WHEN YOU PLACE ORDERS, ARE YOU CAREFUL TO SPECIFY THE DATE OF SHIPMENT AND THE ROUTE EACH IS TO TAKE, INSTEAD OF LEAVING THESE MATTERS TO THE SELLERS?

If not, your goods may not arrive when you need them or you may be paying too much in freight charges. You may not be able to time cash flow to pay for the goods if you have no control over their delivery schedule.

Corrective Measures:

Specify a shipment date. Research the quickest and most cost-effective transportation, and then specify the shipping method and routes on your orders.

#107. DO YOU FOLLOW UP ALL ORDERS TO SEE THAT GOODS ARE SHIPPED AND RECEIVED ON TIME?

If not, vendors may ignore your date-of-shipping requests, so your orders may arrive late. It will be difficult to determine which vendors are giving you the best service.

Corrective Measures:

Follow up orders with a phone call to confirm shipping dates and check to see if orders are arriving on time.

#108. DO YOU CHECK EVERY INCOMING SHIPMENT CAREFULLY AGAINST THE PACKING SLIP AND YOUR ORDER COPY?

If not, you may be receiving goods other than what you ordered, you may be charged for items you didn't get, you may be shorted, or there may be damaged goods.

Corrective Measures:

Always check incoming orders immediately and compare the items received with the packing slip and your original order. Report any discrepancies or damage to your vendor immediately.

#109. DO YOU CHECK THE VALUE OF THE STAMPS ON THE PACKAGE AGAINST THE AMOUNT BILLED BY THE SELLER?

If not, you may be over-billed for freight and you may be paying handling charges of which you are unaware.

Corrective Measures:

Always double-check freight charges to make sure they are fair. If there are hidden charges or overcharges, contact your vendor immediately.

#110. ARE THE TERMS OF SALE YOU OFFER CONSISTENT WITH THE EXPECTED LIFE OF THE SERVICE YOU OFFER?

If not, you may be losing money by offering free service or maintenance beyond the useful life of your product or you may be giving away too much support and losing profit.

Corrective Measures:

Review your service policy and make adjustments to terms as needed. Don't make promises that are impossible to keep or too costly to support.

#111. ARE YOUR CREDIT TERMS SIMILAR TO THOSE OFFERED BY YOUR COMPETITORS?

If your terms do not offer as much credit, your customers may go to the competitor; if your terms offer more credit than your competitors, collecting on this credit may be troublesome.

Corrective Measures:

Change your credit terms to be more competitive. Do not discriminate against any of your customers, and do not extend yourself by being too easy on credit.

#112. Do you check the credit worthiness of your clients or customers when setting up credit terms?

If not, a customer may have a poor credit history and could be a bad risk.

Corrective Measures:

Check credit references and establish a credit limit for each customer. Consider offering different terms for different customers depending on how dependable they are in making payments, and modify the terms as needed.

#113. Do you allow cash discounts for prepayments, or charge penalties for late payments?

If not, customers could decide to pay whenever they like, knowing nothing more will be added or taken away.

Corrective Measures:

Place a penalty on all late payments to make sure your customers get the money to you when you expect and need it. Honor those customers who pay early with discounts. Require a minimum partial monthly payment on new accounts.

#114. Are the terms of sale clearly specified to the buyer at the time of sale?

If not, the sale may be lost if the customer finds out they aren't getting what they were expecting. If misunderstandings keep occurring and customers become aggravated, the reputation of the business will be damaged and goodwill will suffer.

Corrective Measures:

Clearly and concisely specify your terms so that the customer can understand them before the purchase is made. Always be consistent and timely in your response to questions.

#115. Have you attempted to measure the impact of credit on your sales revenues?

If not, you may find later that customer credit is overtaking your regular cash sales. If you are not prepared, cash flow could suffer.

Corrective Measures:

A good liberal line of credit may boost sales if appropriate credit policies have been employed, so determine if credit should be extended or tightened in order to facilitate good sales, and never give bad credit to generate sales.

#116. DOES YOUR FIRM HAVE A STRONG FINANCIAL CONDITION AND WIDE PROFIT MARGINS?

If not and money starts to tighten, you may be caught in a situation in which bills cannot be paid. If you don't have wide profit margins, you could be unprotected against a dip in sales, causing financial difficulties.

Corrective Measures:

Make sure that finances are watched carefully and that financial flexibility is enhanced and maintained. Always maintain adequate profit margins to ensure profit flow.

#117. DO YOU HAVE A SPECIFIC PROCEDURE USED TO CLASSIFY THE RISK INVOLVED IN SELLING TO EACH CUSTOMER?

If not, generic credit procedures may not be flexible enough to spot detailed and specific problems with individual customers or your procedures could be discriminatory and could cause legal action against you.

Corrective Measures:

Develop a flexible credit evaluation procedure. Ensure that your selling policies conform to local, state, and federal laws for differing customers, and apply both generic and flexible evaluation procedures to cover all your bases.

#118. DO YOU TAKE ADVANTAGE OF CREDIT RATING INFORMATION THAT'S AVAILABLE TO YOU FROM YOUR BANKER, TRADE ASSOCIATION, LOCAL CREDIT GROUPS, AND SERVICES?

If not, you may not have factual credit history about a potential or existing customer, or you may not know how to structure your credit for a particular customer.

Corrective Measures:

Ask your banker about credit rating information, research it to its fullest, and use it as a guide. Join a credit bureau so you can have credit checks run on a periodic basis.

#119. Do you request and promptly receive financial statements or similar data from potential and existing customers?

If not, you may be giving credit to firms who could never repay. You cannot head off credit problems in advance, and you may be caught off guard by not evaluating the risks properly.

Corrective Measures:

Require a financial statement and sound credit references before selling on credit. Periodically, obtain this information for existing customers for use in updating their files.

#120. Are there limits to the dollar amount of sales which are approved for credit by some rating system?

If not, you may have people accumulating large debts quickly without realizing their inability to pay. You may need a rating system to extend more credit to good payers.

Corrective Measures:

Set an initial credit limit on the amount of the first sale, require a small down payment, and rate customers as to the amount of credit they can receive.

#121. Do you request some form of protection against default?

If not, bad debt losses will occur and recovery of this debt could be difficult.

Corrective Measures:

Seek legal advice on how to protect yourself against default. Make sure you understand every part of the credit contract, and know what legal remedies may be employed to recover debts.

#122. Do you have an established and progressively stronger collection procedure?

If not, more defaults will occur. A weak collection system may hamper your ability to collect.

Corrective Measures:

Establish and maintain a strong collection procedure. Enforce your system: Pursue and sue where appropriate.

#123. HAVE YOU CONSIDERED USING CREDIT INSURANCE, FACTORING OF ACCOUNTS RECEIVABLE, BANK, OR SIMILAR CREDIT CARD SYSTEMS?

If not, you may be assuming too much risk on the credit you extend, or you may not be aware of ways to reduce your risk.

Corrective Measures:

Explore the use of credit cards as a way of shifting the credit risk away from your business. Examine credit insurance to protect you against any bad customer debt.

#124. DO YOU KNOW HOW MUCH CREDIT SALES ADD TO YOUR GROSS INCOME COMPARED TO THE COST OF SUCH ADDITIONAL INCOME?

If not, extending credit may be costing you more than the sales you bring in, causing losses to occur.

Corrective Measures:

Determine how much of your sales are by credit, what your costs are, and your true margin on such sales, then determine whether you need to change your terms or stop offering credit.

#125. ARE YOU FIRM IN PRESSING FOR PAYMENT ON PAST DUE ACCOUNTS?

If not, many customers may pay irregularly, and that hurts cash flow. You should never fully rely on the income of credit sales payments for use in short-term business planning because it will cause you a payables problem, possibly affecting your own credit.

Corrective Measures:

Make sure your payment terms are shown on all of your sales invoices where credit is given, and on all monthly statements. Consider imposing late charges on your overdue accounts.

#126. DO YOU AVOID BAD CREDIT RISKS?

Your credit-checking procedure may be inadequate, leading to more work in collecting the payments. Your cash flow will suffer and bad debt losses will soar.

Corrective Measures:

Enforce credit-checking procedures such as requiring strict limits, terms of credit and a cash or cash-on-delivery policy for bad credit risks.

#127. ARE YOUR TRADE CREDIT AND PAYMENT TERMS ENFORCED STRICTLY BUT FAIRLY TO ALL CUSTOMERS?

If not, your customers may become angry and take their business elsewhere. Your business will get a bad reputation in the community for being discriminatory. You may be violating the law.

Corrective Measures:

Establish fair, consistent, and flexible terms for all of your customers. Be sure there are solid reasons to make exceptions.

#128. DO YOU HESITATE TO SUE A CREDITOR BEFORE ANALYZING OR WRITING OFF A BAD ACCOUNT?

Your business may get a bad reputation for suing everyone without hesitation when a good customer may simply be having a one-time cash flow problem.

Corrective Measures:

By hesitating and talking to the customer, you may see that this is only a temporary bad time for the customer, and can set up some kind of agreement before prosecuting, saving a good customer.

#129. IF YOU HAVE YOUR OWN CREDIT PLAN, DO YOU HAVE A METHOD OF IDENTIFICATION AND AUTHORIZATION OF CHARGE CUSTOMERS?

If not and your business is somewhat large or busy, it may be difficult to determine the quality customers from the less responsible ones.

Corrective Measures:

Create and use a customer listing system with all pertinent information. Periodically update the system to allow for changes in the individual credit data.

#130. HAVE YOU INTRODUCED A REVOLVING CREDIT PLAN, WHERE IN CUSTOMERS CAN COMPUTE PAYMENT BEFOREHAND?

Consider that many people operate on a set budget and may not be able to afford payments unless they are so prorated, structured, and understood.

Corrective Measures:

Customers will be happier if they can decide and rely on weekly or monthly payments. The introduction of a revolving credit plan may help some customers, giving your business a competitive edge.

#131. IS YOUR FIRM CURRENTLY EARNING A SATISFACTORY RETURN ON INVESTMENT?

If not, you will experience the inability to invest in new plants and equipment, the inability to attract investors, and an inability to grow.

Corrective Measures:

Determine the problem and/or primary cause of your business shortcomings, and correct them by cutting costs wherever possible. Emphasize only profitable operations to maximize your sales.

#132. HAVE YOU COMMUNICATED ON A FREQUENT BASIS WITH YOUR BANKER AND SURETY AGENT?

Tension will result if a good communication is not maintained with your banker. You could lose a source of valuable financing if relations break down.

Corrective Measures:

Maintain good relations with all of your creditors. Keep them informed about your business.

#133. ARE BILLINGS PROMPTLY PREPARED ON THE BASIS OF ADEQUATE INFORMATION?

If not, you could suffer a loss of interest income on monies that are not secured by prompt billings. Past dues can be costly.

Corrective Measures:

Consistently send out your bills at the same time each month with the adequate information included.

#134. ARE CLAIMS FOR EXTRA COSTS BACKED BY SIGNED AUTHORIZATION FROM THE CLIENT OR LEGAL REPRESENTATIVE?

If not, extra costs may not be recovered because of a disputed claim.

Corrective Measures:

Assure that all claims for extras are signed by the appropriate person(s).

Don't Risk the Farm

CHAPTER 8

BE VERY CAREFUL

All entrepreneurs worth their salt will experience at least one major lawsuit in their lifetime. It's an unfortunate state of affairs, but a reality in today's litigious society. I once owned a five-unit apartment building in my hometown of Elkins, West Virginia. A gentleman who lived on the third floor got four or five months behind on his rent. I heard he was a good carpenter, so I approached him with a proposal. The back of the building needed some repair work to meet FHA standards, so I offered him the project in exchange for back rent, in addition to giving him a salary. I procured the building permits and put him to work and he did a good job. The job was inspected and approved by the local building inspector. A year later he fell from the stairs leading to his third floor porch and landed on the second floor porch, and cracked his upper vertebrate. At the time, he attested to his neighbors that it was his own fault. The police report shows that he had been drinking at the time of the fall.

Six months after the accident I was served with a $10 million lawsuit, and accused of negligence. Remember, he did the work! Upon presenting evidence, my insurance company attempted to have the case dropped. Unfortunately, the local court told me that at any given time, half of the state of West Virginia was drunk. They also ruled that I was negligent because I hired a negligent worker to complete the repairs.

I knew I had a problem. First, my insurance covered only up to $1 million, and I was being sued for $10 million. I immediately had the case removed to the United States Federal Court under the right of diversity. If a citizen of one state sues a citizen of another state, the case can be moved to the federal court; or if the amount of the claim exceeds $75,000, the case can also be moved up to the federal court. My case met both criteria.

The defense attorneys tried to stop me from moving the case to the federal court because they knew that a federal court judge would figure out that their claim was frivolous, as happened in my case. He told the other side that unless they limited my liability to $75,000, he was going to keep the case in federal court and probably dismiss it completely. They folded and agreed to his terms, and the case was moved back to the lower court. In other words, my maximum liability was $75,000, well within my insurance coverage blanket. My insurance company finally settled the case for $32,000. The lesson I learned from all of this is that you must protect yourself!

Managing risk

Understanding risk is an important aspect of running any business. Some experts contend that an adequate insurance program designed to reduce risk is vital to the success of a firm. Without question, assets left unprotected could compromise the future existence of the business. Therefore a sound risk reduction plan should be implemented and carefully managed to ensure economic viability in the event of loss due to unanticipated events. The following items should be carefully considered by all existing business owners and prospective entrepreneurs thinking about purchasing a small enterprise:

■ Determine how loss may occur. Recognizing the probability of loss is the initial step in understanding risk. Realistic appraisal is a must in order to protect the firm's assets and livelihood.

■ Seek professional advice. Talk to agents employed by insurance companies and independent agents representing different companies. Ask for their assistance in determining insurance needs. To ensure the credibility of the agents, request references and check them out. In addition, talk to other business owners, as they may provide reliable agent contacts.

■ Shop around for the best buy. Insurance products are subject to competitive forces. Prices will differ among companies.

Following a few simple rules will help to reduce the cost of carrying insurance coverage:

■ Identify risks and the potential for loss.

■ Insure the largest risk factor initially.

■ Try to use deductibles. High deductibles will reduce insurance costs.

■ Eliminate all overlapping insurance coverage. It's a waste of money, because most companies share the burden of loss as opposed to the owner getting extra coverage.

■ Purchase insurance in large units, if possible. Avoid small policies, because they tend to be more expensive for the same coverage.

■ Some insurance companies sell consolidated policies incorporating all coverage into one central agreement. In addition, many professional and trade associations have insurance products at discount group rates. For example, the National Association of the Self-Employed in Dallas, Texas provides some attractive insurance programs at reasonable prices. You can access their Website at *www.nase.org*.

■ Always evaluate the firm's risk exposure on a timely and regular basis for purposes of upgrading or downgrading. This will ensure adequate coverage at reasonable cost, and (in some cases) the phaing out of protection that has become unnecessary.

Structure an insurance program. A formalized plan outlining all aspects of the insurance program should be set forth for management purposes. The plan may include, but is not limited to, the following procedures:

■ State the objective of the insurance plan.

■ Try to deal with only one agent, if possible. Dealing with several may create confusion and disinformation.

■ Assign responsibility for the program to one individual.

■ Prevent or minimize loss through safety and inspection procedures.

■ State the potential for loss candidly. Failure to acquire needed coverage because of disinformation can be a threat to the viability of the firm.

■ No matter how small the chance for loss, all risks should be covered. Avoid underestimation of asset value to save money. If a loss does occur, the firm may not recover its investment.

■ Periodically evaluate the insurance program to determine the need for modification. Some risk programs have automatic cost-of-living increases built in to protect against loss caused by increasing asset value due to inflation. All assets should be appraised occasionally to determine insurance requirement.

■ Always maintain adequate records concerning the risk reduction program. This information may be helpful when attempting to change or modify coverage.

The insurance checklist on page 150 is provided courtesy of the U.S. Small Business Administration; it was written by Mark R. Greene. It is designed to provide insight into the insurance needs of small businesses.

Points reviewed in the checklist are classified into three groups. They are as follows: essential coverage, desirable but non-essential coverage, and employee coverage. After reading each statement, place a check under the column entitled "No action needed" if the statement and how it affects the insurance plan is understood. If it isn't, check the column entitled "Look into this." After completing the study, evaluate existing and/or prospective insurance coverage, keeping in mind the points covered in the checklist. Discuss any problems or concerns with an agent.

Essential coverage

Four kinds of insurance are essential: fire insurance, liability insurance, automobile insurance, and workers' compensation insurance. In some areas and in some kinds of businesses, crime insurance is also essential. Are you certain that all the following points have been given full consideration in your insurance program? Think in terms of the action needed to correct or no action needed for each point reviewed.

Fire insurance

You can add other perils—such as windstorm, hail, smoke, explosion, vandalism, and malicious mischief—to your basic fire insurance at a relatively low additional cost. If you need comprehensive coverage, your best buy may be one of the all-risk contracts that offer the broadest available protection for the money.

Liability insurance

- Legal liability limits of $1 million are no longer considered high or unreasonable, even for a small business.
- Most liability policies require you to notify the insurer immediately after an incident on your property that might cause a future claim. This holds true no matter how unimportant the incident may seem at the time it happens.
- Most liability policies, in addition to covering bodily injuries, may now cover personal injuries (libel, slander, and so on), if these are specifically insured.

Automobile insurance

- When an employee or a subcontractor uses his own car on your behalf, you can be legally liable even if you don't own a car or truck yourself.
- Five or more automobiles or motorcycles under one ownership and operated as a fleet for business purposes can generally be insured under a low-cost fleet policy against both material damage to your vehicle and liability to others for property damage or personal injury.

Workers' compensation insurance

Common law requires that an employer:

- provide his or her employees a safe place to work
- hire competent fellow employees
- provide safe tools
- warn his or her employees of an existing danger.

If an employer fails to provide these, under both common law and workers' compensation laws, he or she is liable for damage suits brought by an employee. State law determines the level or type of benefits payable under workers' compensation policies.

DESIRABLE COVERAGE

Some types of insurance coverage, while not absolutely essential, will greatly add to the security of your business. This coverage includes business interruption insurance, crime insurance, glass insurance, and rent insurance.

Business interruption insurance

You can purchase insurance to cover fixed expenses that would continue if a fire shut down your business—such as salaries to key employees, taxes, interest, depreciation, and utilities, as well as the profits you would lose.

Crime insurance

A comprehensive crime policy written just for small businesses is available. In addition to burglary and robbery, it covers other types of loss by theft, destruction, and disappearance of money and securities. It also covers theft by your employees.

If you are in a high-risk area and cannot get insurance through normal channels without paying excessive rates, you may be able to get help through the federal crime insurance plan. Your agent or state insurance commissioner can tell you where to get information about these plans.

Glass insurance

You can purchase a special glass insurance policy that covers all risk to glass windows, glass signs, motion picture screens, glass brick, glass doors, showcases, countertops, and insulated glass panels.

The glass insurance policy covers not only the glass itself, but also its lettering and ornamentation, if these are specifically insured, as well as the costs of temporary plates or boarding-up when necessary.

Rent insurance

You can buy rent insurance that will pay your rent if the property you lease becomes unusable because of fire or other insured perils and your lease calls for continued payments in such a situation.

If you own property and lease it to others, you can insure against loss if the lease is cancelled because of fire and you have to rent the property again at a reduced rate.

EMPLOYEE BENEFIT COVERAGE

Insurance coverage that can be used to provide employee benefits include group life insurance, group health insurance, disability insurance, and retirement income. Key-man insurance protects the company against financial loss caused by the death of a valuable employee or partner.

Group life insurance

If you pay group-insurance premiums and cover all employees up to $50,000, the cost to you is deductible for federal income-tax purposes, yet the value of the benefit is not taxable income to your employees.

Most insurers will provide group coverage at low rates even if there are 10 or fewer employees in your group. If the employees pay part of the cost of the group insurance, state laws require that 75 percent of them must elect coverage for the plan to qualify as group insurance. Group plans permit an employee leaving the company to convert his group-insurance coverage to a private plan, at the rate for his or her age, without a medical exam, if he or she does so within 30 days after leaving the job.

Group health insurance

Group health insurance costs much less and provides more generous benefits for the worker than individual contracts would. If you pay the entire cost, individual employees cannot be dropped from a group plan unless the entire group policy is cancelled. Generous programs of employee benefits, such as group health insurance, tend to reduce labor turnover.

Disability insurance

Workers' compensation insurance pays an employee only for time lost because of work injuries and work-related sickness, not for time lost because of disabilities incurred off the job. But you can purchase, at a low premium, insurance to replace the lost income of workers who suffer short-term or long-term disability not related to their work.

You can also get coverage that provides employees with an income for life in case of permanent disability resulting from work-related sickness or accident.

Retirement income

If you are self-employed, you can get an income tax deduction for funds used for retirement for you and your employees through plans of insurance or annuities approved for use under the Employees Retirement Income Security Act of 1974 (ERISA).

Annuity contracts may provide for variable payments in the hope of giving the annuitants some protection against the effects of inflation. Whether fixed or variable, an annuity can provide retirement income that is guaranteed for life.

Key-man insurance

One of the most serious setbacks that can come to a small company is the loss of a key man. But your key man can be insured with life insurance and disability insurance owned by and payable to your company. Proceeds of a key-man policy are not subject to income tax, but premiums are not a deductible business expense.

The cash value of key-man insurance, which accumulates as an asset of the business, can be borrowed against, and the interest and dividends are not subject to income tax as long as the policy remains in force.

Checklist for adequate insurance coverage

1. Which of the following risks are applicable to my business, and do I have coverage for them?

    a. property insurance

        ____aircraft damage
        ____civil commotion
        ____commercial property
        ____equipment
        ____explosion
        ____fire
        ____flood
        ____hailstorm
        ____lightning
        ____riot
        ____riot attending a strike
        ____smoke damage
        ____theft
        ____vandalism
        ____vehicle damage
        ____water damage
        ____windstorm

    b. liability insurance

        ____automobile
        ____general liability
        ____non-owned automobiles
        ____product
        ____umbrella coverage

    c. life and health insurance

        ____basic health
        ____disability income
        ____group life
        ____key-man insurance
        ____major medical plan
        ____employee compensation

2. What is my adequacy in coverage?

        ____Check the overall adequacy of your coverage.
        ____Compare coverage against co-insurance requirements, where applicable.

3. Do you review your insurance agent periodically?

_____Take competitive bids on your policies every two years.

_____Check for any instances at which your agent may have neglected to suggest the best possible coverage.

_____Evaluate the effectiveness of your agent in gaining compensation for past losses.

_____Check with your agent for any potential problems relating to settlement of losses as a result of a total insurance package.

_____Evaluate coverage on the most important exposures to ascertain if you are spending your insurance dollar wisely.

_____Evaluate use of deductibles.

_____Review where you can reduce premiums through assuming certain obligations such as an improved burglary system or sprinkler system.

SETTLEMENT OF LOSSES

If you are covered by a reputable insurance company and represented by a competent agent, you will usually obtain a fair and prompt settlement of your claim. All policies do require you, however, to notify the insurer immediately upon the occurrence of a loss.

In order to obtain a fair settlement, it is also necessary for you to provide the documentation that helps the insurance company determine the actual extent of your loss. Accurate accounting records can be very helpful. Records which are necessary to determine losses should be kept in a safe place where they will be protected against fire, vandalism, or water damage.

In many lines of insurance, the insurer has the right to choose whether to make a cash payment, to repair the damage, or to replace the damaged property with goods of similar kind and quality, in a reasonable time. Before an insurance company settles a claim, it uses an adjuster (often an independent firm specializing in evaluation of damage) to review the damage and determine a fair settlement. Most insurance policies specify arbitration procedures if the insured and insurer cannot agree on the amount to be paid for the loss.

Important Questions to Consider

#1. DO YOU HAVE A STABLE RELATIONSHIP WITH AN INSURANCE AGENT?

If not, this could lead to serious mistakes in your insurance planning function. You will not have an agent who understands your particular business and insurance needs on a consistent basis.

Corrective Measures:

Try to maintain at least a five-year relationship with this person or firm, if conditions and costs permit. Don't move to another agent to save a few pennies.

#2. HAVE YOU TAKEN ADVANTAGE OF ALL PREMIUM COST-CUTTING POSSIBILITIES?

Your insurance coverage may be costing more than necessary. You may not be aware of lower risk categories. Insurance coverage may be outdated and need review.

Corrective Measures:

Check into insurance cost-cutting possibilities. Inform your current agent of your specific needs to determine lower costs.

#3. DO YOU PERIODICALLY REVIEW YOUR INSURANCE PROGRAM?

You may not have proper or adequate insurance coverage for your current business needs. You may be paying for coverage that is not needed.

Corrective Measures:

Check whether coverage is adequate to cover your risks. Modify the insurance program if needed, and cut premiums where possible.

#4. DO YOU UNDERSTAND THE RISKS YOUR BUSINESS IS EXPOSED TO AND WHICH OF THEM CAN BE COVERED BY INSURANCE?

If not, you may be underinsured and at risk. You could suffer an unnecessary financial loss on uninsured risks.

Corrective Measures:

Review your risks on a periodic basis with a competent insurance agent or consultant. Determine all risk thresholds, and adequately insure with proper coverage.

#5. IS YOUR INSURANCE MANAGED BY AN AGENT WHO KNOWS YOUR BUSINESS AND HAS A PERSONAL INTEREST IN YOUR SUCCESS?

If your agent can not or has not spent the time to become familiar with your industry and business, you have the wrong agent. You're going to get bad advice; and you can't afford bad insurance advice.

Corrective measures:

Find an agent who may specialize in your field of business, if possible. You will find more agents are starting to specialize in particular fields of coverage. Always review your insurance needs.

#6. DOES YOUR AGENT WORK CLOSELY WITH BROKERS WHO CAN PROVIDE SPECIAL INSURANCE COVERAGE WHEN IT'S NEEDED?

If not, special insurance coverage may not be available when needed. Loss may be incurred before special coverage can be found.

Corrective Measures:

Review and anticipate any special insurance coverage needs, including when they occur. Ask your existing agent to find an agent or broker that can insure your special needs should these special risks materialize.

#7. DO YOU DISCUSS WITH YOUR AGENT THE WAYS IN WHICH INSURANCE COVERAGE AND EXPENSE CAN BE REDUCED?

If not, your payments may be excessive for the existing coverage. Excessive or outdated policies may be in force. Your agent may not be aware of current insurance needs.

Corrective Measures:

Discuss ways of reducing your insurance costs with your agent. Eliminate excessive or outdated policies. Make your agent aware of current insurance needs and situations on a regular basis.

#8. DO YOU KNOW IF YOUR FIRM IS IN A HIGH RISK FIELD?

Your insurance may not be adequate because risks may not have been adequately determined or were understated; therefore potential claims mat not be fully payable with existing insurance coverage.

Corrective Measures:

Identify and evaluate the real risks your company faces. Seek adequate insurance coverage for these risks. Review all risks periodically and modify coverage if necessary.

#9. DO CLIENTS AND DESIGN FIRMS ASSUME RESPONSIBILITY FOR A HIGH PERCENTAGE OF PROJECT RISKS?

If not, you must assume that risk exposure and related insurance burdens. One large claim could cost you dearly in terms of future coverage.

Corrective Measures:

Determine which risks are yours, and which are not, and then insure yourself appropriately. Your project contracts with third parties should always be specific in terms of insurance issues and define the details.

#10. DO YOU HAVE A RELATIVELY EASY TIME BECOMING BONDED?

If you can not be bonded or it is difficult and/or costly for you to get a bond, and your industry requires bonding, loss of business will occur. You can be forced into the costly sub-prime bond market. You can absorb the increased costs through sharper project management.

Corrective Measures:

Clean up your finances to the degree possible so as to become bondable. Secure grade B or C bonds (sub-prime) in order to capture projects and prove your worthiness the next time around.

#11. ARE YOU PROUD OF EMPLOYEES' SAFETY RECORDS?

It's simple: employees won't care if you don't. Lack of emphasis on safety precautions may result in a laxity of safety measures.

Corrective Measures:

Become safety-conscious and inform employees of safety regulations and records. Make sure employees adhere to all safety regulations. Reward and recognize employees with good safety records.

#12. DO YOU CARRY ADEQUATE LIFE INSURANCE ON YOURSELF AND KEY ASSOCIATES?

If not, your company may not be able to survive in the event of the death of a key individual. The loss of any key associates, including you, may create a hardship that cannot be fixed or managed.

Corrective Measures:

Determine who are the key associates and the financial risks involved in the event of their untimely demise. Carry enough life insurance on yourself, and other important individuals within your firm, to ensure the continuation of the company in the event of death.

The Imperial Customer

CHAPTER 9

THE CUSTOMER IS KING

An important factor that stands out when you are analyzing entrepreneurial success is the emphasis placed on customer sensitivity. This fact was recently borne out in an article in *Success* magazine. Upon reviewing the many elements that contribute to small business success, the one cited in the article as being the most important was closeness to the customer. In other words, it would seem that successful entrepreneurs know who butters their bread. In fact, customer empathy is the one area where small firms can successfully compete with the larger companies. Big corporations normally have a price advantage over their small competitors, but because of their bureaucratic nature, they are substantially displaced from their customers. Smaller enterprises, which can immediately identify with their customers, have the opportunity to empathize with their clientele, which significantly counters the competitive price difference. This factor explains why many small firms can successfully compete against large companies while selling the same products or services.

Several years ago I was in the market for a rather complicated 35mm camera. My search took me to a discount store which was part of a large regional chain. The young man who was working behind the counter, probably for minimum wage, was not familiar with 35mm cameras. He couldn't answer one technical question about the equipment. After experiencing the same conditions at other discount stores, I paid an additional $65 and purchased the equipment and accessories at the local camera shop. The owner was well versed in all the technical aspects of his product. He told me that if I had any problems with the equipment to give him a call or stop back in for a refresher.

Big companies realize the importance of customer empathy. They have been trying to get closer to their markets as of late. For example, IBM proudly proclaims that all of its employees, from top officers to clerical personnel, are salespersons. Some of these giants have adopted the marketing concept as their corporate theme. In other words, all corporate decisions revolve around existing and prospective customers. The marketing departments within these corporations have become the most influential source of internal power. Sometimes they even have the power to dictate corporate goals and policies. Whatever the case, a large company will always have a tough time trying to shed its bureaucratic bias. A wall will always exist between itself (the big company) and the customer. Of course, this is an advantage for the smaller enterprise.

You may think that getting closer to the customer is a simple process for the small business operator—not so anymore! The buying public is becoming increasingly fickle. Consequently, markets change very rapidly. In addition, the previously mentioned and ever-present uncontrollable external forces could impose themselves very quickly, thereby modifying consumer tastes and preferences in short order.

Judging the markets

More than 50 percent of the profits that your business will earn five years from now will be generated from products or services that you are not currently marketing, according to the U.S. Small Business Administration. Consequently, the question becomes: Are you able to absorb a 50 percent or more reduction in revenues? Probably not. So don't make the mistake of assuming that the future will be a repeat of past performance and that profits will be forthcoming from existing customers and marketing practices.

In an attempt to judge and exploit changes in customer behavior, various alternatives will become apparent. Don't take time or invest a lot of money analyzing these alternatives unless you are sure there is a good probability of success. The name of the game is to locate various areas of business opportunities and to judge their commercial feasibility within a reasonable time frame and in a cost-effective manner.

Give them what they want

Your product or service is only great if your customers think it is. Nothing else really matters. Don't get me wrong here. Your opinions and the input of others, including experts, has some relevance in the product/service selection process, but the most important thing is what the existing or prospective customers think. You can use the advice of others or information generated through your own efforts to manipulate consumer beliefs, but what ultimately matters in the buying process is what the customer is thinking.

The key to success in any business venture is the ability to predict what the customer will purchase. Even though buying habits can be manipulated by various stimuli (such as advertising campaigns), the best way to ensure profit fruition is to pinpoint your customer's demands and future needs. After that, you can develop or modify product/service lines in accordance with those desires. This process can entail the application of both technical and non-technical means. In other words, customer needs and desires can be identified by using formal surveys or by playing on hunches.

Technical surveys are conducted by using questionnaires to detect current needs and future desires. These questionnaires are circulated to a well defined—though limited—group of people who are supposed to be a representation and reflection of the entire market you are trying to exploit. After the data on the individual questionnaires are blended and studied, a reasonable estimation of customer demands and needs can be made. Don't get the wrong idea—no procedure is foolproof. There are no guarantees that the application of scientific methods will ensure marketing success. However, it might improve your odds somewhat or put you on notice that marketing mistakes are being made.

Now we come to the non-technical aspects of determining customer wants and desires. Simply put, this amounts to playing on a hunch. It has often been said that good managers have a sixth sense. Without a doubt, intuition is a nice managerial gift to possess, and some entrepreneurs claim that most of their successes are predicated upon it. President Reagan was a perfect example. He made decisions based on his own hunches, often in opposition to a majority of his advisers and in the face of economists who predicted that his decisions would lead our country to economic ruin.

What's interesting is the fact that most of the entrepreneurs that I researched for this book stated that they had not conducted any formal customer or marketing studies before initiating operations. Yet today they are successful in their own right. (For every success there are 2 to 3 failures, and I am not about to interview the failures!) The U. S. Small Business Administration states that 60 percent of entrepreneurial failure is due to inadequate markets for the products and services being attempted in the marketplace. Obviously, being aware of marketing potentials through a properly conducted survey will help reduce the chance of entrepreneurial failure. After employing a reasonable scientific survey questionnaire to determine your customer's wants and future desires, allow your ingrained instincts to guide you the rest of the way. The gut feelings and hunches are an important aspect of the decision-making process, and consequently they deserve consideration. They could mean the difference between success and failure.

Another thing must be considered here. Competitiveness within the entrepreneurial ranks is growing at a feverish rate. Everybody's brother and sister are becoming entrepreneurs. Absolute and comparative advantages in products or services will be reserved only for those companies having proprietary technology in their possession. And that doesn't usually last very long. In other words, competition is the name of the game, and it's only going to get worse. Excessive competition should not scare you. Although in order to thrive in the marketplace, you must do somewhat better than your competition. This might involve lower prices, more efficient service, better guarantees, and more effective management. In my experience as a small business consultant, I have found that most prospective entrepreneurs fail to see or understand the importance of determining customer needs and future wants. They are blinded by what they perceive to be the best product in the world. Then they move into the marketplace unaware, and are surprised when sales do not ensue. You definitely gain the upper hand by knowing in advance what products or services will be marketable. This in itself will lessen the chance of failure and may prevent financial loss and the acquiring of psychological scars.

MARKET RESEARCH

Before embarking on a survey campaign, you will need to identify your market. Few entrepreneurial endeavors have the capability of selling to everybody. Many are limited by the specialized nature of their products/services and/or geographic constraints. In addition, lack of capital and marketing expertise could be factors that might restrict market penetration. At times, the market for a product or service is quite evident and rather general in nature. A drugstore would have as its market almost everywhere, although it would probably serve a specific localized customer base.

Market identification, sometimes referred to as segmentation, is accomplished by studying demographic profiles. In other words, all markets can be segmented into various smaller markets. Some common demographics are:

- age
- income
- education
- marital status
- employment classification
- religion
- race
- geographies
- political affiliations

For example, financial planning services have become very popular lately. Most of these services are offered on a localized basis by individual practitioners who do not have the capability to market on a national or even regional basis. Furthermore, financial planning services are not geared to every household. Evidence has shown that the primary market for this service is urban white-collar professionals who earn in excess of $85,000 per year. The large record companies have as their market the entire country, but even they limit their promotional activities to individuals less than 25 years of age. Almost every major corporation in America is moving away from generalized markets to more segmented ones. This can be observed in the recently reported shift in advertising dollars away from broadcast media to more specialized media outlets, such as cable, satellite television, and the Internet. You can see that it is very important to define your market in very specific terms. Only after you do this can you query your prospective customers in order to determine sales potential.

Now we know the importance of demographics as they relate to the demand and marketing of your products and services. However, customer needs and desires are also affected by other factors as well. Prevailing opinions, media publicity and advertising, fads, and trends can all manipulate demand for your products or services. The name of the game is to pinpoint your market and keep up on those factors that cause your customers to change their attitudes and tastes. Other considerations that you should be aware of include:

- changes in competitor behavior
- alterations in supplier availabilities
- media coverage of your products or services
- changing views of experts in your field or endeavor
- the track record of your competitors

At this point we have determined that you need to adequately identify the segmented market to which you want to sell. Now you must determine why your product/service will sell in the marketplace. Is it unique? Is it more economical than your competitor's? Does it have more attractive features, or is it superior in quality? Will it heighten the customer's feeling of self-worth or ego-status? One thing is sure: Competitors cannot be ignored. To some extent, competition will determine the way you market your product or service and the price you ask for it. Ultimately, competitors will determine the particular products or services you will market. To preserve your position against competitive pressures you will need to stay on guard at all times with the objective of outflanking your competitors. Your product or service must stand out from the others in the marketplace. Of course, this requires constant review of what you're attempting to sell. Updates or modification of product or service lines may be needed periodically in order to beat the competition. Just keep in mind that every product or service goes through a life cycle. From a marketing standpoint, product or service profitability will depend on where it finds itself in the life cycle.

STAGES OF THE LIFE CYCLE

- Introduction stage. This phase exists when the product or service is new and original in the eyes of the buying public. Few competitors are involved in marketing the new product or service, and demand is beginning to become evident. Consequently, profit margins are attractive and the ability to carve out significant market shares is present.

- Growth stage. This phase is characterized by the demand for the product or service exceeding available supply. There are not enough supplies, and profits are soaring at this point. High profits begin to attract competitors. Profits peak at the latter end of this stage.

- Maturity stage. This phase takes place when the demand for the product or service is in equilibrium with available supply. Prices begin to stabilize because there are an increased number of competitors in the marketplace.

- Decline stage. This phase is characterized by an oversupply of products or services. Demand begins to slacken. Competition is fierce, with too many competitors in the marketplaces. Prices are falling at this point. This stage is sometimes referred to as the shakedown.

- Saturation stage. This phase takes place after the market shakedown. Many competitors either fail or diversify out of the product or service. Equilibrium between demand and supply is again achieved, although at a lower price than before. The product or service has run its course and the market is viable only to the degree that consumers want replacements.

It may be worth noting that the death of a product or service can be delayed to some degree by constant modification. For example, the early electronic calculator manufacturers avoided the later stage of the life cycle by periodically adding new function keys to their calculators. In addition, some dead products may find rebirth in a new generation of customer. The skateboard, very popular in the mid-1960s, returned in the 1980s and is today experiencing a comeback yet again. A thorough understanding of the product life cycle is important. Ignoring it could be disastrous to your financial health.

Once you have a product or service that has some merit and potential with a clearly defined market, your next step is to conduct some further studies. Market research is similar to problem resolution, in that you are trying to find the answer to some important questions. This process is very critical to entrepreneurial success because it provides answers and data about the buying habits and motivations of your customers. These answers may be multi-fold, given the fact that you're trying to make complex determinations as to whether your product or service is marketable.

Problem identification

In this phase the research problem is clearly defined. Questions that may need to be answered include, but are not limited to:

■ Who are my customers?
■ Where are they located?
■ Why do they buy my product or service?
■ What will customers pay for my product or service?
■ How much will they buy?
■ How many times will they buy it?
■ Through what outlets will my customer purchase the product or service?
■ Who are my competitors?
■ What advertising media should be used?

Trial and error

All of the entrepreneurs that were researched for this book indicated that they did not conduct a marketing survey prior to going into business for themselves. Consequently, this book has outlined the risks of doing nothing to ensure a market for your product or service. In reality, most entrepreneurs rely mostly on trial and error as a decision-making technique. Dun & Bradstreet recently published statistics that approximately 60 percent of all entrepreneurial failures are due to an inadequate market for products and services.

In other words, the small investment input for a marketing survey and test program may more than offset the loss incurred due to a full-blown marketing campaign that failed. The trial-and-error method may be too costly in terms of losses incurred before rewards are achieved. This is not to suggest that surveying and/or testing will ensure success. On the contrary, there are no guarantees, but it does reduce the risk.

Is it feasible?

It is not enough to have the best product or service in the world. Even if everyone beats a path to your door, it doesn't make sense to sell unless markets can be penetrated at a profit. Herein lies a problem of great proportion. Many prospective entrepreneurs are impulsive and quick to take action without engaging in a comprehensive investigation. Even if your marketing studies indicate that an adequate customer base exists, you still need to conduct a profit analysis. This procedure ensures to some degree that your product or service will generate an appropriate return on investment.

Market promotion and strategy

So far we have been dealing with the particulars of customer identification, buying motivations, competition, market testing, and feasibility analysis. Once you have determined that a market exists for your product or service and that it can be exploited in a profitable manner, your next step is to delineate a marketing strategy. Your overall marketing strategy must take into account the four Ps of the marketing mix:

- product (or service)
- price
- promotion
- place (also known as distribution)

These elements are interrelated; one cannot exist separately without the others. However, each has a different degree of importance depending upon what product or service you are attempting to sell and/or the stage of the life cycle in which the product or service finds itself. For example, if you're selling hand-held electronic calculators, the important elements become price and place. These products are in the saturation phase of their life cycles, at which competition abounds. Therefore, a good price and immediate delivery are the keys to success in marketing these units. Conversely, if you are marketing high-priced industrial equipment, the most important element becomes the product itself. Price, promotion, and place take a subordinate position in this case. However, if you are attempting to sell a brand-new service that is unique in the marketplace, promotion and the product itself become the most important elements. Because it is new, customers will not pay much attention to price and will even wait for delivery.

Customer relations

Once you have mastered the art of satisfying customer needs in a profitable way, the next step is to keep what you have. In other words, make the customer happy. A customer relations policy is the foundation of any successful marketing endeavor. It will help you secure and build long-term sales and profits. Just remember that closeness to the customer is one of the few factors that allow entrepreneurial firms to compete successfully with larger firms that are more cost-competitive in the marketplace. Teaching yourself and your employees to be customer conscious will go a long way toward assuring profits and survival.

Important Questions to Consider

#1. Do you know your customers?

If not, your business may be emphasizing the wrong market segments. Your market segments could be declining or enlarging without your knowledge or the overall market may be shrinking.

Corrective Measures:

Determine who your customers are, and then do some market research and analysis to confirm the size, slope, and characteristics of the market. Keep up to date with market trends and changes in customer tastes. Prioritize and pursue your market opportunities according to profit potential.

#2. Do you maintain a customer and/or consumer profile?

If your customer profile is hazy, your marketing strategy may be out of line with your consumer demographics. You will have no way of knowing any potential or pitfalls. Your profits will suffer because of marketing mistakes.

Corrective Measures:

Do a customer demographic survey and determine your marketing strategy based on the results. Determine your market potential based on this and other consumer survey information (such as trade papers or association reports). Prioritize your market opportunities according to the results of the demographic survey.

#3. Do you analyze marketing data on a regular basis?

If not, your market may be changing without your knowledge. Incorrect decisions may be made based upon outdated market information, or the market may be contracting, thus compromising the future survival of your business.

Corrective Measures:

Analyze market data on a regular basis and adjust your marketing strategy when necessary. Always keep well informed of market trends.

#4. Do you follow a stated credit policy in dealing with requests from customers?

If not, credit may be extended to unworthy customers while denied to worthy customers. A misguided credit policy may result in time-consuming legal battles and financial losses.

Corrective Measures:

Develop a credit policy by setting credit restrictions and limits. Be consistent in its use. Seek legal counsel and comply with all local, state, and federal laws. Pursue deadbeats when necessary.

#5. DO YOU HAVE A STATED ADJUSTMENT POLICY?

If not, improper adjustments may be made or proper adjustments may be disregarded. Unadjusted credit may result in adverse publicity, legal action, and loss of goodwill.

Corrective Measures:

Establish a stated adjustment policy. Issue credit to facilitate proper adjustments and handle improper adjustments diplomatically. Predetermine what legal involvement may arise on unadjusted credits; always be fair and consistent in your adjustment policy.

#6. DO YOU AND YOUR EMPLOYEES KNOW PRECISELY WHAT PRODUCTS AND SERVICES YOUR FIRM WILL OFFER TO CUSTOMERS?

If not, products and services that are needed may not be offered, while products and services that are not needed may be extended. Business loss will occur when a customer demands products or services that were not provided, or were executed improperly.

Corrective Measures:

Determine if your products and services are needed. Eliminate any products or services that are not in consumer demand. Always try to satisfy your customer requests for special products and services when appropriate. Offer only products and services for which an adequate profit margin is assured.

#7. DOES THE CUSTOMER RECOGNIZE HOW YOUR PRODUCTS AND SERVICES ARE DIFFERENT FROM YOUR COMPETITORS?

A lack of customer recognition will result in less than adequate marketing and merchandising results. Competitors may capitalize on your inability to project a different or better product or service, causing your customer goodwill to suffer.

Corrective Measures:

Educate your customers as to your product or service differentiation. Use differentiation tactics to lure customers. In other words, tell why you are different and better.

#8. DO YOU PERIODICALLY REVIEW YOUR FIRM'S LINE OF PRODUCTS AND SERVICES?

If not, consumer preference may have changed, causing your company to emphasize the wrong product or service. Increased demand for some products or services may not be recognized, while some are being offered at a loss.

Corrective Measures:

Keep up to date on consumer preference. Determine which products and services are needed and which are not. Use surveys and other data to determine current consumer demands on a periodic and timely basis. Modify your service mix when market conditions demand it. Eliminate any unprofitable products and services.

#9. ARE CHANGES IN OFFERED PRODUCTS AND SERVICES ADEQUATELY COMMUNICATED TO EMPLOYEES?

If not, your employees may be uninformed of product or service changes, causing confusion for both the employee and your customer. Customers will not get the benefit of any new product or service offers or any changes in existing products and services. The wrong message could be given to the customer resulting in a loss of goodwill.

Corrective Measures:

Inform employees of any change in the products and services offered. Make sure customers are getting the benefit of the new products and services offered or changes in the existing products and services. Effectively communicate all changes to everyone concerned.

#10. HAVE YOU TAKEN A SURVEY OF SIMILAR PRODUCTS AND SERVICES OFFERED IN YOUR GENERAL MARKET AREA?

If not, customer demand for the products and services may not fully be recognized. Your competitors may be offering better customer products and services. Customer demographics may have changed without your knowledge, necessitating a change in the products or services you offer or your marketing approaches.

Corrective Measures:

Determine your customer demands from primary and secondary research, and always offer better customer products and services than your competitors wherever possible. Develop new markets whenever needed.

#11. CAN YOU IDENTIFY SPECIFIC DIFFERENCES IN YOUR PRODUCTS AND SERVICES THAT MAKE IT SUPERIOR/INFERIOR TO THE SAME OR SIMILAR PRODUCTS AND SERVICES OF OTHERS?

If you cannot identify the differences, then neither can your consumers. If you offer the same products and services, it will not sway your customers away from your competitors. Any weaknesses in your offerings will not be corrected, while strengths offered cannot be advertised to their fullest in terms of marketing and selling.

Corrective Measures:

Correct any weaknesses and inferior qualities in the products and services you offer. Emphasize only *your* product and service strengths in your advertising and marketing efforts. Develop a distinct product and service profile to make your customers aware of the distinct and special products and services that you offer. Develop a good customer business relationship based on your distinct products and services.

#12. ARE THERE PRICE OBJECTIVES FOR YOUR PRODUCTS AND SERVICES TO ACHIEVE:

a. a target return on investment?

If not, the needed income level may not be achieved to cover asset utilization and absorption.

Corrective Measures:

Identify a target return on your investment when pricing all of your products and services. Never price the product or service below the target unless other factors, such as volume purchases or repeat business, make it worthwhile.

b. a stabilization of price and gross margin?

If not, it will cause customer confusion and a loss of goodwill. Profits will suffer, in particular when price and/or margins fall in relation to costs. Your accounting functions will become more difficult due to a loss of internal controls.

Corrective Measures:

Seek to stabilize price and gross margins to ensure consistency in costing out your products and services. Change your price and/or margin on a consistent, periodic, and timely basis. Educate your customers as to the need for any change or modification, including interim or unanticipated changes.

c. target market share?

If not, you may be sacrificing more important long-term market goals for short-term profit objectives.

Corrective Measures:

Price your products and services with long-term market share implications in mind. Higher prices in the short term will compromise the ability to penetrate large market share over a longer term, making it more difficult to survive downturns in the marketplace and/or general economy.

d. a maximization of income?

If not, your long-term survival will be compromised. Your owner's equity will suffer, thereby compromising the ability of your company to survive any tough times.

Corrective Measures:

Maximize your income wherever possible, without compromising your long-term market share development. Eventually, your market share dominance will generate any needed income levels.

e. a reduction in or stabilization of competition?

If not, your competition will grow, possibly compromising your market share.

Corrective Measures:

Work toward minimizing the impact of your competition by offering quality products and dependable service at competitive prices. Never move head-on against any competitors who are financially stronger. Instead, beat them on the flanks, a little at a time.

#13. H<small>AVE</small> <small>YOU</small> <small>ATTEMPTED</small> <small>TO</small> <small>TEST</small> <small>OR</small> <small>EXPERIMENT</small> <small>WITH</small> <small>NEW</small> <small>PRODUCTS</small> <small>AND</small> <small>SERVICES</small> <small>OR</small> <small>ITEMS</small> (<small>OR</small> <small>VARIATIONS</small> <small>OF</small> <small>OLD</small>) <small>PRIOR</small> <small>TO</small> <small>A</small> <small>FULL</small> <small>COMMITMENT</small>?

If not, keep in mind that a full commitment of resources may be a costly move to undertake without first experimenting to determine the market acceptance and cost factors, and losses could occur.

Corrective Measures:

Experiment with new services or items or variations of old services prior to a full commitment. Trial and error testing is the best way to cut your losses in the event of a product/service failure in the marketplace.

#14. DO YOU ALLOCATE OVERHEAD COSTS, SUCH AS DEPRECIATION, SPACE, AND ADMINISTRATIVE EXPENSES ON A STANDARD VOLUME OF BUSINESS WHEN SETTING PRICES?

If not, misallocation of your overhead costs, incorrect pricing of your products or services, and losses could occur.

Corrective Measures:

Ensure that all overhead costs are calculated and allocated based on a percentage of your sales or expenses. Allocate the overhead costs on each product or service for each department to ensure the proper costing and pricing. This can be done based on a percentage volume for each product, service, or department.

#15. DO YOU ATTEMPT TO RECAPTURE INITIAL START-UP EXPENDITURES OVER THE LONG TERM INSTEAD OF THE SHORT TERM?

If not, initial prices may be too high, thus impeding your sales. Your short-term goals may defeat the long-term market share objectives. Your product or services may be downright uncompetitive.

Corrective Measures:

Do not attempt to recapture initial expenditures quickly at the expense of adequate market share. Determine your pricing with long-term goals in mind rather than excessive short-term profits as an objective. Plan to recapture startup costs in a patient and timely fashion.

#16. WHEN SETTING PRICES, DO YOU USE THE ESTIMATES OF YOUR FUTURE COSTS RATHER THAN PRESENT ONES WHEN ARRIVING AT THE APPROPRIATE PRICE TO CHARGE?

If not, inflexible and irregular pricing policies will result in losses or a smaller profit during inflationary periods when current prices change quickly. If you are engaged in long-term contracts, your profits will suffer if they are locked into old costs.

Corrective Measures:

Correct your prices to estimate future costs, (such as standard cost of living increases), especially in terms of long-term contracts. When your pricing changes are infrequent, future estimates of costs must be considered to ensure an adequate profit margin.

#17. DO YOU CHARGE YOUR CUSTOMERS DIFFERENT PRICES WITH REGARD TO THE:

a. volume of business?

If not, large accounts will be lost.

Corrective Measures:

Give discounts to your largest buyers.

b. type of buyer (commercial, individual, or other)?

If not, you may lose larger commercial and industrial accounts or other large-volume buyers to your competitors.

Corrective Measures:

Give discounts or extended credit terms to your commercial, industrial, or other large-volume customers.

c. distance from you?

If not, customers that are located at a closer distance may require special services, or at the very least, freight discounts.

Corrective Measures:

Provide special services or freight discounts by way of mileage zones when possible.

d. industry policies?

If not, your customers and potential customers will go elsewhere if not treated in accordance with the established industry standards.

Corrective Measures:

Establish a pricing policy based on the industry standards.

#18. DO YOU AVOID OFFERING DISCOUNTS IN RETURN FOR SERVICES OR PRODUCTS THAT THE BUYER OFFERS YOU?

If not, be aware that in some cases back-scratching may be viewed as kickbacks, which are illegal and could pose accounting problems. Tax liabilities will also be incurred.

Corrective Measures:

Engage only in discount practices that are legal. Establish a rapport with the buyer to ensure that only legal trade discounts will be entertained, and maintain proper records for legal and tax reasons.

#19. Do you periodically re-evaluate and modify your prices?

If not, your prices may be too high, causing your customers to go elsewhere. If your prices are too low, it creates losses and cash flow difficulties. Long-term bad pricing will lead to your business termination.

Corrective Measures:

Research competitive prices and services and establish a price based on the information gathered. Update your prices to correct the percentage of markup to cover your expenses and profit. Constantly review your pricing policy.

#20. Do you know who makes the decision to buy your products/ services?

If not, you cannot target your advertising message to the proper decision-makers. Shotgun advertising approaches are often costly and less effective.

Corrective Measures:

Identify your decision-makers and target them in your advertising campaign.

#21. Do you know how the final decision to buy your product or service is made?

If not, you cannot properly target your advertising message to push the right buttons. Improvising your efforts is costly and not effective. The final decision-making may not involve the person to whom your presentation was geared.

Corrective Measures:

Evaluate and study all emotional and economic buying motives. Determine which motives move your customers, and design your advertising message to capitalize on those motives. Inquire about the decision-making process to find out how the final decision is made.

#22. Do you have a clear purpose in mind for your advertising?

If not, then your advertising lacks short-term and long-term goals, resulting in a misguided advertising message. This could lead to customer confusion and excessive cost without a proper focus.

Corrective Measures:

Establish advertising goals, both short and long term, and focus your advertising message. Evaluate the results and modify your advertising strategy if necessary.

#23. Is personal selling a part of the firm's promotional efforts?

If not, the loss of a personal touch with your customers leads to a detachment from your individual customer. Difficulty in understanding your products/services will make them more difficult to sell.

Corrective Measures:

Blend a degree of personal selling in all of your marketing efforts. Allocate all personal selling techniques to all products/services that are difficult to market otherwise. Determine the profitability of the personal selling approach.

#24. Do you know which part of the market your firm should be serving?

If not, you may be trying to reach the wrong market segment. There may no longer be a market for the service/product that you provide, or the market may have shifted in a negative way, resulting in a misallocation of marketing resources. The market may also have shifted in a positive way, but you are not aware of it, resulting in lost opportunities.

Corrective Measures:

Use research to determine your correct overall market, and use current demographic surveys to determine your best market segments, and then penetrate those market segments that offer you the best profit opportunities. Study your market consistently to ensure a proper posture in terms of the products/services offered.

#25. Do you attempt to sell differentiated products and/or services that carry a different price/value relationship?

If not, then meeting your competitors head-on may result in a divided market share, which can be very costly and generally leads to market failure in the event that your competitors are financially stronger.

Corrective Measures:

A differentiated product/service market may result in a larger market segment for your company. It is less costly to penetrate a differentiated market. Market niches are more profitable for you and less attractive to your larger competitors.

#26. ARE YOUR MARKETING AND PROMOTION EFFORTS HONEST AND STRAIGHTFORWARD?

If not, dishonest or misleading marketing will damage your business. You may be sued for false advertisement.

Corrective Measures:

Keep marketing and promotional efforts honest and ethical. Always promote your company as honest and trustworthy.

#27. IS YOUR FIRM GROWING AND BECOMING BETTER ESTABLISHED AS A RESULT OF YOUR MARKETING AND PROMOTIONAL EFFORTS?

If not, your marketing and promotional efforts are incorrect or less than adequate, or your marketing and promotional efforts may be okay, but your competitors are doing it better.

Corrective Measures:

Let experts review your marketing and promotional efforts. Do some trial and error experiments to find the best approach. Review your more successful competitors and improve upon their strategies.

#28. ARE ALL ASPECTS OF MARKETING AND SALES PROMOTION COORDINATED WITH PRODUCTION PLANNING AND SCHEDULING?

If not, your money may be spent on sales promotion without having a product to sell, causing your customer goodwill to suffer. Your production may be ahead of marketing and sales promotion, creating costly storage, insurance, and security problems.

Corrective Measures:

Coordinate your marketing, sales promotion, and production planning. Pay extra attention to the potential problem areas in your scheduling process that could cause bottlenecks.

#29. ARE YOUR MARKETING AND PROMOTIONAL EFFORTS CONTROLLED BY BUDGETS, WHICH ARE CHANGED ONLY FOR COMPELLING REASONS?

If not, the budgets for marketing and promotional efforts may get out of hand, costing you more money than is necessary. A loss of control related to overall finances may result in large marketing expenditures. A mistake here can affect finances elsewhere.

Corrective Measures:

Review your marketing and promotional budget constantly. Stay within your marketing and promotional budgets except for compelling reasons. Regain control over your promotional budget to control your overall expenditures.

#30. DO YOU SUBSCRIBE TO OR HAVE ACCESS TO A SALES PROMOTION SERVICE, AND DO YOU USE IT IN PLANNING AND EXERCISING YOUR PROMOTIONAL EVENTS?

If not, you may be passing up a relatively inexpensive source of assistance. No one is available to review and comment on your planned strategy, and without that input, you will lack any diversified expertise.

Corrective Measures:

Look for a sales promotion service that caters to your type and size of business. Use only a reputable sales promotion firm that employs personnel with marketing and sales promotion experience. Always check their references.

#31. DO YOU USE CO-OP ADS WITH OTHER MERCHANTS IN THE COMMUNITY?

If not, you may be paying too much for overall advertising while other merchants may be benefiting and paying less to do so. Customers may be drawn to larger co-op ads and may miss your smaller ads.

Corrective Measures:

Use co-op ads with other merchants in your community whenever feasible. Remember, larger co-op ads are more eye-catching and promote a cooperative attitude among merchants.

#32. DO YOU CONDUCT A CONTINUING EFFORT TO OBTAIN FREE PUBLICITY IN THE LOCAL PRESS OR BROADCAST MEDIA?

If not, more money will be spent on advertising. Information about your business may not get to the public if there is no money available for advertising, and free publicity is not continual. A lack of continual publicity results in lost business opportunities.

Corrective Measures:

Save your advertising dollars, or use your available ad dollars more wisely by obtaining free publicity on a continuous basis. Continually provide free publicity to enhance your business image by establishing a close working relationship with the media.

#33. ARE YOU ACQUAINTED WITH THE FEDERAL TRADE COMMISSION STANDARDS FOR TRUTH AND ACCURACY IN ADVERTISING AND DO YOU ADHERE TO THEM CAREFULLY?

If not, you will lose customers over advertising practices and claims that are not truthful. Your company may be fined or have restrictions imposed due to inaccurate advertising practices.

Corrective Measures:

Become acquainted with the FTC truth-in-advertising laws and adhere to them. Always back all of your advertising claims.

#34. DO YOU REGARD CUSTOMERS AS FRIENDS WHO ARE ENTITLED TO THE BEST MERCHANDISE VALUES AND SERVICES YOU CAN GIVE THEM?

Potential customers may look elsewhere for values. Your customers may look to your competitors for better service, resulting in a loss of your customer goodwill.

Corrective Measures:

Provide your customers with the best merchandise values possible. Provide them with better service than your competitors. Constantly seek to upgrade your merchandise and service. Request feedback from your customers about your merchandise and service, and modify your approach predicated upon the feedback you receive.

#35. DO YOU PURPOSEFULLY CATER TO ALL GROUPS RATHER THAN SELECTED GROUPS OF CUSTOMERS?

If not, certain groups of customers may be slighted and shop elsewhere while the select customer group chosen may not be your best customer.

Corrective Measures:

Treat all customers equally. Don't cater to selected groups of customers, unless your product/service requires you to do so. Determine your trade discounts by company policies rather than customer grouping. Be consistent in your customer policies whether you're catering to select groups or more diverse markets.

#36. DO YOU HAVE A CLEAR PICTURE OF THE STORE IMAGE YOU SEEK TO IMPLANT IN THE MINDS OF YOUR CUSTOMERS?

If not, there is no real directional plan for your store's image. Your customers may receive a negative image.

Corrective Measures:

Establish a directional image plan. Steer all of your business facets towards the desired image. Develop your niche through this image and constantly modify the image as market conditions and your customer tastes demand.

#37. DO YOU EVALUATE YOUR OWN PERFORMANCE BY ASKING CUSTOMERS ABOUT THEIR LIKES AND DISLIKES, AND BY SHOPPING COMPETITORS TO COMPARE THEIR ASSORTMENTS, PRICES, AND PROMOTIONAL METHODS TO YOUR OWN?

If not, your directional image may be wrong while your competitors are doing it better than you are. Your assortments, prices, and promotion methods may be in a rut and not appropriate given current market conditions.

Corrective Measures:

Seek feedback from your customers. Shop your competitors for ideas, and use the best ones through trial and error methods that will allow you to identify the best strategies for your company. Keep up to date with assortments, competitive prices, and promotional methods.

#38. DO YOU ATTEMPT TO APPEAL TO YOUNGER CUSTOMERS BOTH IN THE MERCHANDISE AND SERVICES YOU OFFER, AS WELL AS IN THE ATMOSPHERE YOU CREATE?

Neglecting a very important buying group results in a loss of current and potential business.

Corrective Measures:

Treat all customer groups equally, establish a good rapport, and offer your services and up-to-date merchandise to the younger customer. Nurture them as future customers.

#39. DO YOU ADD VALUE TO YOUR MERCHANDISE OR SERVICES BY DEVELOPING CUSTOMER CONFIDENCE IN YOUR JUDGMENT AND READINESS TO ENSURE SATISFACTION?

If not, customer confidence may be eroded and too many dissatisfied customers will lead to a loss of business.

Corrective Measures:

Readily assure customer satisfaction. Develop customer confidence in your judgment and truthfulness through advertising and customer relation policies. Always follow through on all guarantees whether direct, implied, or verbal.

#40. DO YOU FREQUENTLY SUPPLEMENT YOUR ROUTINE DAY-BY-DAY SELLING OPERATIONS WITH SPECIAL PROMOTIONS?

If not, your business's selling volume will become stagnant or even decline when newness and excitement is gone from your business atmosphere. Your sales team may lack personal enthusiasm.

Corrective Measures:

Create special promotions, and stimulate your sales personnel with new selling tactics and promotions, making selling and shopping fun. Review and act on your customer feedback. Change any special promotion strategy based on customer feedback and market conditions.

#41. DO YOU ADVERTISE CONSISTENTLY IN AT LEAST ONE APPROPRIATE MEDIUM?

If not, your customers will not know of any special promotions. Your business name recognition may be poor and customers will not be aware of any new or different services you offer. The lack of a consistent market presence will result in stagnant sales.

Corrective Measures:

Advertise your special sales and promotions. Stimulate your business name recognition and educate your customers to new services and merchandise offers through advertising. Initiate public relations (free advertising) whenever the opportunity presents itself.

#42. DO YOU PLAN YOUR ADVERTISING AT LEAST FOUR WEEKS AHEAD?

If not, your merchandise may not arrive in time for your planned advertising campaign. Your sales personnel may not be properly informed of merchandise advertised in time for an effective sales promotion effort. Rushed advertising campaigns often fail to generate the needed sales volume.

Corrective Measures:

Plan your advertising well in advance. Coordinate your advertising with your merchandise arrival. Inform your sales personnel of promotions prior to the advertising campaign. Train your employees on your current promotional strategy.

#43. DO YOU APPROVE ALL ADS BEFORE THEY ARE RELEASED, REVIEWING THEIR CONTENT AND MAKING SURE THAT THE GOODS MENTIONED WILL BE READY FOR SELLING?

If not, your ads may be unsuitable and poorly prepared. Merchandise and advertising may become uncoordinated. Your chosen advertising medium may not be appropriate.

Corrective Measures:

Review your ads for the highest-impact results and modify if necessary. Coordinate your merchandising and advertising. Make the effort to determine the best medium prior to advertising.

#44. DO YOU CONSISTENTLY CHOOSE ITEMS OR SERVICES FOR ADVERTISING THAT ARE TIMELY, HAVE EXCEPTIONAL VALUE, OR OFFER EXCLUSIVE FEATURES TO HELP BUILD YOUR STORE IMAGE?

If not, the items chosen may not build needed volume traffic. Your image and profits will suffer.

Corrective Measures:

Choose items that will build a consistent volume of traffic. Use *advertiming* instead of just advertising. Timing is important nowadays, so review your advertising and value the quality of your merchandise to ensure a positive business impact. Constantly modify or change your product mix to reflect changes in customer tastes.

#45. DO YOU FOLLOW THE ADS OF STORES IN LARGER CITIES CATERING TO CUSTOMERS SIMILAR TO YOUR OWN IN ORDER TO FIND OUTSTANDING ITEMS TO ADVERTISE?

If not, many new advertising and marketing ideas may be missed, and outstanding volume and profit building items may be overlooked.

Corrective Measures:

Check your competitor's ads for good advertising and marketing ideas and learn to recognize all of the high-impact advertised items that you can use. Become the advertising leader within your area with new merchandise, advertising, and ideas.

#46. DO YOU TELL NEWSWORTHY AND READABLE STORIES RATHER THAN TRUMPETING PRICE APPEAL ONLY?

In many cases, trumpeting prices may turn customers off, especially if they're too commonplace. Your customers may be attracted to your competitor's ads that are more colorful and educational.

Corrective Measures:

Gear your ads to catch the attention of your customers. Create newness and differential in advertising, and educate your customers when appropriate.

#47. ARE ADVERTISEMENTS FACTUAL, PROVIDING ALL PERTINENT DETAILS ABOUT THE ITEMS YOU ARE OFFERING?

If not, customers will become confused about your advertised items and possibly seek more information about those advertised items from your competitors. You may be breaking the law.

Corrective Measures:

Adhere to all legal regulations. Provide pertinent details in your ads, and make them clear and simple to understand.

#48. DOES EACH OF YOUR ADS SPECIFICALLY SELL YOUR STORE, IN ADDITION TO THE MERCHANDISE ADVERTISED?

If not, your advertisement does not give any business name recognition to potential or even existing customers, causing your customers to possibly recognize the merchandise as being sold in your competitor's business and shop there. Your advertising budget may be increasing with no tangible results.

Corrective Measures:

Use business name recognition throughout your ads. Sell not only the merchandise, but also the store as a friendly place to shop, so as to develop the store image along with the advertised specials.

#**49.** WHEN YOU PLAN TO ADVERTISE GOODS THAT ARE CARRIED BY YOUR COMPETITORS, OR THAT ARE COMPARABLE TO THEIRS, DO YOU CHECK THESE COMPETITORS' PRICES AND ASSORTMENTS BEFORE RELEASING YOUR AD?

If not, your competitors may be breaking an ad at the same time with a lower price. They may have comparable merchandise at a better value, or a better assortment of the goods advertised.

Corrective Measures:

Check your competitor's prices prior to advertising. Check your competitors for comparable merchandise value, or for assortment of the merchandise that you will be advertising, and make appropriate adjustments in your merchandise, price, and advertising approach to reflect the above observations.

#**50.** DO YOU REGULARLY AND SYSTEMATICALLY FAMILIARIZE YOUR SALESPEOPLE WITH YOUR PLANS FOR ADVERTISING AND PROMOTIONS?

If not, your salespeople will not be familiar with the overall advertising campaign. This will give your customers a sense of disorganization, causing them to become irritated and go elsewhere.

Corrective Measures:

Familiarize your salespeople with the overall advertising and promotional campaign and specially advertised and/or promotional goods. Alert your salespeople to any change in price or service in the merchandise to be advertised. Eliminate any potential misunderstandings and mistakes through an informative sales advertising and promotion SOP.

#**51.** DO YOU CONSULT YOUR SUPPLIERS ABOUT DEALER AIDS HELPFUL TO THE PROMOTION OF THEIR MERCHANDISE IN THE STORE?

If not, helpful dealer sales aides may be missed, causing your promotional effort to cost more, resulting in a potential loss of sales.

Corrective Measures:

Consult your suppliers about any free promotional sales aids. Seek co-op advertising from suppliers or ask for better prices or terms on larger-volume purchases of their merchandise.

#52. Do you insist that your salespeople treat each of your customers as an individual rather than one of the crowd?

If not, your customers may feel slighted or ignored and cease to buy. The individual needs of your customer may not be met. The friendly atmosphere of your business may be jeopardized.

Corrective Measures:
Treat all customers as welcome individuals in your business. Determine the individual needs of your customers and seek to satisfy them. Make your entire customer base feel important to your business by adequately training your employees in the art of salesmanship.

#53. To resolve a serious disagreement with a customer over a purchase or bill, do you ever try arbitration, rather than going to court or simply giving in to a customer who you feel is wrong?

If not, the customer may become irritated and take their business elsewhere. Court action can take up a considerable amount of your time and expense.

Corrective Measures:
Determine beforehand the upper limit of the legal cost and time you are willing to spend; if excessive in either respect, consider arbitration. To avoid a direct, irritating confrontation over a customer's bill or purchase, it may be better to seek out a third party to settle the dispute. Try to identify an unbiased person, acceptable to both parties involved, to make the final decision.

#54. In planning displays, do you devote the same care to the selection of merchandise, the use of effective lighting and arrangement, the evaluation of results, and the use of outside displays?

If not, your displays may create an adverse image effect. The lighting may not be effective or the merchandise may not be highlighted to your best interest. Advertising dollars will be wasted if these other factors are not given adequate consideration and coordinated with the overall advertising campaign.

Corrective Measures:

Assess these elements and make improvements as necessary to create a more attractive shopping environment. Coordinate your overall display strategy with your advertising and promotional strategy.

#55. Are your window displays planned to attract attention, develop interest, create desire, and prompt a customer to enter your store for a closer inspection?

An unplanned, hodge-podge window display may turn off a potential customer. Without feedback, ill-planned window displays may continue, resulting in a poor image and ultimately lost business.

Corrective Measures:

Plan your window displays to best enhance your business image. Turn on customer interest with attractive, desire-prompting windows, and monitor all customer feedback on your displays.

#56. Have you prepared particular employees to act as marketing agents for the firm?

If not, your company will lack a proper marketing focus and suffer a loss of sales due to confusion among employees and a loss of organizational productivity.

Corrective Measures:

Choose only employees with the best sales ability. Promote marketing understanding in every aspect of your business operation; even non-sales employees should understand the basic sales tactics and market focus. Use incentives to promote sales.

#57. Are employees aware of the importance of good client relations?

If not, an enhanced number of customer complaints, dissatisfied customers, and a loss of sales opportunities and profits will result.

Corrective Measures:

Hold training sessions to make all of your employees aware of the importance of customer relations. Establish a reward system for fostering good customer relations and immediately remove inappropriate employees from direct contact with your customers.

Research and Development

CHAPTER 10

THE INNOVATIVE AND CREATIVE ENVIRONMENT

Many people do not distinguish between creativity and innovation, but there is a difference. Creativity is the process of creating something new or looking at things in a non-traditional way. Innovation deals with applying what has been created or identified in this process. For example, you can invent a new process to reduce manufacturing costs in your plant—this is a creative endeavor. However, innovation is not advanced unless you apply the new process to your operations.

America is viewed throughout the world as the most creative and inventive nation on the planet. On the other hand, we do not apply all of our creative output to innovative processes. Other countries procure our creative discoveries and use them in their industrial applications more effectively than we do. Countries such as China, India, and Japan are relieved of the research and development cost burdens, yet they can claim to be more innovative.

Here are some techniques that can be used to assist you in safely converting your new ideas into entrepreneurial innovations:

- Scrutinize any new idea to the maximum degree possible. Don't leave any stone unturned. This provides for peace of mind.

- Determine and record all of the negative and positive aspects of any new idea. What benefits can be expected in terms of improved marketing, lower costs, or enhanced productivity? Who will receive them? Are there any risks associated with implementing the new idea? If so, what are the risks? Can a mistake be absorbed? Good managers always visualize the worst-case scenario and then make a determination as to whether they can survive that possibility. If they think not, a new idea will be forthcoming.

- Once the new idea has been analyzed for possible flaws, restructure it so that the idea is simple to understand and interpret. This will help you to clear your thinking about the new idea.

- Review your idea with other people who may have already utilized a similar approach. Customers, competitors, consultants, accountants, and other experts could provide input. Idea weaknesses must be candidly admitted and addressed. The idea may need to be modified or even eliminated in favor of a new approach.

- Execute the idea at the proper time. Wrong timing may cancel out the benefits of a good idea. For example, trying to execute productivity improvements using new techniques could result in a morale backlash unless employees have been properly prepared for the introduction of new methods. This orientation might take several weeks or months.

- Evaluate the results of implementing your idea. Without proper feedback, you may never know whether an idea is working until a lot of damage has been inflicted.

Letting it rip

You can have all the best ideas in the world, but if you don't convert those ideas into actions, nothing will be accomplished. Even if your idea turns out to be something less than a winner, at least you experimented with that particular approach and the results can be recorded for future reference. So take the initiative and direct your creative energies into tangible innovative results. Just remember the words of Jack Paar, who said, "Life is a series of obstacles, and we ourselves are the largest obstacles." Don't fall prey to inaction. If you are willing to experiment and learn, your ability to successfully convert ideas to innovation will increase.

Keep in mind that your survival in your present and future entrepreneurial environments will depend upon your ability and willingness to apply new ideas in a changing marketplace. Many small companies are reporting that they are diversifying their product and service lines in order to stay afloat. You must keep abreast of your market and know when to change. Without ideas in hand ready to go, you may miss the boat. Even if the market for your products or services is growing, you still may have to engage in creative and innovative endeavors to thrive. Why is this the case? Because we find ourselves in a highly competitive economy, in which everybody and his brother is trying to start a business. Attraction of future customers will depend upon your success in standing apart from your competitors. In other words, doing something different, such as surprising your customers with a new product or service, will help you in the game of entrepreneurship.

GOVERNMENT HELP

In 1952, Congress and the president signed into existence the Small Business Innovation Development Act which authorized the Small Business Innovation Research Program, also known as SBIR. This program affords entrepreneurial firms the opportunity to promote and fund their creative and innovative ideas. These ideas must meet the research and development needs of the federal government while potentially opening the door to future commercialization. The SBIR program consists of three phases. They are:

- Phase I: to evaluate the scientific/technical merit and feasibility of an idea.
- Phase II: to expand on the results of and further pursue the development of Phase I.
- Phase III: for the commercialization of the results of Phase II, requiring the use of private or non-SBIR federal funding. The program will provide funding up to $100,000 for Phase I and up to $750,000 for Phase II, if your idea has merit in terms of helping the government in research and development efforts. More information about SBIR can be obtained by writing or calling:

U.S. Small Business Administration
Office of Technology
409 Third Street, S.W.
Washington, DC 20416
Phone: 202–205–6450
Website: *www.sba.gov/SBIR*

Now don't get the wrong idea! The SBIR program is not for everybody. Only ideas of a technical nature that will help the government's research and development efforts will be considered. Also, the idea must stand a chance of commercialization in the private marketplace.

CREATIVE FOCUS AND IDEA GENERATION

Entrepreneurship and the creative spirit

There is one thing that definitely separates the entrepreneur from the typical small business owner, and that is creative spirit. Entrepreneurs love to be creative. They strive to invent, innovate, change, experiment, and modify. Unfortunately, those entrepreneuring souls within the corporate ranks who are often faced with unappreciative bosses and jealous peers are seldom given the chance to be creative. Many of these internal entrepreneurs, now referred to as intrapreneurs in the business world, are suppressed. Some are pigeonholed rather than promoted.

However, many giant companies that are facing contracting markets and falling profit margins are calling upon the creative spirits of these intrapreneurs in an attempt to secure their future. The traditional small business owner is also finding the going tough. Entrepreneurial competition is growing in leaps and bounds. The baby boomers are starting all kinds of businesses in record numbers. Even the tiny mom-and-pop grocery store on the corner will need to be creative and idea-oriented in order to survive.

An example of this creative spirit involved an entrepreneur who was having some trouble with his employees on Monday mornings. He was experiencing a 10 percent absentee rate. The entrepreneur decided to change the payday from Friday to Monday. Bingo! Absenteeism dropped by 60 percent and stabilized in a normal range.

One of my personal ventures entails the ownership of a newsstand/convenience shop in Winchester, Virginia that was failing when I bought it in November of 2002. Sales were approximately $6,000 per month. As of April 2006, the sales are $27,000 per month. One of the creative sales measures I used was to offer everyone a free $1 lottery ticket for every 10 packs of cigarettes they purchase. Cigarette sales rose from 300 packs a month to more than 4,000 per month, to the regret of my competition.

The point to ponder here is that in any given problem situation your number of remedial alternatives will increase as the breadth of your thinking expands. In other words, creative thinking increases your options. Here are some techniques that can be applied to help you enhance your creative thinking skills:

- be open to new ideas
- problem empathy
- prepare yourself
- initiate new ideas
- creative germination
- expand your ideas

No PROFITS WITHOUT RISK

If you are looking for total security in an environment without risk, don't expect any dividends in the form of entrepreneurial returns. You must take a risk in order to generate revenues. The more you are willing to risk, the greater the possibility of profits. If you want all of your money protected by the FDIC, or if you are losing sleep over a $500 investment in the stock market, forget about entrepreneurship as a viable employment alternative. You may gripe and complain about your boss and the lousy pay, but you will be happier employed by somebody else as opposed to working for yourself.

Calculating the risk factor

It is known from many research studies that successful entrepreneurs are moderate risk-takers. They are not the dice rollers that many purport them to be. The Center for Entrepreneurial Management (CEM) found that of the 2,500 entrepreneurs responding to their research, 40 percent would take 3-to-1 odds at a racetrack. Almost 15 percent would try 2-to-1 odds, while 23 percent would opt for a 10-to-1 shot. Approximately 22 percent indicated they would go for the daily double and a chance of making a bundle.

If you are an acute risk-taker and in any way have gambling fever, don't take the entrepreneurial plunge, because you will probably lose your shirt. Even if you are a moderate risk-taker, caution is still needed. You must analyze all deals in terms of risk versus reward before making a decision.

Innovate or cease to exist

You might think you are too small or your product/service too common to invest in research and development. Most people think of R&D as strictly a function of big or highly technical companies. But R&D leads to innovation, not just in your product or service offerings, but also in your methods of operation and delivery. Innovation leads to efficiency and efficiency leads to lower costs and higher profits. Simply speaking, research and development for a small business is nothing more than paying attention to trends, maybe spending a little money for information and advice from professionals, and then acting on the information received.

For a small clothing shop on the corner it may be nothing more than changing merchandise stock to meet the latest fads or styles. For a retail tire distributor it may be taking on a new line of tires that have been technically improved to last longer. For a management consultant it may be learning new cutting-edge techniques and methods to offer their existing and/or potential client base. These are examples of R&D in action.

In any business, upgrading your fax machine from the old rolled paper units to a plain paper fax is a form of innovation. Somewhere along the line you read or heard about the cost-effectiveness of plain paper faxes—that's research and development—and you acted on that information.

It's really that simple and quite inexpensive for most entrepreneurial firms. But it must be ongoing, or your products, services, and methods of operation will become obsolete and compromise your continued existence.

Important Questions to Consider

#1. DO YOU ENCOURAGE CREATIVE THINKING WITHIN YOUR COMPANY?

If not, you are losing out on some very inexpensive and valuable sources of brainpower both in terms of output (new ideas) and input (critical review of existing business operations).

Corrective Measures:

Let your employees know that free thinking and the expression of the output and/or input generated because of this environment of free thinking is important to you and will be taken seriously.

#2. DO YOU ENCOURAGE CALCULATED RISK-TAKING WITHIN YOUR COMPANY?

If not, your business will die of boredom and lack of new markets. Experimentation with new ideas, products, and services is good and sets the tone for a dynamic and growing company.

Corrective Measures:

Create an internal environment within your business that encourages well-thought-out risk-taking. It doesn't even have to be an expensive undertaking. An inexpensive evaluation here and there is all that is needed for most small firms to gain valuable insight into new methods of operation, or new products and services. It is money well spent.

#3. DO YOU ENCOURAGE IDEA GERMINATION WITHIN YOUR COMPANY?

If not, you risk organizational stagnation in reference to operational and marketing issues. Markets will disappear and operational efficiencies will be compromised. Profits will eventually suffer.

Corrective Measures:

It's one thing to allow creative thinking; it is another to allow the seeds of creative thinking to take hold and sprout. Take new and creative ideas seriously. Try a few out and have patience while they germinate within your business. Some will pan out, others won't. But generally, the benefits to the company of new and unique ideas that work far outweigh the costs of those new and unique ideas that fail to generate the desired results.

#4. DO YOU ENCOURAGE INNOVATION WITHIN YOUR COMPANY?

If not, why expend the money, time, and effort in creating a free-thinking, creative, risk-taking internal environment within your company? Innovation is nothing more than taking and applying the aforementioned resources into a workable stream of events that produce the desired results, be it a new product or service, a better way to deliver said product or service, or more productive internal methods of operation.

Corrective Measures:

Take what you've invested in (creative thinking, idea germination, risk taking) and run with it. Don't sit there like a bump on a log! Convert those efforts into real and tangible company results that put money in your pockets.

#5. ARE YOUR RESEARCH AND DEVELOPMENT ACTIVITIES FUNDED AND SUPPORTED ON A REGULAR BASIS?

Without research and development activities you will not develop upon and/or improve your market position. Products, services, and methods of operation will become stagnant and obsolete. Your sales will eventually deteriorate. Without appropriate budgeting for research and development funds there will always be an excuse for not innovating.

Corrective Measures:

Review budget expenditures regularly and allow for some research and development funds to be set aside, no matter the size of your business. This will allow you to keep up with current trends and ideas in order to maintain competitiveness. If appropriate funding has not been allowed for research and development, it may be necessary to borrow money for this purpose. Given the constantly and rapidly changing competitive environment for all products and services, you will have an advantage if you do a little studying (research) and then act on those findings (development).

#6. ARE THE FEATURES OF YOUR PRODUCTS OR SERVICES REVIEWED AT REGULAR INTERVALS TO ENSURE THAT THEY ARE NOT BECOMING OBSOLETE?

If not, the product or service may be losing its economic appeal and value. Eventually the market will reject your offerings and compromise your survival.

Corrective Measures:

Keep accurate data on trends that concern your products and services. Confer with marketing experts regularly to ensure proper market fit. Check with employees, vendors, and customers for their input. Change or modify your product/service line when the market demands it.

#7. DO YOU ASK VENDORS TO OFFER SUGGESTIONS ON HOW TO IMPROVE YOUR PRODUCTS OR SERVICES?

If not, you are avoiding and ignoring a creative, valuable, and unbiased opinion of your products and/or services. What is not apparent to you may be quite clear to your vendors. Remember, if you are successful, so are your vendors. Not only that, your vendors may provide you with vital information on your competitors.

Corrective Measures:

It's simple. Take the time and listen to your vendors. Spring for a lunch or dinner and you will be surprised at what you hear. Don't be stubborn about their suggestions and opinions. They're in business to help you generate sales. Keep an open mind and change or modify your product/service line if it makes sense.

#8. ARE YOU CONTINUOUSLY WORKING ON RESEARCH AND DEVELOPMENT PROJECTS THAT WILL IMPROVE YOUR PRODUCTS, SERVICES, MANUFACTURING PROCESSES, AND PRODUCTIVITY?

Products and services can become obsolete. Production processes may become obsolete. Competitors will move ahead because of newer and more innovative products and services. You may not be taking advantage of improved productivity methods.

Corrective Measures:

Keep accurate reports on all equipment in use and the need for potential improvements. Provide for funding and implementation of upgrades when appropriate. Hold frequent meetings for updating reports on improvements. Start a detailed research and development program directed toward product, service, and productivity enhancement.

#9. Do you maintain research and development efforts that are balanced among your markets, your products/services, and your people?

If not, concentrating on only one area, or the wrong areas, may allow other more critical areas to fall behind. Too much or too little research and development effort in any area can be costly or detrimental to your business.

Corrective Measures:

Maintain an even balance of control over all areas receiving R&D input. Determine which areas need what level of input. Then invest your research and development dollars optimally, meaning putting those funds in the most critical areas first.

#10. Do you encourage your employees to help in research and development efforts?

If not, your employees may feel disenfranchised. Since R&D activity is cutting-edge stuff that may involve new innovations, ignoring your employees will increase their suspicions of you and create mistrust.

Corrective Measures:

Encourage employee input at all levels of R&D activity. Reward employees for good research and development suggestions, particularly the ones that are accepted and implemented by you.

#11. Are you benefiting from the research and development efforts of other firms and organizations?

If not, you may be losing free or inexpensive sources of valuable research and development input.

Corrective Measures:

Subscribe to business journals that will keep you updated on new research ideas and thrusts. Join associations that will help with you retrieve vital research data. Establish networks and relationships with competitors concerning research efforts.

International Trade

CHAPTER 11

Globalization and the integration of the world economy is becoming increasingly evident. The total value of international trade equaled $3.3 trillion in 2005, or 30 percent of the total U.S. economy. Of the total amounts, imports accounted for the fastest growth at a 13.2 percent annual rate, thereby complicating the U.S. trade deficit, which stood at $725.8 billion dollars in 2005. But exports are also growing very rapidly. The large consumer markets developing in Asian nations, Latin America, and the European Union will provide vast opportunities for American businesses, both large and small.

BECOMING AN EXPORT SUCCESS STORY

Making the export decision

Exporting is crucial to America's economic health. Increased exports means business growth, and business growth means more jobs.

Yet only a small percentage of potential exporters take advantage of these opportunities. It is critical for U.S. businesses to think globally. Your decision to read this book indicates an interest in exporting; however, you may have discovered your company is already competing internationally—foreign-owned companies are competing with you in your domestic markets. The division between domestic and international markets is becoming increasingly blurred. Your business cannot ignore international realities if you intend to maintain your market share and keep pace with your competitors. Making the export decision requires careful assessment of the advantages and disadvantages of expanding into new markets. Once the decision is made to export, an international business plan is essential.

Advantages and disadvantages of exporting

Consider some of the specific advantages of exporting. Exporting can help your business:

- enhance domestic competitiveness
- increase sales and profits
- gain global market share
- reduce dependence on existing markets
- exploit corporate technology and know-how
- extend the sales potential of existing products
- stabilize seasonal market fluctuations
- enhance potential for corporate expansion
- sell excess production capacity
- gain information about foreign competition

In comparison, there are certain disadvantages to exporting. Your business may be required to:

- develop new promotional material
- subordinate short-term profits to long-term gains
- incur added administrative costs
- allocate personnel for travel
- wait longer for payments
- modify your product or packaging
- apply for additional financing

These disadvantages may justify a decision to forgo exporting at the present time. For example, if your company's financial situation is weak, attempting to sell into foreign markets may be ill-timed. On the other hand, some companies have been successful selling abroad before they have made any sales domestically.

The need for an international business plan

Behind most export success stories is a plan. Whether formally written down or sketched out informally at a meeting of your management team, an international business plan is an essential tool to properly evaluate all the factors that affect your company's ability to go international. An international business plan should define your:

- commitment to international trade
- export pricing strategy
- reason for exporting
- potential export markets and customers
- methods of foreign market entry
- exporting costs and projected revenues
- export financing alternatives
- legal requirements
- transportation method
- overseas partnership and foreign investment capabilities

The first draft of the plan may be short and simple, but it should become more detailed as the planners learn more about their company's competitive position. These questions should ultimately be addressed:

- What products are selected for export development? What modifications, if any, must be made to adapt them for overseas markets?
- What countries are targeted for sales development?
- In each country, what is the basic customer profile? What marketing and distribution channels should be used to reach customers?
- What special challenges pertain to each market, and what strategy will be used to address them?
- How will the product's export sales price be determined?
- What specific operational steps must be taken and when?
- What will be the time frame for implementing each element of the plan?
- What personnel and company resources will be dedicated to exporting?
- What will be the cost in time and money for each element?
- How will results be evaluated and used to modify the plan?
- Do you agree on the export plan?

A clearly written marketing strategy offers immediate benefits:

- Because written plans display their strengths and weaknesses more readily, they are of great help in formulating and polishing an export strategy.
- Written plans are not as easily forgotten, overlooked, or ignored by those charged with executing them. If deviation from the original plan occurs, it is likely to be a deliberate choice to do so.
- Written plans are easier to communicate to others and are less likely to be misunderstood.
- Written plans allocate responsibilities and provide for an evaluation of results.
- Written plans can be of help in seeking financing. They indicate to lenders a serious approach to the export venture.
- Written plans give management a clear understanding of what will be required and thus help to ensure a commitment to exporting. In fact, a written plan signals that the decision to export has already been made.

SAMPLE OUTLINE FOR AN EXPORT PLAN

This export plan has been recommended by the U.S. Department of Commerce:

Table of contents
Executive summary (one or two pages maximum)
Introduction: Why this company should export
Part I—Export policy commitment statement
Part II—Situation/background analysis
        Product or service
        Operations
        Personnel and export organization
        Resources of the firm
        Industry structure, competition, and demand
Part III—Marketing component
        Identifying, evaluating, and selecting target markets
        Product selection and pricing
        Distribution methods
        Terms and conditions
        Internal organization and procedures
        Sales goals: profit and loss forecasts
Part IV—Tactics: action steps
        Primary target countries

Secondary target countries
Indirect marketing efforts
Part V—Export budget
Pro-forma financial statements
Part VI—Implementation schedule
Follow-up
Periodic operational and management review
Addenda—Background data on target countries and market
Basic market statistics: historical and projected
Background facts
Competitive environment

Creating an international business plan is important for defining your company's present status, internal goals, and commitment, but is also required if you plan to seek export financing assistance. Preparing the plan in advance of making export loan requests from your bank can save time and money. Completing and analyzing an international business plan helps you anticipate future goals, assemble facts, identify constraints, and create an action statement.

Identifying international markets

To succeed in exporting, you must first identify the most profitable international markets for your products or services. Without proper guidance and assistance this process can be time-consuming and costly. The federal and state governments, trade associations, exporters' associations, and foreign governments offer low-cost and easily accessible resources to simplify and speed your foreign market research.

FEDERAL GOVERNMENT RESOURCES

Many government programs are dedicated to helping you assess whether your product or service is ready to compete in a foreign market. Many small firms have found the counseling services provided by the SBA's Service Corps of Retired Executives (SCORE) particularly helpful.

Two other SBA-sponsored programs are available to small businesses needing management and export advice: Small Business Development Centers and Small Business Institutes affiliated with colleges and universities throughout the United States. Small Business Development Centers (SBDCs) offer counseling, training, and research assistance on all aspects of small business management. The Small Business Institute (SBI) program provides intensive management counseling from business students who are supervised by faculty.

The U.S. Department of Commerce

The U.S. Department of Commerce's (DOC) International Trade Administration (ITA) is a valuable source of advice and information. In ITA offices throughout the country, international trade specialists can help you locate the best foreign markets for your products.

District Export Councils (DECs) are another useful ITA-sponsored resource. The 51 District Export Councils located around the United States are composed of 1,800 executives with experience in international trade who volunteer to help small businesses export. Council members come from banks, manufacturing companies, law offices, trade associations, state and local agencies, and educational institutions.

The U.S. & Foreign Commercial Service (US&FCS) helps U.S. firms compete more effectively in the global marketplace with trade specialists in 69 United States cities and 70 countries worldwide. US&FCS offices provide information on foreign markets, agent/distributor location services, trade leads, and counseling on business opportunities, trade barriers, and prospects abroad.

The United States Department of Agriculture

If you have an agricultural product, you should investigate the U.S. Department of Agriculture's (USDA) Foreign Agricultural Service (FAS). With posts in 80 embassies and consulates worldwide, the FAS can obtain specific overseas market information for your product. The FAS also maintains sector specialists in the United States to monitor foreign markets for specific U.S. agricultural products.

Port Authorities

Port Authorities are a wealth of export information. Although traditionally associated with transportation services, many port authorities around the country have expanded their services to provide export training programs and foreign-marketing research assistance. For example, the Port Authority of New York and New Jersey provides extensive services to exporters, including XPORT, a full-service export trading company.

Private sector resources

In addition to government-supported resources, private sector organizations can also provide invaluable assistance.

> ■ Exporters' associations. World Trade Centers, import-export clubs, and organizations such as the American Association of Exporters and Importers and the Small Business Exporter's Association can aid in your foreign market research.

■ Trade associations. The National Federation of International Trade Associations lists more than 150 organizations. Many of these associations maintain libraries, databanks, and established relationships with foreign governments to assist in your exporting efforts. More than 5,000 trade and professional associations currently operate in the United States; many actively promote international trade activities for their members.

■ Chambers of commerce. State chambers or chambers located in major industrial areas often employ international trade specialists who gather information on markets abroad.

Exporting

Of the various methods of foreign market entry, exporting is most commonly used by small businesses. Start-up costs and risks are limited, and profits can be realized early on. There are two basic ways to export: direct or indirect. The direct method requires your company to find a foreign buyer and then make all arrangements for shipping your products overseas. If this method seems beyond the scope of your business' in-house capabilities at this time, do not abandon the idea of exporting. Consider using an export intermediary.

Indirect exporting

There are several kinds of export intermediaries you should consider.

Commissioned agents

Commissioned agents act as brokers, linking your product or service with a specific foreign buyer. Generally, the agent or broker will not fulfill the orders, but rather will pass them to you for your acceptance. However, they may assist, in some cases, with export logistics such as packing, shipping, and export documentation.

Export management companies (EMCs)

EMCs act as your off-site export department, representing your product to prospective overseas purchasers. The management company looks for business and takes care of all aspects of the export transaction. Hiring an EMC is often a viable option for smaller companies that lack the time and expertise to break into international markets on their own. EMCs will often use the letterhead of your company, negotiate export contracts, and then provide after-sales support. EMCs may assist in arranging export financing for the exporters but they do not generally assure payment to the manufacturers. Some of the specific functions an EMC will perform include:

- conducting market research to determine the best foreign markets for your products
- attending trade shows and promoting your products overseas
- assessing proper distribution channels
- locating foreign representatives and/or distributors
- arranging export financing
- handling export logistics, such as preparing invoices, arranging insurance, and customs documentation
- advising on the legal aspects of exporting and other compliance matters dealing with domestic and foreign trade regulations

EMCs usually operate on a commission basis, although some work on a retainer basis and some take title to the goods they sell, making a profit on the markup. It is becoming increasingly common for EMCs to take title to goods.

Export trading companies (ETCs)

ETCs perform many of the functions of EMCs. However, they tend to be demand-driven and transaction-oriented, acting as an agent between the buyer and seller. Most trading companies source U.S. products for their overseas buyers. If you offer a product that is competitive and popular with the ETC buyers, you are likely to get repeat business. Most ETCs will take title to your goods for export and will pay your company directly. This arrangement practically eliminates the risks associated with exporting for the manufacturer.

ETC cooperatives

ETC cooperatives are United States government-sanctioned co-ops of companies with similar products who seek to export and gain greater foreign market share. Many agricultural concerns have benefited from ETC cooperative exporting, and many associations have sponsored ETC cooperatives for their member companies. The National Machine Tool Builders' Association, the Outdoor Power Equipment Institute, and the National Association of Energy Service Companies are a few examples of associations with ETC co-ops. Check with your particular trade association for further information.

The Export Trading Company Act of 1982

This legislation encourages the use and formation of EMCs/ETCs by changing the antitrust and banking environments under which these companies operate. The Act increases access to export financing by permitting bank holding companies to invest in ETCs and reduces restrictions on trade finance provided by financial institutions. Under the Act, banks are allowed to make equity investments in qualified ETCs.

Foreign trading companies

Some of the world's largest trading companies are located outside the United States. They can often be a source of export opportunity. U.S. & Foreign Commercial Service (US&FCS) representatives in embassies around the world can tell you more about trading companies located in a given foreign market.

Exporting through an intermediary

Working with an EMC/ETC makes sense for many small businesses. The manufacturer should carefully weigh the pros and cons before entering into a contract with an EMC/ETC. Some advantages include:

- Your product gains exposure in international markets—with little or no commitment of staff and resources from your company.
- The EMC/ETC's years of experience and well-established network of contacts may help you to gain faster access to international markets than you could through establishing a relationship with a foreign-based partner.
- Using an intermediary lowers or eliminates your export start-up costs, and, therefore, the risks associated with exporting. You can negotiate your contract with an EMC so that you pay nothing until the first order is received.
- Your intermediary will guide you through the export process step-by-step. Over time, you will develop your own export skills.

Some disadvantages of exporting through an intermediary include:

- You lose some control over the way in which your product is marketed and serviced. You will want to incorporate any concerns you may have into your contract, and you will want to monitor the activities of your intermediary.
- You may lose part of your export-sales profit margin by discounting your price to an intermediary. However, you may find that the economies of scale realized through increased production offset this loss.
- Using an intermediary can result in a higher price being passed on to the overseas buyer or end-user. This may or may not affect your competitive position in the market. The issue of pricing should be addressed at the outset.

Export merchants/export agents

Export merchants and agents will purchase and then re-package products for export, assuming all risks and selling to their own customers. This export intermediary option should be considered carefully, as your company could run the risk of losing control over your product's pricing and marketing in overseas markets.

Piggyback exporting

Allowing another company, which already has an export distribution system in place, to sell your company's product in addition to its own is called piggyback exporting.

Piggyback exporting has several advantages. This arrangement can help you gain immediate foreign market access. Also, all the requisite logistics associated with selling abroad are borne by the exporting company. Oklahoma-based DP Manufacturing's winches were attached to another product and sold abroad by another company. DP Manufacturing now handles its own exports and reports that 15 percent of its sales come from international markets.

How to find export intermediaries

Small businesses often report that intermediaries find them—at trade fairs and through trade journals where their products have been advertised—so it can often pay to get the word out that you are interested in exporting.

One way to begin your search for a U.S.-based export intermediary is in the Yellow Pages of your local phone directory. In just a few initial phone calls, you should be able to determine whether indirect exporting is an option you want to pursue further.

The National Association of Export Companies (NEXCO) and the National Federation of Export Associations (NFEA) are two associations that can assist in your efforts to find export intermediaries. The Directory of Leading Export Management Companies is another useful source.

The U.S. Department of Commerce's Office of Export Trading Company Affairs (OETCA) can also assist in providing information on how to locate ETCs and EMCs, as well as ETC cooperatives in the United States. The office, under a joint public/private partnership, compiles the Export Yellow Pages, which provides the names and addresses of EMCs/ETCs, as well as other export service companies, such as banks and freight forwarders. Contact your local U.S. Department of Commerce district office for information on being listed or for a free copy of the directory. Locating the best export intermediary to represent you overseas is important. Do your homework before signing an agreement.

Direct exporting

While indirect exporting offers many advantages, direct exporting also has its rewards: Although initial outlays and the associated risks are greater, so too can be the profits.

Direct exporting signals a commitment on the part of company management to fully engage in international trade. It may require that you dedicate a staff person or even several personnel to support your export efforts, and company management may have to travel abroad frequently.

Selling directly to an international buyer means that you will have to handle the logistics of moving the goods overseas.

DIFFERENT APPROACHES TO DIRECT EXPORTING

Sales representatives/agents

Similar to manufacturers' representatives in the United States, foreign-based representatives or agents work on a commission basis to locate buyers for your product. Your representative will most likely handle several complementary (but non-competing) product lines. An agent is generally a representative with authority to make commitments on behalf of your firm. Be careful, therefore, about using the terms interchangeably. Your agreement should specify whether the agent has the legal authority to obligate the firm.

Distributors

Foreign distributors, in comparison, purchase merchandise from the U.S. company and re-sell it at a profit. They maintain an inventory of your product, which allows the buyer to receive the goods quickly. Distributors often provide after-sales service to the buyer.

Your agreement with any overseas business partner—whether a representative, agent, or distributor—should address whether the arrangement is exclusive or non-exclusive, the territory to be covered, the length of the association, and other issues.

Finding overseas buyers for your products need not be more difficult than locating a representative here in the United States. It may require, however, an investment of time and resources to travel to your target market to meet face-to-face with prospective partners. One way to identify those interested in your product is to tap the DOCs Agent/ Distributor Service. This program provides a customized search to identify agents, distributors and representatives for United States products based on the foreign companies' examination of the United States product literature.

Other sources of leads to find foreign agents and distributors are trade associations, foreign chambers of commerce in the United States, and American chambers of commerce located in foreign countries. Many publications can be useful as well. The Standard Handbook of Industrial Distributors lists agents and distributors in more than 90 countries. The Manufacturers' Agents National Association also has a roster of agents in Europe.

Foreign government buying agents

Foreign government agencies are often responsible for procurement. Some countries require an in-country agent to access these opportunities. This can often represent significant export potential for U.S. companies, particularly in markets where U.S. technology and know-how are valued. Foreign country attachés in the United States can provide you with the appropriate in-country procurement office.

If you produce consumer goods, you may be able to sell directly to a foreign retailer. You can either hire a sales representative to travel to your target market with your product literature and samples and call on retailers, or you can introduce your products to retailers through direct-mail campaigns. The direct-marketing approach will save commission fees and travel expenses. You may want to combine trips to your target markets with exploratory visits to retailers. Such face-to-face meetings will reinforce your direct marketing.

Direct sales to end-user

Your product line will determine whether direct sales to the end-user are a viable option for your company. A manufacturer of medical equipment, for example, may be able to sell directly to hospitals. Other major end-users include foreign governments, schools, businesses, and individual consumers.

BECOMING AN IMPORT SUCCESS STORY

Importing, for our purposes, is the shipping of products or services into the United States (or any other country for that matter). Although importing is generally looked down upon by our government because it contributes to our trade deficit (little assistance is available to importers), the United States is the largest importing nation in the world. And because of that fact, vast opportunities are waiting for importing firms, both large and small.

As with exporting, you must develop an import plan. Here are the key components of the import plan:

■ analyze marketing opportunity
■ watch for present/future market trends
■ identify key market segments

- follow import restrictions/government regulations
- identify competitor market shares
- compare competitor products
- determine the type of competitor support facilities
- identify competitor distribution channels
- identify competitor problems/difficulties
- identify competitor credit terms, commissions, or other incentives
- identify competitor promotions
- identify degree of competitor pre-sale and post-sale service
- identify how long each competitor has been associated with foreign suppliers

Assess product potential

- identify product
- identify future competition
- identify product competitive strengths and weaknesses
- identify the needs the product fulfills
- identify special skills and training needed
- identify product options and accessories currently available
- identify installation and maintenance requirements
- identify adaptation for U.S. market
- identify how product is marketed abroad

Make a firm commitment

- list reasons for interest in U.S. market
- assess existence of adequate financial base
- assess ability to maintain continuing support for market penetration
- determine if using market share or profit orientation
- determine expected payback across time

Allocate adequate resources

- establish personnel responsibilities and roles
- estimate personnel time and resources needed
- devise appropriate organizational structure to develop U.S. market
- analyze how the organizational structure may need to change over time
- analyze ability of current production capacity
- identify fluctuations in production
- identify minimum order requirements
- determine the willingness to adapt products for U.S. market
- identify capital limitation for handling inventory
- determine the ability to cover market development costs

Identify technical issues

- import documentation
- documents required by U.S. customers
- flexibility in payment methods
- legal procedures
- product classification options
- duty assessment
- marking/labeling requirements
- product registrations

Draft a marketing plan

- executive summary
- introduction
- statement of commitment
- situation analysis
- market opportunity
- target market segments
- competitive analysis
- assessment of product potential
- operational strengths and weaknesses
- resource allocation
- organizational structure
- marketing plan
- marketing goals
- product analysis and selection
- warranties and services
- pricing and terms of sale
- shipping and transportation
- warehousing and logistics
- information systems
- advertising and promotion
- budget and pro-forma financial statements
- implementation schedule and milestones

SOURCES OF IMPORTING HELP AND ASSISTANCE

Banks

Banks are integral in the payment process, but can also be an important tool in accessing supplier relationships.

Freight forwarders

Freight forwarders in the import process are foreign firms responsible in many situations for packaging, documenting, consigning for carriage, insuring, and assuring that the product you ordered is received in good condition at a U.S. port for clearance by U.S. Customs.

Carriers

Carriers may operate in any mode depending on where you source your product and how it's transported. No matter how it's shipped, the carrier is interested in your repeat business and the success of your venture.

Customs House Brokers

Customs House Brokers are U.S. firms specializing in clearing import shipments through U.S. Customs. They are licensed and regulated and bonded by the Federal Maritime Administration.

U.S. Customs

Now known as the U.S. Bureau of Customs and Border Protection (*www.customs.ustreas.gov*), a part of the newly formed Department of Homeland Security, U.S. Customs is the lead agency in enforcing myriad regulations regarding the importation of your potential shipment and charging the appropriate duties and taxes.

Foreign embassies and consulates

The commercial section of Foreign Embassies and Consulates can be found in Washington, D.C. as well as many major cities. An excellent Internet source is the Electronic Embassy. Go to their Website at *www.embassy.org*. The site has business directories which allow companies serving the international community, and those working, living, and traveling internationally, to find their audience. Most embassies and consulates also have Websites. One of the functions is the promotion of their country's products and services.

Sourcing your import needs

Sourcing your import needs has never been easier. In addition to the Foreign Embassies and Consulates previously mentioned, virtually ever major trading partner has an online directory promoting their exports. Use these Web URLs to access the appropriate directory:

Australia	*www.austrade.gov.au*
Austria	*www.austria-export.at*
Brazil	*www.braziltradenet.gov.br*
Canada	*www.strategis.ic.gc.ca*
China	*www.ccpit.org*
France	*www.ubifrance.fr*
Germany	*www.bfai.com*
Ireland	*www.itw.ie*

Italy	*www.italtrade.com*
Japan	*www.jetro.go.jp*
Korea	*www.kotra.or.kr*
Mexico	*www.mexico-trade.com*
Netherlands	*www.hollandtrade.com*
Spain	*www.icex.es*
Sweden	*www.swedishtrade.com*
Taiwan	*www.taiwantrade.com.tw*
U.K.	*www.uktradeinvest.gov.uk*

Alibaba.com (*www.alibaba.com*) is the world's largest marketplace for global trade and is the leading provider of online marketing services for importers and exporters. Alibaba is the number one destination for buyers and sellers to find trade opportunities and promote their businesses online. Alibaba's has more than 4,830,000 registered members from more than 240 countries, growing at a rate of over 18,740 members each day. A few other resources include:

- CustomsClearance (*www.customsclearance.net*)
- How To Import (*www.tradeport.org*)
- U.S. Bureau of Customs and Border Protection (*www.customs.ustreas.gov*)
- U.S. Import Requirements (*www.cbp.gov*)
- Import Resources (*www.itds.treas.gov/Import2.html*)
- Vehicle Importation Regulations (*www.nhtsa.dot.gov*)

The granddaddy of international trade information

These two Websites have the most information concerning how to engage in international business. They review the assistance and information available from all state and federal government agencies in very great detail along with contact information. The Websites also provide helpful articles and guidelines for both exporting and importing.

- *www.itds.treas.gov*
- *www.export.gov*

Important Questions to Consider

#1. HAVE YOU CONSIDERED SELLING YOUR PRODUCTS OR SERVICES IN INTERNATIONAL MARKETS?

If not, you may be missing out on new markets for your products/ services. Sales and profit opportunities may pass you by as more attuned and progressive entrepreneurs seek out international markets within your industry.

Corrective Measures:

Call the field offices of the U.S. Department of Commerce and the U.S. Small Business Administration. Set up an appointment and visit with them to discuss the possibility and potential of selling your products/services in international markets.

#2. HAVE YOU TAKEN ADVANTAGE OF GOVERNMENT EXPORT PROGRAMS AVAILABLE FROM FEDERAL AND STATE GOVERNMENTS?

If not, you may be missing out. Federal and state governments are coming to the aid of both small and large companies that have the potential for international trade. These government entities are the prime source of international trading information and assistance.

Corrective Measures:

Call the U.S. Department of Commerce and the U.S. Small Business Administration; set up an appointment and visit with them to discuss the possibility of selling your product on the international market.

#3. HAVE YOU CONSIDERED REPLACING OR SUPPLEMENTING YOUR PRODUCT WITH CHEAPER IMPORTS WITHOUT COMPROMISING QUALITY?

If not, you may be ignoring sources that could produce both enhanced sales and profits. Many firms, both large and small, are now actively contracting abroad to secure higher margin goods.

Corrective Measures:

Don't be left behind, because your competitors won't slow down for you. Investigate which nations produce your products. Call their embassies in Washington, D.C. and inform them of your desires. They will put you in touch with manufacturers and suppliers, and in many cases even act as the go-between. Some of these foreign governments will even finance your imports.

#4. DO YOU KEEP UP WITH THE LATEST LAWS AND REGULATIONS AFFECTING IMPORTING AND EXPORTING?

If not, you're making a big mistake. These laws change more frequently than those here in the United States, with stiffer penalties.

Corrective Measures:

Stay on top of all domestic and foreign laws related to your international activities. Remember, regulations differ among nations. You must keep and abide by them separately, depending on the country.

#5. IF ALREADY ENGAGED IN IMPORTING OR EXPORTING, DO YOU KEEP UP WITH THE LATEST INTERNATIONAL TRENDS AND FADS?

You will have major problems if you do not stay on top of the latest international trends and fads that affect your international operations.

Corrective Measures:

International trade journals and publications, state and federal government agencies, foreign governments, and the Internet are just a few of the many reservoirs of information available.

#6. IF ALREADY ENGAGED IN IMPORTING OR EXPORTING, ARE EMPLOYEES INTERNATIONALIZED?

If not, mistakes will occur. And in international marketing, mistakes are more costly than in domestic marketing.

Corrective Measures:

You must engage in proper and appropriate training. The rewards of international trade can be great, but so can the risks and losses.

#7. DO YOU INTERACT WITH OTHER COMPANIES THAT ARE INVOLVED IN INTERNATIONAL TRADE?

If not, you may be losing out on important information relating to international marketing. Networking with others in the same industry can be the best and most accurate source of information.

Corrective Measures:

Seek out other entrepreneurs involved in international trade, especially those within your industry. Network with these individuals on a frequent basis. Valuable insight will be achieved.

Human Resources

CHAPTER 12

YOUR MOST IMPORTANT ASSETS

Employees are your most important resource. As an entrepreneur, you will soon realize that salary and wages will be your single largest expense factor. The way in which you manage your human resources will determine the degree to which you are successful as an entrepreneur. In other words, human productivity will make or break you. It's not an easy resource to manage; research has shown that about 75 percent of all workers are unhappy with their jobs. In addition, entrepreneurial firms have fewer resources per employee than do larger companies. Consequently, this complicates the employee morale problems for small enterprises.

Once you realize that employees are income generators after reaching a certain level of output, you will note that it is impossible to survive without them. Another factor you must consider is the growing employee shortages that are starting to appear throughout the country in all occupational classifications. This is due to the accelerating economy. Enhanced employment-related competition among all employers will make it difficult and costly to keep good employees. That doesn't make life any easier for the new or existing entrepreneur.

Building a positive environment

"Happy employees are productive employees." The old adage is true. If you treat your employees fairly and give them the respect they deserve, only positive results can ensue. As a management consultant, I have found that in many troubled companies the difference between profit and loss is not so much material in nature as it is human. Most successful entrepreneurs know this to be a fact.

You will find that employee management can be a challenging affair. Here are some helpful ideas that may assist you in fostering a productive and profitable employee relations program:

- communication
- delegation of authority
- organizational hygiene
- incentives
- employee alliances
- orientation programs
- forget about foreign models of management

HERE ARE SOME TIPS

To improve human relations within the entrepreneurial firm:

- Improve your own general understanding of human behavior.
- Accept the fact that others do not always see things as you do.
- In any differences of opinion, consider the possibility that you may not have the right answer.
- Show your employees that you are interested in them and that you want their ideas on how conditions can be improved.
- Treat your employees as individuals; never deal with them impersonally.
- Respect differences of opinion.
- Insofar as possible, give explanations for management actions.
- Provide information and guidance on matters of employee security.
- Make reasonable efforts to keep jobs interesting.
- Express appreciation publicly for jobs well done.

- Offer criticism privately, in the form of constructive suggestions for improvement.
- Train supervisors to be concerned about the people they supervise, the same as they would be about merchandise or materials or equipment.
- Keep your staff up-to-date on matters that affect them,
- Quell false rumors, and provide correct information.
- Be fair!

Look at the difference

The following comparison is interesting in terms of the difference between how employees think versus how managers think. Noting these variations will help you understand your employees' motivations. A rank of 1 is considered extremely important, while 10 is considered least important.

Ranking by Management		Ranking by Employees
1	credit for work done	7
2	interesting work	3
3	fair pay	1
4	understanding/appreciation	5
5	counsel on personal problems	8
6	promotion on merit	4
7	good working conditions	6
8	job security	2

CONCLUSION

Please understand that many theories have been advanced concerning how to best manage employees. You have Theory X and Y of the late 1970s. You have management-by-objectives, also known as MBO, and management-by-exception, known as MBE, in the 1980s, not to mention the One Minute Manager Series. And, of course, the theories advanced by Steve Covey in the 1990s and early 2000s. They all had relevance for their respective times in business history, and some principals of each theory can be applied even today.

Do some research and analyze the results against the backdrop of unique features about your business. Then take the best of what you find and experiment! Some of the applications will work and some will not. An application may work in your friend's business but not in your business, for whatever reason. The name of the game is trial and effort!

Important Questions to Consider

#1. Do you use job specifications when hiring workers?

If not, you will not be protected against discrimination suits. Also, you will not know the values of particular positions to your business, and you will not be able to identify and describe the physical and mental qualifications needed to perform the tasks in question.

Corrective Measures:

Develop job specifications for each job to determine the physical and mental capabilities needed to perform the jobs. Write a job specification for each job so that the employee will know what is needed to perform the job and whether they are qualified to do it.

#2. Do you have a written statement of policies (company handbook) concerning items of interest to employees?

If not, your employees will not be informed as to sick leave, holidays, and what they can or cannot do while on the job. The employees will experience a decline in morale if they feel they are not being treated fairly.

Corrective Measures:

All employees are entitled to know in writing about sick leave, holidays, standard operating procedures, and so on. Issue a written statement to each employee explaining this, and also what they can or cannot do while on the job. A written statement will set guidelines so employees will know what limitations and/or privileges they can expect. A written statement will clarify necessary procedures for effective operations.

#3. Are employee benefits described in a company handbook?

If not, your employees will not have a clear understanding of their health plans, retirement, or sick leave. This can lead to misunderstandings and cause a misinterpretation of the benefits. Inconsistency in this regard can result in morale problems and even discrimination lawsuits.

Corrective Measures:

Develop policies concerning employee benefits and put them in the company handbook. Benefits are usually of major importance to all employees, and a handbook will provide necessary information pertinent to all areas. A handbook will let your employees know that they are important to you and that you have their best interests in mind.

#4. HAVE YOU PREPARED AN OPERATIONAL MANUAL THAT PROVIDES THE INFORMATION YOU FEEL ESSENTIAL TO ANYONE WHO MIGHT HAVE TO STEP IN TO MANAGE YOUR COMPANY?

Your company could suffer severely, even to the point of failure, if you or key managers become ill and/or need to be away from the business for a while. The company may not be able to maintain its present level of performance. Lack of an operational manual could impose excessive responsibilities on other management personnel.

Corrective Measures:
Prepare an operational manual that will provide pertinent information relating to all aspects of operations within your company. Distribute and review the manual to all key personnel. Make sure they understand the manual and its purpose.

#5. DO YOU HAVE AN ADEQUATE TRAINING PROGRAM, AND DO YOU BASE YOUR TRAINING NEEDS ON JOB DESCRIPTIONS?

Investing in personnel training is saving for the future. If you don't constantly upgrade the skills of your employees to meet the challenges of the competitive marketplace, then you are slowly losing the battle. Also, if you don't target your training efforts to the right people and/or jobs, valuable time and money will be wasted on repetitive training and unqualified personnel. Additionally, be aware that new employees are usually uncomfortable during the first few weeks on the job and many leave early on without an initial training/orientation program.

Corrective Measures:
Develop ongoing training programs. Choose employees that are qualified and train them appropriately. Use an orientation program to acquaint new employees with all facilities, procedures, and other employees. Develop precise job descriptions for all employees and train them according to the exact parameters of those job descriptions.

#6. HAVE YOU COMPARED THE WAGE AND SALARY SCALES WITH OTHER COMPANIES IN THE SAME INDUSTRY, AND ARE THEY CONSISTENT WITH COMPANY OBJECTIVES?

If not, you may be overpaying your employees, which will result in unnecessary expense. Conversely, you may be underpaying your employees, which will cause your better personnel to seek employment elsewhere, and also lead to overall morale problems with your company. Inappropriate salary scale may make your company unattractive to potential good employees.

Corrective Measures:

Investigate other competitive organizations within your industry to be certain you are paying comparable wages. Adjust any wages and salaries when necessary and appropriate. However, there may be situations in which the rules must be bent.

#7. Are employee benefit programs a part of the total compensation package?

If not, your employees will perceive that benefits are not something to expect. You may be unable to attract and retain good employees. Never pass out traditional benefits as part of an incentive program. It may be perceived as discriminatory or illegal.

Corrective Measures:

Inform all employees exactly what benefits they are entitled to receive. Employees usually perform more efficiently if they feel you are concerned for their welfare. A well-suited compensation package (including a few benefits) could entice your better employees to remain and work on the firm's behalf as well as their own. If no benefits currently exist in your business, do not make promises about future benefits! There is nothing worse than breaking promises to employees.

#8. Have you investigated initiating a retirement program?

Everybody is worried about retirement income. Even as a one-person business operating out of your home office, you must give some consideration to your future. If you don't have a retirement program in place, your existing employees may not be enticed to remain. Also, the company would be less appealing to potential employees. Retirement programs are expensive, so you may want to have a program that is tax sheltered and partially or fully funded by the employee.

Corrective Measures:

Investigate retirement program options with your insurance agent. A retirement program would stimulate employment commitments and boost morale, increasing the possibility of attracting competent employees. And don't forget about yourself when investigating retirement programs. And remember, if you are not serious about a retirement program, do not make promises.

#9. DO YOU MEET FREQUENTLY WITH YOUR KEY EMPLOYEES TO COORDINATE YOUR EFFORTS?

If not, organizational inefficiency will occur. Duplication of effort may ensue due to a lack of communication among key individuals. You will lose the advantage of obtaining a constant flow of new ideas from these important employees. Most importantly, lines of communication may become blurred or crossed, causing confusion.

Corrective Measures:

Determine a suitable time (at least twice a week) to meet with your key employees. Keep the meetings on a regular basis. Make every effort to be present at the designated time. Listen to what they have to say. Use their recommendations if they make sense.

#10. IS EACH PERSON PROPERLY SUPERVISED?

A loss of individual and overall company productivity will occur if proper supervision is not instituted. Individual employees could assume too much or too little responsibility. Lines of authority may become blurred and/or overlap.

Corrective Measures:

Make sure that each employee is supervised and they know to whom they must answer. Also, be certain that each employee knows and adheres to their job description and job specifications. This will make supervision easier. Define lines of authority in a clear fashion.

#11. DO YOU GIVE YOUR EMPLOYEES REASONABLE FREEDOMS TO WORK THE WAY THEY FEEL THEIR JOBS CAN BEST BE ACCOMPLISHED, LET THEM MAKE THE DAY-TO-DAY DECISIONS NECESSARY TO CARRY OUT THEIR WORK, AND AVOID LIMITING ANY OF THEM TO REPETITIVE TASKS?

If not, you will lose worker productivity within your business. Employee morale will suffer. In addition, your company will forfeit the opportunity to allow creative input from your employees in terms of managing and directing their individual work environments.

Corrective Measures:

Incorporate trial periods of increasing employee freedoms and decision-making in their daily work. Avoid limiting your employees to routine tasks where possible. Know when to give and take. If this approach works, it would have the effect of reducing the time and cost associated with constant supervision.

#12. DO YOU SEEK YOUR EMPLOYEES' OPINIONS OF STOCK ASSORTMENTS, CHOICE OF NEW MERCHANDISE, LAYOUT, DISPLAYS, AND SPECIAL PROMOTIONS?

Mistakes will occur when you are too far removed from the ultimate customer. If you don't seek out your employees' opinions on a regular basis, you will lose valuable customer input that is always transmitted through your employees. Also, it could lead to a general feeling of disenfranchisement among your employees.

Corrective Measures:

Confer with employees on an individual and group basis and ask for their input and opinions about inventory and floor plan issues. Reaffirm employees' feelings of importance.

#13. DOES YOUR COMPANY HAVE AN EMPLOYEE SUGGESTION SYSTEM?

If not, you may be giving up some very creative input from your employees. Sometimes they see things that are not apparent to you.

Corrective Measures:

Incorporate an appropriate suggestion system. Solicit employee opinions as to the system. Give them input in the decision-making process related to the suggestion system. And most importantly, reward them for good ideas, particularly if you want your suggestion system to have ongoing credibility with the employees

#14. DO YOU SET WORK GOALS FOR YOURSELF AND FOR EACH EMPLOYEE AND THEN CHECK THE ACTUAL PERFORMANCE AGAINST THESE GOALS, DEFINED WITHIN A SPECIFIC PERIOD OF TIME?

If not, you will be unable to determine what each employee can and cannot achieve, much less yourself. You can not establish performance goals for your company, or have achievement benchmarks.

Corrective Measures:

Set individual goals for each employee for a specific period of time and tie those goals to the overall objectives of the firm. Make sure you communicate with each employee and get their input about these goals. At the end of the specified period, check their performance.

#15. Do you turn to schools (both high school and college) for part-time and full-time help?

If not, you could be losing a valuable source of help as well as obtaining individuals who might possibly be willing to accept a lower wage while in school. Loss of community goodwill may occur if you don't support local educational institutions.

Corrective Measures:

Utilize the talents and opportunities provided by your local educational establishments. They could be a good source of cost-effective labor. In addition, a two-way street of cooperation between your company and the schools can pay real tangible benefits in terms of public relations, access to useful research information not otherwise available, and first choice on a quality and trained labor pool.

#16. Do you have an incentive plan that recognizes the personal needs of your employees and rewards unusual productive and innovative methods?

If not, low employee morale will ensue, especially among your most productive workers. Loss of valuable employees will also occur. Additionally, overall company productivity will be negatively impacted.

Corrective Measures:

Question employees to find out what incentives would most effectively motivate them. Experiment with their suggestions. After a reasonable time period check, to see if productivity has increased. Based on your findings, incorporate a permanent cost effective incentive program that works best for both the company and employees.

#17. Are you acquainted with the standards of OSHA that apply to your industry, and do you meet them?

If not, fines could be imposed on your business, if not outright closure. The downtime that results from closure for OSHA noncompliance is costly, if not deadly. The safety of your employees could be at stake.

Corrective Measures:

Become acquainted with the standards of OSHA within your industry and comply with the rules. Also, acquaint yourself with and conform to state laws relating to safety standards within your industry for your business. Many states combine their efforts with OSHA.

#18. Have you established good relationships with local unions?

If not, you could be excluded from top-grade employees, particularly when you may need them the most.

Corrective Measures:

Take steps to develop good relationships with the unions. Establish this close relationship only to the extent that you need trade employees to function, and it is beneficial to your firm. This is most important in union shop states and of less importance in open shop states where right-to-work laws exist.

#19. Do you support industry efforts to establish local apprenticeship and/or internship training?

Not supporting appropriate training programs could impede efforts to foster a pool of trained employees within your industry or community. You may be denied access to existing talent pools by those organizations taking a more active approach in this regard.

Corrective Measures:

Consider supporting your industry's efforts with an open mind and positive approach towards internships and apprenticeship programs. Look into the possibility of opening or sponsoring apprenticeship or internship training programs if they apply to your business, particularly in cooperation with your local educational institutions.

#20. Do you take time to get to know your employees?

If you do not make an effort to get to know and communicate with your employees, they may feel ignored and unimportant, resulting in low morale. The employees will not talk openly with you about potential problems. By not getting to know your employees, particularly in reference to their respective talents, you may give them responsibilities beyond their capabilities, or you may underestimate their abilities and not allow them to manage projects they could handle. In either case it will result in lost productivity and declining morale.

Corrective Measures:

Knowledge of your personnel will allow you to reduce employee turnover, which can be expensive. Periodically analyze and evaluate all personnel. Have an open door policy about employees' ideas and needs. Organize and execute company picnics or parties. Communicate on a regular basis, on an individual and/or organizational basis.

Time Management

CHAPTER 13

THE TIME FUNNEL

Effective management of your time is the key to ultimate entrepreneurial success. Whether you run a large or small company, or work on one project or multiple projects, effective management of your time will help you stay focused and organized so as to complete the needed tasks in a timely and effective matter. This chapter will assist you in understanding the importance and challenges of effective time management, particularly in today's increasingly complex and competitive entrepreneurial marketplace. It will define specific methods you can employ to better manage your limited time and paper burdens. In addition to improving your skills in terms of setting the correct priorities and identifying and eliminating time-wasting behavior, you should walk away from this chapter with a better sense of time perspective and how it impacts your operation. Hopefully, as a result, you and your company will both experience increased productivity, reduced stress, and (most importantly) enhanced profitability.

221

Interruptions

Many factors can affect your productivity as an owner-manager. None more so than unwanted and unimportant interruptions. You will find that as your business grows, so does the number of questionable interruptions, particularly those that deal with your employees. Telephones calls are a close second, followed by unwanted guests and friends who just drop by to say hello.

You must set standards in reference to these issues, or you will soon find yourself using an increasing amount of your valuable time engaged in unproductive endeavors. Your more productive side will cease to be a factor in the business, and eventually sales and profits will suffer as a result.

R<small>ESULTS</small> <small>VERSUS</small> <small>TASKS</small>

Many entrepreneurs are task-oriented to a fault. They forget that a result is more important than a task. That is not to suggest that tasks in and of themselves are unimportant; obviously, you must engage in tasks in order to achieve results. The trick is to maximize a particular set of tasks to achieve a result in the most optimum and efficient way. Some people just keep doing tasks and achieving nothing in return. You know these types of people. They're a dime a dozen and just keep chasing their tails throughout life.

High pay-off actions

Now that we have traded off tasks versus results, we must trade off results versus results. Yes, there is a hierarchy of results. Some results are better than others. You must concentrate your activities and energies, producing those results that will provide the maximum benefit to your business. Anything less is cheating your business and yourself.

Fall in love with the waste basket

It's not a pleasant thought, but at times your trash can be a good management tool. Famed author and organization expert Barbara Hemphill put it plainly in her book, *Taming The Paper Tiger*, by suggesting "the art of waste basketry." In other words, immediately toss out the papers you don't need. Ask yourself these questions:

- What do I need to keep?
- In what form do I need to keep it?
- How long do I need to keep it?

Without a doubt, paper and documents can quickly accumulate and entirely consume you, creating a sense of personal and organizational paralysis.

TIME-WASTERS

Time is money, and the proper use of time is essential. Management consultant R. Alee MacKenzie has identified 15 time wasters that can cost you in terms of lost productivity and profits. As an entrepreneur, you must deal with them in an effective manner in order to ensure efficient operations:

- telephone interruptions
- visitors dropping in without appointments
- meetings, both scheduled and unscheduled
- crisis situations for which no plans were provided
- lack of objectives, priorities, and deadlines
- cluttered desk and personal disorganization
- failure to set up clear lines of responsibility and authority
- inadequate, inaccurate, or delayed information from others
- indecision and procrastination
- lack of or unclear communication instruction
- inability to say no
- fatigue

WHAT TO DO

- Contract out tasks. Contract out tasks you do not have the expertise to complete. Your client will appreciate your honesty and effort to get the best result.
- Start with the most worrisome task. Start the morning, afternoon, or evening with the most worrisome task before you. This will reduce your anxiety level for the next task.
- Complete deadline work early. Not only will this reduce stress and lighten your work schedule, but it will also give you more self-confidence about managing your schedule.
- Know your capacity for stress. When you are hitting overload, take the break you need (even if it is a short one) when you need it.
- Stay organized. Take time at the end of each day to briefly organize your desk and make reminder lists of tasks for the next day or week.
- Take advantage of down time. Allow yourself some down time between busy periods to review your schedule and reevaluate your priorities.
- Have fun. Be sure to have some fun while working or playing; a good sense of humor can keep most problems in perspective.

■ Build flexibility into your schedule. Your availability to family and friends depends on the flexibility you build into your schedule. Get to know your neighbors so you know who to call on for help.

In the bigger picture, consider the relationship between your business life and your personal life. Be as realistic as possible when answering the following questions, keeping in mind what is most important to you:

■ What are your long-term goals? Your partner's goals?

■ Where are the conflicts and where are the similarities?

■ What is it that you really want to do? List all possible ways to accomplish this.

■ How long will it take you to reach your goal?

■ How do your time line and goals affect your family (parents, siblings, partner, children)?

■ How do your personal goals conflict with or match your business goals?

■ How much time can you donate to community programs?

■ Have you talked about your personal goals with your business partner?

■ Have you talked about your business goals with your personal partner?

Don't underestimate the toll that emotional stress takes on your physical health and your ability to concentrate on your work or enjoy time with your family. Make sure you have time for the important people and events in your life.

Technology time management

Let's not forget that box sitting on your desk and/or in your lap, called a computer! Proper file management is just as important as managing your desk and paper trail. Keeping those computer files in organized folders in an easily accessible and organized fashion is very important to personal productivity and prudent time management. Disorganization can be just as destructive to organization and personal effectiveness as pure paper issues.

Important Questions to Consider

#1. DO YOU POSSESS GOOD TIME MANAGEMENT SKILLS?

If not, you might be disorganized and confused. This will cause costly procrastinations and lead to frustration due to your inability to get things done on an efficient and timely basis.

Corrective Measures:

Get organized. Take some workshops in time management. It can be hard for those of you who have possessed poor time management skills over a long period of time. However, now is the time to change. If you acquire good time management skills (which can be learned relatively quickly) the results of good organization will show immediately.

#2. DO YOU DEMAND EFFECTIVE EMPLOYEE TIME MANAGEMENT SKILLS?

Good time management skills on the part of your employees are important. Lacking these skills will produce disorganization, lack of achievement, and overall inefficiency within the company.

Corrective Measures:

Emphasize to your employees that now is the time to change. Encourage them to attend seminars and workshops to improve their time management skills.

#3. DO YOU MAINTAIN COMPANY-WIDE SCHEDULES AND BENCHMARKS?

If not, you will have difficulty achieving key targets, goals, and objectives within specific time frames. Delays are costly in terms of lost sales and negative customer goodwill. If performance contracts are involved, there could be penalties involved.

Corrective Measures:

Set up broad and specific organizational schedules and benchmarks on a regular basis. Communicate these to all of your employees within the business. See to it that time frames are successfully met.

#4. HAVE YOU AND YOUR EMPLOYEES TAKEN A SEMINAR IN TIME MANAGEMENT LATELY?

Possessing good time management skills is not enough. As with anything in the business world, constant updating is required to stay ahead of the competition. You can rest assured that if you don't get the latest in educational applications relating to time management skills, your competition will, and then beat you over the head with them.

Corrective Measures:

You and your employees must constantly update your time management skills on a regular basis. There are many inexpensive time management courses offered by community colleges and vocational schools. Take advantage of what they have to offer.

#5. IS YOUR DESK A MESS?

This may sound as though it's a stupid question, but it does tell a lot about you. A constantly messy desk suggests a constantly messy person in terms of personal and business time management skills.

Corrective Measures:

You may want to seek help from the many professional consultants and coaches that assist entrepreneurs and business executives in organizing their personal and professional lives.

#6. DO YOU THROW AWAY UNIMPORTANT MAIL, PAPERS, AND DOCUMENTS QUICKLY?

Don't throw away any paper that comes across your desk for two weeks. Then stand back and observe. How much of the important stuff has been lost in the pile that has accumulated? And how many important matters have been delayed for fear of jumping into that pile?

Corrective Measures:

Clean off the desk now. Every piece of paper coming across your desk on a daily basis, including the mail, should be processed without hesitation. Disregard the junk and unimportant items the same day you receive them.

#7. IS YOUR COMPUTER, PALMPILOT, AND CELL PHONE DATA STORAGE BEING USED EFFICIENTLY?

If not, this can be just as costly to your personal productivity as a constantly messy desk.

Corrective Measures:

Get those data files organized and prioritized for fast and easy access. You may want to rely on some professional assistance for this endeavor—the miracles of modern technology can leave us all a little behind the curve at times.

Technology in Small Business

CHAPTER 14

IT'S A REQUIREMENT

In today's business world, any serious attempt at a successful venture needs to include computerization, or you may as well just keep the doors locked. Technology advances to make life easier, get simple tasks done faster, and make complex situations easier to manage. Without spreadsheets to see where your finances are, databases to keep track of inventory, and a computerized register that can show you sales at the push of a button, you may as well go back to the dark ages of a 20-pound ledger and an inkwell to run your business.

Technology is only as good as its uses and its users, so judge according to your capabilities as to what computerized capital you bring in to your enterprise. The best computer setup in the world does nothing for your business if you can't get it to do what you want, and it's not worth the price you paid for it if you only need it for a few small functions. However, as with anything else you will decide upon during your initial setup phase and later restructuring, leave room for upgrading your technology.

There are several types of technology and applications that you can use for your business depending upon your situation, and I am going to break them down into six main groups for you. They are record keeping, inventory control, sales, distributing and marketing, security, and communications. There are more, of course, and these categories will intersect and overlap with each other, but these six will open the door to just about any other way technology comes into contact with your business. These are just the basic categories that every entrepreneur needs to have a firm understanding of, and have the ability to maximize them to increase your profits.

RECORD KEEPING

There are few things more frightening in the world than having a sit-down with an IRS agent when your records are incomplete or incorrect! As a business owner, you need to know where your capital is going; how much your business is earning, and how much you're paying employees, vendors, and municipal fees. Of course, you'll need to pay taxes on just about everything you do, so you need to have a way to put it altogether. This sounds as though there are a lot of different tasks to accomplish which may require several programs, but for a small business these tasks can be performed quite easily with a bare-bones computer setup, an office suite program, and an accounting application.

An excellent office suite program is OpenOffice.org. It's a freeware program, meaning it won't cost you a dime to use it keep track of your businesses finances. It is completely compatible with the Microsoft programs that would cost you a few hundred dollars, and is just as easy and intuitive to use. The OpenOffice.org suite contains a word processor, database, spreadsheet, slide show presenter (similar to PowerPoint), and even templates to design your company's letterhead and business cards. A few minutes of setting up these powerful applications to suit your needs, and all your daily record keeping can be accomplished in the time it takes you to drink your morning coffee.

It is so simple to design a spreadsheet or database format using fixed columns and mathematical formulas that all you have to do after that is just type the numbers in to calculate anything from daily to yearly results for your business. What once required new ledgers and logbooks and took untold hours compiling to truly get a grasp on your business standing, can now be compiled, recorded, and stored on a CD-ROM.

Another important aspect of business expenses is who the money is getting paid to and how you are getting it to them. A program like Quicken or QuickBooks can handle your company's check writing, payroll calculation, and payment, as well as maintain all your vendor and supplier payments. It also gives you the ability to print out your own invoices, as any professional business should. Most accounting programs come with tax calculation capability, so you'll know how much of your hard-earned money Uncle Sam is entitled to.

INVENTORY CONTROL

What good is a warehouse if you don't know what's in it, or where a particular item is? With a good database and consistent usage of it, then this won't be a problem for you. A portable barcode reader linked to the master inventory database can let you know what's come in, what's going out, what needs to be reordered, and what's not selling. If you're dealing with time-sensitive goods, you can keep on top of the dates you need to know. A computerized cash register can keep track of every barcode scanned, giving you an accurate and reliable sales tracking system. Instead of having to log every delivery manually, wouldn't it be easier and better to just scan a barcode and use that time and space in a more profitable manner?

SALES

If you are a retail business owner, then a computerized cash register is a must, but your register doesn't have to *be* a computer. Let me explain: You could get a register that is a computer to keep track of all related files for you. This is the route you would want to go if you have more than one register operating at one time. However, you could also go with an inexpensive register such as a Sharp that allows you to hook into a computer and pull the records out of its memory. This will make logging your daily numbers more reliable, because it doesn't depend on the human element. Either solution will allow you to keep an eye on your sales, what merchandise is moving, and track the time of your sales so you know when you are the busiest.

DISTRIBUTING AND MARKETING

If you ship or receive items through UPS or FedEx, just go to their Website and keep tabs on where your goods are at any time. If you're doing retail sales online, of course you'll need a company Website for your customers to place orders, and you'll need to be able to assure them their goods will be delivered on time. Your company Website could be the biggest marketing tool you have, as it could bring you customers from around the globe. Knowing how to set up a site that pulls people in can make the difference between decent sales and early retirement. You might need to bring in a professional for this, but the potential for new clients and sales is almost always worth the cost.

E-mail marketing is one of the most effective ways to keep in touch with customers. It is generally cost-effective, and if done properly, can help build brand awareness and loyalty. At a typical cost of only a few cents per message, it's a bargain compared to traditional direct mail at $1 or more per piece. In addition, response rates on e-mail marketing are strong, ranging from five to 35 percent, depending on the industry and format. Response rates for traditional mail averages in the 3 percent range. One of the benefits of e-mail marketing is the demographic information that customers provide when signing up for your e-mail newsletter. Discovering who your customers really are—age, gender, income, and special interests, for example—can help you target your products and services to their needs. These are a few points to consider when creating your e-mail newsletter:

- HTML versus plain text. Response rates for HTML newsletters are generally far higher than plain text, and graphics and colors tend to make the publications look more professional.
- Provide incentive to subscribe. Advertise the benefits of receiving your newsletter to get customers to sign up for your newsletter, such as helpful tips, informative content, or early notification of special offers or campaigns.
- Don't just sell. Many studies suggest that e-newsletters are read far more carefully when they offer information that is useful to the customers' lives rather than merely selling products and services.

ESTABLISHING AN INTERNET PRESENCE

Even if you choose not to sell your goods or services online, a business Website can be a virtual marketing brochure that you can update with little or no cost. Your presence on the Internet can be a useful marketing tool by providing richer presale information or post-sale support and service. This might temporarily differentiate your product or service. E-marketing has lessened the disadvantage that small businesses have faced for years when competing with larger businesses. E-commerce has redefined the marketplace, altered business strategies, and allowed global competition between local businesses. Electronic commerce has evolved from meaning simply electronic shopping to representing all aspects of business and market processes enabled by the Internet and other digital technologies.

Today's business emphasis is on e-commerce—rapid electronic interactions enabled by the Internet and other connected computer and telephone networks. Rapid business transactions and unparalleled access to information are changing consumer behavior and expectations.

Many small businesses assume that the Internet has little value to them, because they feel that their product or service cannot be easily sold online. But inexpensive information processing and electronic media can help most small businesses provide better, faster customer service and communication.

According to the OPEN Small Business Network Semi-Annual Monitor from American Express, small companies are increasingly using the Internet as a business tool. Overall, 71 percent of the small businesses surveyed reported using the Internet, up from 66 percent in March of 2002. The American Express study discovered that small businesses use the Internet for a wide variety of tasks, including:

- making travel plans (38 percent)
- purchasing supplies (37 percent)
- servicing customers (36 percent)
- making marketing or advertising purchases (35 percent)
- conducting market or industry research (33 percent)
- making purchases from wholesalers (25 percent)
- networking with other small businesses owners (24 percent)
- managing accounts and bill payments (22 percent)

The study also revealed that younger companies (those in business for 5 years or less) were more likely to use the Internet than older small businesses (78 percent versus 69 percent).

SECURITY

Whether your business is in retail sales or not, or whether you even handle money or merchandise in your business or not, you need to keep track of everything that goes on. From cameras on the sales floor or in the warehouse to hanging over your employees' desks, you need to make sure that your time and money are not wasted. Your business depends on the people you have working for you doing their jobs during the time they are there, and one person sitting around playing solitaire when he or she should be typing up a contract can be a huge financial blow.

Relax, you don't need to have your eyes glued to a little monitor watching over everything all the time. With a few cameras and a hard-drive recorder you can check in whenever you want. If you set up your security with Webcams you don't even have to be there to know what's happening at work. If your business involves people using computers with Internet access, a monitoring program can keep them on task and out of chat rooms.

COMMUNICATIONS

This is where technology has grown the most over the years, and it seems that every upgrade to communications impacts other areas of the technological world over time, so keeping on top of this is a must. Cell phones can keep you in touch. Personal Data Assistants (PDAs) can keep you up to date on your clients, your inventory, your e-mail, and your schedule. As I said earlier, your Website is seen around the world, so it's a huge tool to communicate with your potential client base. E-mail has become the lifeblood of internal and external business communication, and is slowly replacing the fax machine. Of course, the fax is still necessary for some documents, and you will probably need to have access to one.

Obtaining, maintaining, and marketing a Website for your business is relatively easy to do. The first thing your site needs is its own URL or Web address. GoDaddy.com or NetSolutions.com can register the domain name for your site for a small fee and reserve it until you are ready to open the site to the public. Next you need a Web hosting service. ValueWeb.com and iPowerWeb.com both offer plenty of space and tools for designing sites, including e-mail accounts, file transfer capability, and streaming audio and video. Of course, the most well-designed and user friendly site in the world is no help to you if customers can't find it. The next step is to register your site with search engines such as Google and Yahoo. They allow you to put any relative terms to your business into their search engine so when a customer is looking for something relating to the words you entered, your site is listed for them.

Any business that is worth starting is worth investing in the right technological capital. Of course, the most important piece of technology you're going to need is a computer. The work to be done determines what type of machine you need. If you just need a simple record-keeping machine, you can get a bare-bones box for a few hundred dollars. If your work involves architecture or graphic-intensive work, then you'll need a workhorse. Internet connectivity is a must in this day and age, and you should get the best connection speed and performance that your business can comfortably afford.

Keeping up with technology is just another burden on you as an entrepreneur, but keeping up with it, maximizing usage, and minimizing costs will definitely increase your firm's bottom line.

In reference to your computer hardware and software system, you have undoubtedly been faced with using a prepackaged system verses a custom system. If all you truly need is just an office machine, then by all means go with the mass-produced deal of the week, but if you need more power and capability, go custom. Yes, it will cost you a little more to go custom with your hardware, but at least you will get a system built to the exact specifications of your business. Also, servicing your system will be a lot easier, given that local hardware vendors usually service what they sell. As far as software is concerned, developing custom software is just too cost prohibitive nowadays for most small firms. The prepackaged stuff on the market today is hard to beat.

There may come a point in your business life where customized software makes sense and you can afford it. Generally, the bigger and more complex a business becomes, the more you need customized software.

The need to take bids

It is advisable to request bids from several vendors located close to you. Don't jump at the lowest price. Issues such as system expandability, compatibility to existing systems, reputation of the vendor, customer service, servicing of the product, replacement units, and trade-in allowances are all important elements of your decision. Talk to some of your entrepreneur friends for guidance in this decision. You won't be disappointed.

How to acquire a system

Once you've decided to acquire a computer system, how do you go about it? Here are the general steps:

- determine your requirements
- prepare a request for proposal
- ask for proposals and bids
- evaluate the system proposals

Important Questions to Consider

#1. HAVE YOU CONSIDERED BUYING A COMPUTER SYSTEM FOR YOUR BUSINESS?

If not, you are definitely being left in the dust. Given the level of technology within most industries (not to mention recent office and clerical technical advances), your more computerized competitors will eat you alive. Their ability to develop new products/services will become increasingly obvious to you as well, as their ability to deliver their wares faster and cheaper than your operation develops.

Corrective Measures:

If you are computer shy, take an introductory computer course from your local community college or vocational school. You may want to consider hiring at least one employee with computer knowledge. Whatever the case, you must start the process now before it's too late. Even the holdouts will be forced to computerize, lest their businesses become obsolete—both in terms of products/services offered and internal operations—and eventually cease to exist.

#2. DO YOU HAVE A COMPUTER SYSTEM?

If not, then you are way behind the curve in terms of lost organizational productivity and profitability.

Corrective Measures:

Despite the cost of computers and technology training, the system will more than pay for itself very quickly. Hire a computer consultant.

#3. IS YOUR EXISTING HARDWARE SYSTEM ADEQUATE ENOUGH FOR YOUR OPERATION?

If not, you may be limiting your ability to take on new computer tasks as demanded by the growth of your business. Accounting, inventory, payroll, and job-costing efforts could be compromised at some point, leading to costly errors in reporting.

Corrective Measures:

On a periodic basis, evaluate your computer hardware needs, taking into consideration your company's current growth and future expansion plans. You may want to consider getting some advice from several hardware vendors or outside computer consultants.

#4. ARE YOU AWARE OF YOUR COMPUTER SYSTEM'S CAPABILITY?

If not, you may be misapplying the system's capability and not receiving vital reporting that could be useful to you as the owner-manager in the decision process. That would be a wasteful display of existing resources. Additionally, you will not be in a good position to determine when and if a system's modification is needed.

Corrective Measures:

When you purchase or modify your system, investigate and get to know its abilities and limitations upfront. Knowledge is key here. Demand that the vendor explain the system thoroughly and completely. You may want your computer consultant present at the time of the vendor explanation. Or bring in the consultant later, if you are still not sure of what you have on your hands.

#5. ARE YOU AND YOUR EMPLOYEES PROPERLY TRAINED IN COMPUTER OPERATIONS?

If not, mistakes will occur that will cost you in terms of time and money. Poor and inaccurate reporting can even compromise the very existence of your operation.

Corrective Measures:

Get some computer education. Courses and seminars may be readily available from the vendors where you purchased your hardware and software, often for free. Community colleges and vocational schools routinely run inexpensive computer courses as well.

#6. DO YOU MONITOR YOUR COMPUTER'S PERFORMANCE IN TERMS OF MEETING ALL YOUR INFORMATION OBJECTIVES?

If not, you will not be aware if you are getting the right kind of information and in the correct form. You may be receiving either too much or too little of what you really need.

Corrective Measures:

Evaluate and determine your informational objectives relating to your business. Modify your existing computer system to accommodate and meet these objectives. Professional assistance may be needed here; bring in a competent computer consultant.

#7. ARE YOUR TELECOMMUNICATION FUNCTIONS UP TO DATE, AND DO THEY STACK UP IN TODAY'S MARKETPLACE?

Don't you hate watching a new movie and seeing an old telephone system or cell phone brick used as a prop? Not keeping up with the latest telecommunications technology is costly both in terms of operations and lost organizational efficiency.

Corrective Measures:

Make sure you are using the correct mix of telecommunication technology. Similar to insurance, you can use too much technology for your own good. That's also expensive and counterproductive. Do an IT audit. You may want to consider a good IT consultant. Check with your local chamber of commerce. Make sure you have the right combination of technology that is right for your particular business.

Ripe for the Picking

CHAPTER 15

HELP GALORE

Few individuals are aware of the reservoir of assistance available from public and private organizations directed to the small business community. Taking advantage of these services may mean the difference between success and failure for many struggling businesses and entrepreneurs. Many of these informational outlets will help when evaluating business opportunities and specific propositions.

U.S. Small Business Administration (SBA)

One of the primary objectives of the U.S. Small Business Administration is to promote the economic well-being of small firms and entrepreneurs. This is partly accomplished by providing an array of business and managerial assistance programs that are available upon request. Keep in mind that the SBA offers valuable financial assistance programs as well, both in terms of direct and guaranteed loans programs.

The best way to assess the capability of the SBA is to access its primary Website at *www.sba.gov* and go from there. Also, you can call the SBA in Washington, D.C., but the best approach is to call the SBA office closest to you. The SBA maintains an office in every state capital. In larger states there may be more than one office.

University Business Development Centers (UBDCs)

These organizations are established in tandem with the U.S. Small Business Administration to provide additional counseling services to the small business community. UBDCs are college- or university-based counseling centers utilizing institutional resources, including faculty and students. In addition, these centers muster community involvement and volunteers to accomplish their task of providing help to small firms and people wanting to start businesses. This is the strongest assistance program provided by the SBA. A UBDC close to you can be found on the SBA Website.

SCORE and ACE

The Service Corps of Retired Executives (SCORE) and the Active Corps of Executives (ACE) provide one-on-one counseling to business operators. SCORE is a group of retired businesspeople who volunteer their services to small businesses through the SBA. ACE is a group of active managers who counsel small-business owners on a volunteer basis. ACE volunteers come from major corporations, trade associations, educational institutions, and professions. The SCORE Website (*www.score.org*) will help you identify local chapters and counselors simply by entering your zip code or by the type of expertise. Nowadays, most SCORE and ACE chapters work directly with the UBDCs to provide a coordinated approach to the delivery of assistance services.

Small Business Institutes (SBIs)

The SBI program was launched in 1972 by the SBA and eventually contracted with more than 500 colleges and universities to establish small business institutes. As of 1996 it is independent of the SBA and still operates in approximately 250 universities throughout the nation. This program, although similar to the UBDC approach, does have distinct differences. Counseling services provided by SBIs are limited in one respect, but more extensive in others. SBI student and faculty counselors are assigned to certain projects with the objective of providing detailed verbal and written recommendations to specific problem areas that a prospective entrepreneur or business owner may face. This approach enables students to experience real life business situations. The cost for this service has historically been free to individuals or businesses seeking assistance. But some SBIs are now charging for their services. You can find out more about SBIs by surfing their Website at *www.smallbusinessinstitute.org*.

Management and Technical Assistance Program

This SBA-financed program is designed to give free professional advice and expertise to small firms and individuals who qualify. The agency contracts with reputable and reliable accounting and/or consulting firms to carry out the objectives of this program. Generally, problems of a very difficult or technical nature are handled under call contracting. More detailed information can be retrieved at the following Website: *www.sba.gov/gcbd*.

Department of Commerce

The U.S. Department of Commerce is another federal agency that puts vast assistance resources at your fingertips. I believe that, in some cases, the DOC provides better help than the SBA. This agency maintains an array of informational resources that are available to anyone. This department is constantly collecting economic, financial, and business data relating to the economy, different industries, slates, and, in some cases, individual firms. Many companies rely of the very detailed census data provided by DOC when doing consumer- and commercial-related marketing studies. Over the last decade, the Department of Commerce has been heavily involved in the promotion of American products abroad. It has enormous amounts of data that can be used by domestic exporters when studying overseas markets. In addition, the department gets actively involved in setting up channels of distribution for any business (new or existing) wanting to exploit foreign market potentials. The Department of Commerce field offices can be contacted for details concerning their assistance programs and publications. As with the SBA, the DOC generally maintains a field office in every state capital. A list of these can be obtained by accessing the DOC primary Website at *www.commerce.gov*.

The Minority Business Development Agency (MBDA)

Part of the Department of Commerce, this office provides basic assistance services to minority-owned firms. This agency maintains regional and district offices. These offices can be found at the following Website: *www.mbda.gov*.

Federal Trade Commission (FTC)

The FTC was set up to protect consumers and businesses against firms that would promote restraint of trade and use unfair competitive methods. It publishes much material on what constitutes illegal practices when conducting business. It also investigates claims made against firms and will take action should the need arise. FTC information can be accessed at the following Website: *http://www.ftc.gov*.

Internal Revenue Service (IRS)

The IRS provides a lot of information valuable to the small business community. Yes, it has a tax collecting slant, but a lot of the information is useful. Go to the IRS Website specific to small companies and see for yourself at: *www.irs.gov/business/small*.

Uncle Sam

If you want to do business with the federal government, there is money to be made. Go to the following Website and look around; it has a wealth of information: *www.sba.gov/gcbd*. Other useful Website addresses related to federal assistance and information are as follows: *www.business.gov* and *www.firstgov.gov*.

State governments

Most state governments are realizing the importance of small business activity to their economy. Many have developed assistance programs aimed at helping prospective entrepreneurs and existing small firms. Services may include managerial, procurement and/or funding help. The degree of assistance varies from state to state. All states have economic development departments that can lead you in the right direction. The following Website address will lead you to any specific state and then you can surf for the particular department you seek: *www.statelocalgov.net*.

Local governments

Most municipalities maintain records in reference to local economic activity. Statistics dealing with retail sales, personal income, construction permits, traffic counts, and growth patterns can be obtained and are useful when analyzing general business prospects or specific propositions. For example, when evaluating several possible store locations, traffic counts and area growth patterns should be carefully reviewed. You can also access local government programs by clicking on the state you want, and then surfing the various cities, towns, and counties.

Accountants

In addition to their traditional role as bookkeepers and auditors, many accountants provide invaluable information and assistance relative to decisions concerning business propositions. Here are some of the more common services that can be expected from most accountants:

■ record keeping and auditing
■ corporate and individual tax planning
■ overall financial analysis

It is wise to consult a banker, attorney, or business consultant when seeking a suitable accountant. Bankers and lawyers are in constant contact with the accounting profession and they generally know the accountants that can provide adequate help at reasonable cost. A good approach is to seek out owners in similar lines of business and ask for advice. This can be the best source of reference available because of the direct contact between accountant and owner. In addition, there are two national, professional accounting associations that may provide referrals upon request: the American Institute of Certified Public Accountants (*www.aicpa.org*) and the National Society of Public Accountants (*www.nsacct.org*).

Accountants can save you a tremendous amount of pain and expense if they are used wisely. Always have an accountant explore a prospective business proposition before purchasing, for obvious reasons cited earlier in the book. If already in business, you need accountants to evaluate any large investment decision contemplated. Even if a business has an internal accountant, outside opinion should be sought. It can be helpful in spotting difficulties that may not be apparent from the inside. The small price paid for the information is an investment if it helps avoid a bad deal which potentially could cause severe losses. Remember, it's better to pay a little now than a whole lot later.

Advertising agencies

Generally, small advertising accounts will have to pay for the additional services rendered over and above the cost of media purchased from the agency. However, larger accounts can expect some, if not all, of the following services to be included as a part of the media fee paid. In other words, these services may be performed free of charge if large amounts of media are purchased:

■ planning of advertising strategy and tactics
■ selection of correct media outlets
■ production of ad layouts and commercials

- coordination and execution of strategy and tactics
- evaluation of advertising results

Advertising agencies are located in the Yellow Pages. In addition, talking to various media and other businesses may provide information concerning the services and reputation of various agencies. Also, several professional advertising associations might provide referrals upon request, such as the American Advertising Federation (*www.aaf.org*) and the American Association of Advertising Agencies (*www.aaaa.org*).

Associations (trade and professional)

Trade and professional associations represent a specific group of businesses or individuals that find themselves in the same or a similar line of business. Many trade associations maintain assistance programs designed to help and serve the firms they represent. Newsletters, seminars, and toll-free numbers are but a few services offered by many of these trade organizations. In addition, quite a few associations collect and analyze financial data in reference to the whole industry it serves, as well as individual firms. This information is organized, and in many cases made available to members and prospective entrepreneurs wishing to enter the industry through a start-up operation or by purchasing an existing firm.

A list of trade and professional associations can be found by referring to the Encyclopedia of Associations, published by Thomas-Gale Publishers. It can generally be found in most libraries. If not, you can find it at *www.gale-edit.com.*

Chambers of commerce

Local chambers of commerce can provide valuable assistance to prospective entrepreneurs and existing small businesses. Besides facilitating interaction between local businesspeople, civic groups, and professionals, CCs can be an important source of community contacts that could help any business. In addition, many chambers of commerce maintain small business committees that are used to promote and/or assist small firms within the area they serve. Also, some chambers have strong ties to the U.S. Small Business Administration and other governmental bodies, including state and local agencies that represent the interests of small enterprises. Some chambers collect statistical data on the communities they serve and make this information publicly available. Facts concerning sales, income structure, and growth patterns may be acquired to assist in the planning function.

Competition

Competitors are almost always looked upon as the enemy. However, with a little creative thinking, competitors can be viewed as a source of vital information. Some will candidly provide useful data upon being asked and others will not. Even if some competitors are strict about conveying ideas and information, their actions in the marketplace can reveal interesting particulars worth noting. For example, an unanticipated price hike may indicate that a competitor is experiencing unusually strong demand, falling profit margins, or increasing cost pressures. It may also signal a shift in marketing strategy or tactics. So, always ask questions, listen, and observe.

Customers

Customers can yield valuable tips about the firm's image to the public at large. Many small business entrepreneurs have been shocked to hear the comments about their business from their clientele. Before starting a small business, it is wise to speak with potential customers. They might reveal some pros and cons that may not have been apparent upon initial or later evaluation. In reference to buying a going concern, seeking out current and potential customers could be an excellent way to gauge the viability of the enterprise being considered for acquisition.

Financial institutions

Local financial institutions have an intimate knowledge of the community they serve. Therefore, they can be an important source of information concerning business prospects. Many will help in analyzing financial data concerning the local economy and specific business opportunities. Most know what businesses can work in the community and which ones have a high chance of failure. Some even know which locations are good or bad for particular types of businesses.

Family and friends

U.S. presidents have been known to call on family members and friends when delineating major policy directions: John Kennedy constantly consulted his father on civil rights issues and Jimmy Carter drew on his mother and friends for advice. Even his daughter, Amy, was consulted on nuclear arms questions. And Bill Clinton consulted with Richard Nixon several times a week.

Soliciting advice can be like picking peaches. Generally a yield of good, average, and rotten fruit is collected. Therefore, when absorbing advice from friends, family, and/or associates, consider the source very carefully. Was previous advice and information solid and sound? If so, to what degree? If not, watch out.

Insurance companies

Insurance companies and their local agents can provide useful information relating to the reduction of liability under a number of conditions. Besides providing the traditional business insurance services such as casualty, health, and life protection, many are involved in the reduction of risks relating to defective products or services, nonpayment of client accounts, or international transactions.

To find out which companies are involved in comprehensive risk reduction programs may require some time and energy. It may take time in finding the right kind of insurance combination required at a good price. Generally, calling local agents will reveal vital and necessary information. Again, talking to bankers, attorneys, accountants, and consultants will usually provide insight into the types of insurance required and where to find it.

Some insurance companies provide additional services to small firms and prospective entrepreneurs. These services can range anywhere from setting up pension and profit-sharing plans to providing in house consulting services on such things as cash-flow and resource management.

Attorneys

Attorneys are listed in the Yellow Pages. In addition, calling or writing the state bar association, which is usually located in the capital city of a particular state, will yield a list of lawyers located in a given area of that state. However, the best source of contact information concerning competent legal help will come from bankers, accountants, and business consultants. Most work with legal experts on a regular basis and are in a position to know the best lawyer for a given situation. Also, try other businesses in a related field. Some good legal contacts may surface.

You can also do a national search of qualified legal counsel by referring to the Martindale-Hubbell Legal Directory, the listing of all attorneys in the country. That directory can be accessed for a quick search at *www.lawyers.com*. There is also another Website, at *www.lawyer.com* that could be helpful as well. Attorneys can assist you in the following areas:

- analysis and evaluation of contracts
- negotiation with investors, lenders, and suppliers
- compliance with legal statutes and codes
- defense in legal matters
- identification of capital sources

Libraries

Most large and medium-sized libraries maintain an array of business books and periodicals that can be helpful, but college and university libraries tend to be the best for business research purposes. Many of the large universities collect, assimilate, and publish an array of economic information on local areas. The quality of this data tends to be very high and can provide a small firm or prospective entrepreneur with valuable information when planning or analyzing opportunities.

Planning districts

Many localities belong to planning districts. These districts maintain offices and are funded by one or more communities for the purpose of coordinating growth objectives. They gather, disseminate, organize, and publish an array of data about the areas they serve. The information tends to be somewhat technical, but it can prove helpful to any firm or individual examining potential within a locality. Market trends, population shifts, income patterns, and activity in certain lines of business are but a few of the types of information available from the office of a good planning district. Call the municipal manager of the local government to find out if such an organization exists in your area.

Management consultants

Every business occasionally finds itself in a management situation that it cannot directly control or correct. When this condition prevails, a management consultant can be hired to help with the difficulties. In addition, a prospective entrepreneur may want to use a consultant to assist in the start-up phase of a new enterprise. Keep in mind that most of these consultants specialized in particular segments of management, although some generalists remain.

Bankers, lawyers, and accountants can be excellent sources in providing contact with management consultants. Also, talking with potential or existing competitors may reveal some consultants willing to provide services in the area of business contemplated or currently being exploited. Another source of referrals are the professional associations that represent management consultants. Some maintain codes of ethics to enhance the credibility of their membership.

- Association of Management Consulting Firms (*www.amcf.org*)
- Institute of Management Consultants (*www.imcusa.org*)
- Society of Professional Consultants (*www.spconsultants.org*)

Marketing consultants

As with management problems, marketing difficulties can also surface, demanding the attention of outside expertise. Marketing consultants can help handle the following:

- mail order
- direct mail
- distribution
- market testing
- merchandising

Keep in mind that marketing consultants tend to specialize in a particular field, and a generalist may be difficult to locate. Checking the Yellow Pages in larger cities will reveal some prospects. In addition, bankers, accountants, and attorneys may provide good contacts. The best leads are generally given by firms that are currently using or have employed a marketing consultant. When initially talking to consultants, always ask for background information and client references. Check out the information carefully to ensure credibility. A bad consultant can be costly in terms of loss of time, markets, and money. Marketing consultants can also be located by accessing the management consulting associations listed in the previous section. Many marketing consultants also join management consulting associations.

Periodicals

There are several excellent periodicals that serve the small business community. Reading and studying the contents contained within their covers can prove to be helpful to the individual wishing to start or buy a business. Also, existing enterprises can find useful material relating to operational matters. Some of the information to be found in these publications includes, but is not limited to, the following:

- dealing with lenders and investors
- sources of capital
- government assistance programs
- marketing techniques and tips
- bartering of goods and services
- exporting
- creating an image and/or generating sales

Public relations

Public relations firms and consultants are listed in the Yellow Pages in large and medium-sized cities. However, the best sources of contacts include business consultants, bankers, accountants, lawyers, and other businesses that have used PR services. In addition, contacting the professional association listed here might provide some referrals. When talking to potential firms or consultants, always ask for background information and investigate thoroughly. Also, it is important to remember that many advertising agencies perform public relations services. When searching for advertising expertise, ask about PR functions as well.

Suppliers

Some vendors provide a wealth of information and help to new or existing businesses in the field they serve. A few suppliers will even go so far as to set up an entrepreneur in business by providing location, inventory, and financial assistance. Most do not go to those extremes, but many will help in one or more vital areas.

Constantly search for new suppliers. Evaluate their services and credit terms carefully. It is not unethical to play them against each other. In fact, it makes good business sense. Tell one or more suppliers that a better deal can be obtained elsewhere. Watch for their reactions. Some will bend and others will not.

Colleges and universities

These institutions offer numerous classes which may provide helpful information. Currently, more than 300 business schools offer courses in small business management and/or entrepreneurism. The U.S. Small Business Administration is compiling a list of these colleges. A call to the regional SBA office may reveal how to get the list. Also, many business professors moonlight as freelance, part-time consultants offering their expertise at rates normally below those charged by established consulting firms. They can be a source of valuable information.

Some business schools want their students to work on outside projects so as to allow them real-life experiences. Many schools make it a requirement. These colleges are always looking for challenging situations that can be used as a proving ground for their students. Generally, no fee is charged to the entrepreneur or small firm, and these students can provide valuable talent in most problem situations.

Seminars and workshops are additional services provided by some institutes of higher education to existing businesses of all sizes and to prospective entrepreneurs. Topics can cover the entire business spectrum and the fees are normally low. Many of these interaction meetings are held in unison with the U.S. Small Business Administration, U.S. Department of Commerce, state or local chambers of commerce, or other bodies representing business interests.

Important Questions to Consider

#1. ARE YOU AWARE OF THE PUBLICATIONS SPECIFICALLY WRITTEN ABOUT SMALL BUSINESS MANAGEMENT AND OPERATIONS?

If you do not keep up with the trends in business management techniques, your business will falter. New techniques emerge all the time that should be considered. Not paying attention could be costly in terms of mistakes. Eventually, you may have to pay for corrective advice that would otherwise be available free or at nominal cost.

Corrective Measures:

Visit your local bookstore and browse through the business books for those that might be useful to you. Go to your local library and look at the business books and periodicals. Check the list of government publications; there are many available which offer helpful basic information for specific businesses.

#2. DO YOU REGULARLY READ AT LEAST THREE PERIODICALS THAT RELATE TO YOUR BUSINESS ACTIVITIES?

If you are not reading any materials relating to your business or industry, you may be missing out on important information. While business books are useful for general reference, periodicals are more timely, and contain more current and topical information.

Corrective Measures:

Keeping up with current events within your field will keep you informed and make you aware of other businesses with similar problems and opportunities and may be useful to you in resolving those problems and charting new directions.

#3. DO YOU HAVE A BASIC REFERENCE LIBRARY COVERING AREAS SUCH AS ACCOUNTING, MARKETING, MANAGEMENT, AND SIMILAR GENERAL PUBLICATIONS?

If you lack informational resources to help you with minor problems, you will end up paying for that information by employing experts. You will also lack the ability to make quick reference checks relating to your operation.

Corrective Measures:

Many times reference books or notes can supply you with some small pieces of information that can answer a question quickly, explain why something is happening, or help you in problem recognition and resolution.

#4. DO YOU PARTICIPATE IN AND MAKE USE OF YOUR INDUSTRY'S TRADE ASSOCIATIONS?

If you are not a member of your industry trade association, you may not be keeping up with industry trends. You may also be missing out on trade shows, seminars, and other valuable exposures such as knowledge of new technologies and information that may applicable to your business.

Corrective Measures:

Join at least one trade association related to your industry. If there is more than one, you may want to join both if they offer different types of information and support services.

#5. ARE THERE MARKET LETTERS OR ECONOMIC REPORTS THAT CAN HELP IN YOUR REGULAR OPERATIONS?

If you are not keeping up with the economic climate surrounding your business and industry, you will not be making the best business decisions. Business mistakes will ensue that will hurt sales and profits.

Corrective Measures:

Through your trade association magazines or newsletters, you should be able to obtain such information. Many trade associations offer special reports on market and economic trends within the industry they represent. *The Kiplinger Report* is a great publication that reports weekly on numerous political, economic, and business issues of a general nature. The U.S. Small Business Administration and the U.S. Department of Commerce also publish numerous economic reports.

#6. DO YOU USE YOUR LOCAL OR REGIONAL LIBRARY?

Sometimes it is not economically sensible or feasible to buy every business book or periodical you want or need. If you do not visit your local library, you may not be aware of new and important publications which could be of assistance to your business.

Corrective Measures:

Visit the local library. You can check out the books you need, thereby obtaining helpful information without having to spend a lot of money buying these publications.

#7. IS YOUR LOCAL LIBRARIAN AWARE OF YOUR NEED FOR REFERENCE MATERIAL AND GOVERNMENT PUBLICATIONS?

If your librarian is not aware of your need for certain resources, he or she may not spend the budgeted monies in your area of interest. Very few people ask for expenditures in particular fields of interest.

Corrective Measures:

Alert the librarian to your informational needs. Periodically remind your librarian of your field of interest. Make purchase suggestions to the librarian. You might be surprised at the response!

#8. DO YOU BELIEVE THAT YOUR BUSINESS WILL NEED HELP FROM AN OUTSIDE PROFESSIONAL SOMEDAY?

Every business, no matter how good a business person you fashion yourself, will need help along the way. Whether it's to manage growth or deal with human resources problems, don't be so stubborn that you can't seek out and ask for assistance from the professional community.

Corrective Measures:

Seek help early on if your business is struggling in any area of operation. This will give you time to work on solutions and probably save you money in the long run, as well as saving your business. Be candid and reveal all pertinent information to outside professionals.

#9. DO YOU RELY ON YOUR FIRM'S ATTORNEY, ACCOUNTANT, AND INSURANCE AGENT FOR RECOMMENDATIONS?

If not, you may not have the best information for making optimal business decisions. Not paying attention to the advice of these professionals may be expensive to you and the business in terms of making mistakes that could otherwise be avoided.

Corrective Measures:

Your professional team may be able to spot potential trouble areas before you do and provide solutions. Sometimes both problems and opportunities are more apparent to outsiders than the owner-manager. Periodically changing professionals is a wise decision as well.

Conclusion

Today's competitive world leaves very little breathing room for making mistakes. Markets and financial centers are not very forgiving of those who err in the business community. Therefore, be prepared! Do your homework! Research everything! And most importantly, ask questions.

I hope this book has forced you to think about the most important aspects of business operations, and to dwell on problem resolutions. Please reread the book, not once, but numerous times. As time passes, you will find yourself answering more and more of the questions in the affirmative as opposed to the negative. At that point, you are increasingly insulating yourself from the threats imposed by a hostile economic environment.

Good luck to you—the risk-takers of the world and the true heroes of our collective economic realm in America!

Index